MW01059979

THE CROSS
& HUMAN
TRANSFORMATION

THE CROSS
& HUMAN
TRANSFORMATION

Paul's Apocalyptic
Word in 1 Corinthians

Alexandra R. Brown

FORTRESS PRESS
Minneapolis

THE CROSS AND HUMAN TRANSFORMATION
Paul's Apocalyptic Word in 1 Corinthians

Fortress Press ex libris publication 2008

Library of Congress Cataloging-in-Publication Data

Brown, Alexandra R.
    The cross and human transformation: Paul's apocalyptic work in 1 Corinthians / Alexandra Brown.
    p.   cm.
    Includes bibliographical references and index.
    ISBN: 978-0-8006-2677-8
    1. Bible. N.T. Corinthians, 1st—Criticism, interpretation, etc. 2. Holy Cross 3. Apocalyptic literature.   I. Title.
BS2675.2.B76 1995   227'.206—dc20

Manufactured in the U.S.A.

For my mother
BERYL STOKER BROWN
and
in loving memory of my father
MILTON HAYNES BROWN
1916–1994

Contents

Abbreviations

CBQ	*Catholic Biblical Quarterly*
HUCA	*Hebrew Union College Annual*
JBL	*Journal of Biblical Literature*
JSJ	*Journal for the Study of Judaism in the Persian, Hellenistic and Roman Periods*
NovT	*Novum Testamentum*
NTS	*New Testament Studies*
SBL	Society of Biblical Literature
SBLASP	SBL Abstracts and Seminar Papers
SBLDS	SBL Dissertation Series
SNTS	Society for New Testament Studies
TDNT	*G. Kittel and G. Friedrich, eds., Theological Dictionary of the New Testament*
TZ	*Theologische Zeitschrift*
USQR	*Union Seminary Quarterly Review*
ZNW	*Zeitschrift für die neutestamentliche Wissenschaft*

Preface

The twentieth-century painter Wassily Kandinsky worked among a generation of artists in Europe whose productive years were just prior to, during, and after World War I. In those ominous, apocalyptic times Kandinsky and others rejected the forms of the past which they found outdated and impotent[1] and so thrust their energy into the expression of new aesthetic and professedly spiritual (although not necessarily Christian) values. In an essay written in 1912, Kandinsky seems to echo the apostle Paul who wrote in 1 Corinthians 7:31 that "the form of this world is passing away."

> At some predestined hour the time is ripe for decisions. That is to say, the creative spirit (which one may call the abstract spirit) finds access to a single soul, and later on to many, and sets up a yearning therein, an inner urge.
>
> When the necessary conditions for the ripening of a precise form are fulfilled then this longing, this compulsion, gains the power to create new values in the human spirit, values which—consciously or unconsciously—begin to come alive.
>
> From this moment on one is constantly trying—consciously or unconsciously—to find material form for the new values that live in spiritual form within.
>
> This is the search for the materialization of spiritual values. Material is here a kind of stockpile from which the spirit draws what it needs at any given time, just as the cook does from the larder.[2]

---

1. Paul Klee: "The streams of yesterday's traditions have really run dry. . . . [They are] in the last stages of exhaustion," from Paul Klee's diary, no. 903, Autumn 1911, and no. 905, January 1912, in *The Blue Rider*, ed. and trans. Hans K. Roethel (New York: Praeger Publishers, 1971), 75.
2. Wassily Kandinsky, "Über die Formfrage," in *Almanach der blaue Reiter* (Munich, 1912), 75; quoted in Roethel, *The Blue Rider*, 63.

> There are whole epochs that deny the spirit, because the eyes can-
> not see the spirit at those times.[3]

This book concerns in part that "inner urge" of the apostle Paul which originated in the "apocalypse of Jesus Christ" (Gal 1:12,16) and moved him to express new spiritual realities in new "material" forms. Long before the artist Kandinsky, the Christian apostle Paul saw the "ripeness of time" and the necessity of expressing a truth that had newly arrived on the scene. Indeed, he found himself thrust into the critical moment in human history when conditions were set for the advent and realization of the "new creation."

Yet the apocalyptic force of Paul's rhetoric is seldom felt even where scholars note its apocalyptic motifs. Nor has the radical percep-tual shift that is anticipated by Paul's rhetorical strategy been ade-quately explored. In this book, I hope to demonstrate the vital connection so often overlooked in studies of 1 Corinthians 1–2 be-tween Paul's apocalyptic rendering of the message of the cross and his intent to promote reconciliation among the Corinthian Christians.

In our time, the cross is often more a source of controversy than a sign of peace. Feminist theologians in particular claim negative pow-ers for the cross when it is used to support rather than to undermine an ideology of oppression. We cannot escape the fact that the cross has been used to "justify, even glorify, suffering in ways that are dam-aging to persons."[4] Nor can we forget the horror of its image burned into the earth by the Ku Klux Klan or the painful paradox of the crosses marking graves in Nazi death camps.

I hope that by presenting Paul's argument within its original con-text, and yet with awareness of its distortions in more recent times, I may make a case for reclaiming the liberating power of his message. Because the church today, like the ancient Corinthian church, is so often in conflict, divided by ego and ideology, resistant to transfor-

---

3. Kandinsky, "Über die Formfrage," 74, in *The Blaue Reiter Almanac*, ed. and trans. Klaus Lankheit (New York: Viking Press, 1974), 147.

4. In her book on the cross and feminist ethics, Sally B. Purvis summarizes the problem: "Contemporary feminists, including Christian feminists, have been wary of the cross as a symbol for community. As several scholars have cogently and persuasively argued, the cross has been used to justify, even glorify, suffering in ways that are dam-aging to persons. It has also distorted persons' understanding of responsibility, guilt, sin—that is, the cross is theologically and ethically dangerous." Beyond the wariness she notes, Purvis offers an alternative reading of the cross as power and reclaims it as "an intellectual, spiritual, and communal resource for radical change." See Sally B. Purvis, *The Power of the Cross: Foundations for a Christian Feminist Ethic of Community* (Nashville: Abingdon Press, 1993), 14.

mation by the Word of the Cross, Paul's message is still urgently relevant. Above all else, 1 Corinthians teaches us that nothing short of the radical challenge of the cross to every mere ideology stands a chance of converting us from worldly to godly wisdom, from the dominion of Satan to the reign of God, from our self-absorption and egotism to that ministry of reconciliation to which we are called not only within but especially *beyond* church walls.

Acknowledgments

I wish to acknowledge with deep gratitude my teachers and others who inspired, advised and encouraged me at various stages along the way from the conception of this book to its publication. I am especially grateful to Robin Scroggs, who advised the dissertation on which this book is based, and to J. Louis Martyn, Raymond E. Brown, Barney L. Jones, Carl Holladay, Luke T. Johnson, Abraham J. Malherbe, Celia Deutsch, Susanne Lehne, Susan Schaeffer, Claudia Setzer, Sara B.C. Winter, Richard Sturm, Mary Foskett, Russell Davis, the late Minor Rogers, Louis Hodges, Harlan Beckley, Richard Marks, John W. Elrod, Karen Lyle, Cecile West-Settle, Peter Dunleavy, Walapa Marks, Martha Brown Stromberg, Suzanne Brown Sumrall, and Kirk Follo.

It was my good fortune to spend much of my sabbatical year at the Institute for Ecumenical and Cultural Research in Collegeville, Minnesota where this book took its present form. I am grateful to the Institute staff, Patrick Henry, Dolores Schuh, CHM, and Wilfred Theisen, OSB, to colleagues there who have become dear friends, to the Benedictine Monks of St. John's Abbey and the Sisters of Saint Benedict's Convent whose hospitality so enriched that year, and to Washington and Lee University who sponsored the sabbatical leave. Finally, I wish to thank Karen Lyle for her tireless hours of typing and technical assistance and the editorial staff, especially Director of Publishing Marshall Johnson, of Fortress Press, for expertly seeing the book through to publication.

For all these named, and for many unnamed but remembered, I give thanks.

Introduction

I appeal to you, brothers and sisters, by the name of our Lord Jesus Christ, that all of you be in agreement and that there be no divisions among you, but that you be united in the same mind and the same purpose. (1 Cor 1:10, NRSV)

For the word of the cross is folly to those who are perishing, but to us who are being saved, it is the power of God. (1 Cor 1:18, RSV)

"For who has known the mind of the Lord so as to instruct him?" But we have the mind of Christ. (1 Cor 2:16, RSV)

Saying what is can effect a set of circumstances with every bit of transformational impact that Austin first invoked to show that words do things other than what they say.[1]

In 1 Corinthians 1–2, Paul strikes at the heart of schism in the church. His principal weapon is the Word of the Cross (1:18)[2]; with it he breaches the barriers of ego and ideology—even Christian ideology—that divide believers at Corinth. His battleground is the realm of human perception; wielding the Word of the Cross, he invades the perceptual landscape of his hearers, cutting across their accustomed (and, he believes, false) ways of knowing with the sharp expression of a new reality. The effectiveness of this strike, Paul's letter suggests, rests in the power of the Word he preaches to liberate both minds and bodies from the grasp of the false world to which he elsewhere refers as "the present evil age" (Gal 1:4). Paul's discourse is aimed toward reconciling the Corinthian church, but it reaches beyond the

---

1. Sandy Petrey, *Speech Acts and Literary Theory* (London: Routledge & Kegan Paul, 1990), 27.

2. Throughout I refer to the Word of the Cross capitalized and without quotation marks, using Word to indicate the message communicated by Paul's words.

historical contingencies of ancient Corinth, revealing the power of the cross proclamation to address and transform succeeding generations of readers and hearers. How the words of the text work to reveal the Word that transforms life is the subject of this study.

Our text reveals both that the transformation in view is a perceptual one—it concerns the way one sees the world—and that it is governed by the cross. The perceptual focus is established by Paul's opening appeal for unity of mind, by the density of perceptual language (especially wisdom terminology) in the text, and by the culminating noetic claim of the argument in 2:16: "But we have the mind of Christ." As we will see, perceptual terminology is especially prevalent in the part of the discourse devoted to the cross where it is also strikingly intertwined with apocalyptic language and image. The way these themes—perception, cross, and apocalypse—combine in our text leaves little doubt that Paul's aim in preaching the cross is to alter his hearers' perception of the world in such a way as to alter their experience *in* the world. In the preaching of the cross, something is unveiled that moves the one who perceives it from one world to another, from the divided mind to the "mind of Christ" (2:16).

There were other apocalyptic visionaries before Paul from whom he learned the rich images and expectations of the messianic age, others who taught him to look for a perfect world to come where the righteous are vindicated and the wicked destroyed. Yet Paul saw more than his apocalyptic forebears had prepared him to see; while others looked into a future world, a world distinct temporally and spatially from the present world, Paul saw the advent of a new reality here and now—a life "in the Spirit," as he put it—full of the limitations and sufferings common to bodily existence and yet made free to engage passionately in and for the creation. While he remains in essential ways a Jewish apocalypticist, the categories and language of his apocalyptic heritage have now been radically transformed. The long-awaited messiah has indeed come, inaugurating the new world, drawing the old to a close. But this advent has not met traditional expectations; the messiah has, in fact, been crucified, and the world remains, to all appearances, unredeemed. The announcement of a new creation whose founding event is the crucifixion of its messiah met then as now with incredulity. It was, as it is, a scandal: in Paul's words, "a stumbling block to Jews and folly to Gentiles" (1 Cor 1:23).

Paul's burden, then, is to proclaim his unlikely vision—the advent of the new creation in a crucified messiah—in language that will compel others to see it too. The task is daunting and the stakes are high. Paul cannot afford to deal abstractly with his vision; he will not avoid its rough, unpalatable images. Nor is he able to treat it as a private religious experience, an event that happened to strike him personally as redemptive. Rather, the cross is at the very center of his preaching. His message is grounded in the stark reality of the Christ, condemned by the law and hung to die outside the walls of all that is considered sacred.

What, then, becomes of the resurrection? Does not the crucifixion too much dominate Paul's word? We hear overtones of such questions in 1 Corinthians, and in this letter too we hear his answer: "If Christ has not been raised, then our preaching is in vain and your faith is in vain" (1 Cor 15:14). But if we read the letter's final chapter *in light of its first*, we see that, for Paul, the resurrection is never the "answer" to the crucifixion.[3] For Paul, rather, the resurrection bears out, brings to full fruit, the saving conditions already effected by the death itself. In other words, for Paul, only the cross can adequately explain the resurrection; the rising of Christ confirms the victory accomplished already by his dying act. To imitate Christ is to carry this victorious death in the body, to live its negation of the world's wisdom and thereby to proclaim the victory of the cross over powers that are now, since that death, passing away.

Here, then, is the "folly" of what Paul preaches: Christ's death brings to nothing all that the world associates with the godly hero—success, power, wisdom, even righteousness—and in this negation it brings to birth a new reality.

But this new reality is revealed as yet in mystery, hidden in the Word of the Cross; it is therefore vulnerable to grave misinterpretations. Two of these are evident in Paul's letters to Galatia and Corinth: in Galatia, we meet the offense of the cross to the salvation schema of the legalists; in Corinth, we meet the shining faces of the spiritualists, for whom the cross and the *future* resurrection of the dead are but afterthoughts to the enthusiasm of the *present* resurrection. In the one case we hear a *pre*-cross soteriology; in the other, a *post*-cross spirituality. In both, the possibility of self-justification is assumed, whether through law observance or perfection in wisdom; in both, therefore, the cross is emptied, for the cross, in Paul's view at least, is God's final, saving response to the incapacity of human beings to save themselves.

---

3. Käsemann writes, "Before Paul, the cross of Jesus formed the question which was answered by the message of the resurrection. The apostle decisively reversed this way of looking at things." Ernst Käsemann, "The Saving Significance of the Death of Jesus in Paul," in *Perspectives on Paul*, trans. Margaret Kohl (Philadelphia: Fortress Press, 1969), 57.

Continuing Conflict in Corinth

The history of the Corinthian church suggests that Paul was not entirely successful in his attempt to reconcile the fractious congregation. In the collection of letters that we call Second Corinthians, he is forced to respond to further community problems. The letters reveal that although there had been a shift in the *direction* of the dissent that flowed so freely among believers in Corinth, the underlying *pathology* of their discontent remained, finding expression in their desire to identify, elevate, and boast in authorities that demonstrated recognizable prestige and power. Whereas in 1 Corinthians Paul had been forced to distance himself from misplaced claims on his authority by some (1 Cor 1:12-14), in 2 Corinthians he must defend himself against charges of weakness in the face of his more "polished" opponents (e.g., 2 Cor 10:7-18). In both cases, the need to define one's own power by denigrating another's eclipses the true power of the cross and disintegrates the body of Christ. In both, the clamor of self-promotion deafens the ear to the Word with power to pierce and unite human hearts.

The Present Study

What frustrates Paul's communication with the Corinthian church? What prevents the positive reconciling effects of his preaching there? These questions have dominated scholarly research into our letter for several decades, much of it driven by history-of-religions concerns to determine the position that Paul encounters and opposes in Corinth.[4] Typically in these studies, an effort is made to separate Paul's theology from that of his opponents and to show how he adopts, adapts, or rejects available traditions in the service of the "core" of this thought, namely, the "theology of the cross." While

---

4. In addition to the several important studies that locate Gnosticism in our text (W. Lutgert, R. Bultmann, W. Schmithals, U. Wilckens, P. Winter), there are others who employ similar methodology (research in the history of religions) and find the text's determinative background in Jewish wisdom traditions (H. Conzelmann, J. Dupont, A. Feuillet, H. Windisch), in combinations of wisdom and apocalyptic traditions (R. Scroggs), or in certain strains of Hellenistic Jewish philosophy (R. Horsley, B. Pearson), specifically Philo. These studies have yielded tremendous insight into the complexity of the Corinthian milieu and into Paul's own theological and philosophical depth. They have not yielded consensus either on the precise identity of Paul's Corinthian opponents or on the operative background for Paul's own formulations in 1 Corinthians. For a selected bibliography, see Alexandra R. Brown, "Paul's Apocalyptic Word of the Cross: Perception and Transformation in 1 Corinthians 1–2," (Ph.D. diss., Columbia University, 1990), 6–8 nn. 6–10.

these studies have made valuable contributions to understanding the text's "background," they have tended to eclipse certain rhetorical aspects of Paul's discourse on the cross, especially the function of the cross in promoting the cognitive transformation that Paul strives for in the letter.

I depend on those "background" studies but go beyond them to explore how Paul's preaching on the death of Jesus—his Word of the Cross—works in a particular social and linguistic context toward the perceptual transformation of his hearers. Faced with disintegration in the community, Paul writes a letter that he intends to have reconciling effect. As active agent of this reconciliation, he introduces in forceful, indeed apocalyptic, language the Word he expects to have power to reconcile its hearers. The force of the Word he brings is apparent in the internal workings of the text itself; we will see that its entry into the discourse causes a disruption of the conventions of language that both shape and reflect the world of ordinary perception. In its capacity to disrupt perceptual structures, the Word has destructive force; but this is not its only force. The discourse ends with the announcement of a newly created perceptual organ, the "mind of Christ." True to its apocalyptic setting, the Word of the Cross creates anew in the rubble of destruction.

1

Paul as Apocalyptic Preacher

DEFINING APOCALYPTIC

No term is more central to our concerns, nor more elusive, than "apocalyptic." Since the nineteenth century, when it was taken up by scholars such as F. Lücke (1832), Johannes Weiss (1892), and R. Kabisch (1893), apocalypticism has been the subject of considerable scholarly attention. In 1901, Albert Schweitzer published a polemical and influential book, *The Quest of the Historical Jesus,* in which he argued that neither Jesus nor the early church could be properly understood apart from the apocalyptic sensibilities and expectations by which they were driven. By the late twentieth century, Schweitzer's thesis has been found wanting in many respects, but his principal insights live on as the body of literature on apocalyptic in early Christian thought grows.

But what do scholars mean by "apocalyptic"? The question does not have an easy answer. While the Greek word group *apokalypsis/ apokalyptō* is satisfactorily translated "unveiling"/"unveil" (rendering *apo* as "out from" and *kalypso* as "veil"), or more commonly, "revelation"/"reveal," the criterion by which a text, a movement, or a thinker can be sensibly designated "apocalyptic" is complicated by historical, literary, and theological matters that extend well beyond lexical meanings.

Apocalyptic as Genre

Because the last book of the Christian canon, self-described as "The revelation (*apokalypsis*) of Jesus Christ," records the "unveiling" of end time events, this document has set the unofficial standard for defining apocalyptic. While in the popular imagination the standard is a conceptual one—depicting the drama of the end time in images of earthly cataclysm and heavenly triumph—in the scholarly imagination the standard is formal and literary. According to the latter, "apocalyptic" describes a literary genre, often pseudonymous, in the form of narrative about heavenly ascents, visions, or auditions of persons to whom divine secrets about the end time are unveiled. The genre, it is generally recognized, first appeared in pre-Christian texts of Second Temple Judaism, beginning with the Book of Daniel, and was adapted by Christian writers, most notably the writer of the Book of Revelation.

Research on the apocalypse genre has yielded consensus on its principal characteristics as a literary form, its major themes, and, to some extent, the social and historical circumstances out of which it arises. But, as Richard Sturm has noted in his comprehensive review of research on apocalyptic, the genre approach to defining apocalyptic has serious limitations, chief among them the fact that not every work bearing apocalyptic *ideas* follows the *form* prescribed for the genre.[1] "If one approaches apocalyptic primarily as a literary genre," Sturm asks, "must persons who did not write apocalypses, like Jesus or Paul, be neglected or ignored? Would their omission mean that it is improper to refer to their ideas and images as 'apocalyptic'?"[2] Sturm goes on to trace the development of another, more fruitful approach to defining apocalyptic by those who treat it as a theological concept whose boundaries are not limited by genre.[3]

Apocalyptic as a Theological Concept

Increasingly, the presence of certain theological motifs in a work, regardless of its formal features, has come to signal its apocalyptic identity.[4] From the cumulative research on apocalyptic as a theological

---

1. Richard E. Sturm, "Defining the Word 'Apocalyptic,'" in *Apocalyptic and the New Testament, Essays in Honor of J. L. Martyn,* ed. Joel Marcus and Marion Soards (Sheffield: JSOT Press, 1989), 24.
2. Sturm, "Defining the Word 'Apocalyptic,'" 25.
3. For a full analysis of the literature, see the remarkably comprehensive and efficient review of the major arguments and contributions to the theological understanding of apocalyptic in Sturm, "Defining the Word 'Apocalyptic,'" 25–42.
4. Sturm attributes to Johannes Weiss (1892) the first effort to define apocalyptic primarily as a concept, namely, in his designation of Jesus' teaching of the "kingdom of God" as primarily "eschatological-apocalyptic." Sturm, "Defining the Word 'Apocalyptic,'" 26, citing Johannes Weiss, *Jesus' Proclamation of the Kingdom of God,* trans. Richard Hyde Hiers and David Larrimore Holland (Philadelphia: Fortress Press, 1971; reprint, Chico, Calif.: Scholars Press, 1985),78–79.

concept, Sturm derives the following list of motifs whose presence in a work signals the theological perspective typical of apocalyptic: "(1) the idea of two aeons, (2) the embattled sovereignty of God over time and history, (3) the revelation of an imminent eschaton."[5]

PAUL AS APOCALYPTIC THINKER

Using these concepts as measures of apocalypticism, we find that many texts and authors that were once omitted from apocalyptic bibliographies on formal grounds now seem to belong there. Both Jesus and Paul, for example, express views conforming to these convictions, and some of Paul's letters are so permeated with them that the letters themselves seem justifiably classified as "thoroughly apocalyptic."[6]

But we must press for more clarity on precisely how Paul's thought conforms to the apocalyptic perspective outlined above. Already certain Pauline texts that exhibit these theological convictions leap to mind, but ambiguities still remain about what apocalyptic theology really entails for Paul. Revelation and eschatology have emerged as central features of our definition, but in what sense is the end time revealed to Paul and how does that revelation serve to order his view of self, God, and the world? *Where* does Paul's thought reflect the embattled sovereignty of God over time and history? In *what sense* does it rely on the doctrine of the two aeons? And, perhaps most critically, what, precisely, does Paul find "revealed" in Jesus Christ and how is that revelation related to eschatology? Only when we turn to Paul for the *internal* criteria that give substance and shape to the more generally derived (and ambiguous!) *external* criteria listed above may we begin to fathom what it means to call him, his thought, his way of arguing, or the effects of his argument "apocalyptic."

Pauline Apocalyptic: Discovery and Debate

We are helped in our quest for the distinctiveness of Paul's apocalyptic thought by three modern biblical theologians: Ernst Käsemann, J. Christiaan Beker, and J. Louis Martyn. Each goes beyond the earlier insights about the place of *future* eschatology in early Christian thought to show that early Christian apocalyptic, especially in Paul,

---

5. Sturm, "Defining the Word 'Apocalyptic,'" 36.
6. See the treatment of Galatians as apocalyptic in J. Louis Martyn, "Apocalyptic Antinomies in Paul's Letter to the Galatians," *NTS* 31, no. 3 (1985): 410–24.

while keeping the eschaton fully in view, radically redefines the relation between the end time and the present.[7]

Ernst Käsemann.   Käsemann's greatest contribution to the study of
apocalyptic may be his observation that apocalyptic has to do fundamentally with what he called "lordship," and therefore with the question, "To whom does sovereignty of the world belong?" The
apocalyptic battle being waged and won for the reign of God, he argued, is a battle that claims allegiances in the present. In Christian
apocalyptic, what is being revealed is that powers of the world which
are inimical to God are being subjected to him as the realm of this
world gives way to the "reign of Christ" (*basileia tou Christou*). In this
realm, which is coterminous with the church, says Käsemann, "the
powers, except death, . . . have lost the lordship to Christ, whereas
they still reign in the world which surrounds the Church."[8]

Life in the present remains "a stake in the confrontation between
God and the principalities of the world" which will finally be decided
at the parousia (second coming). Because the reign of Christ (*basileia
tou Christou*) which reflects God's sovereignty awaits completion in the
coming reign of God (*basileia tou Theou*), present existence can be understood only apocalyptically:[9]

> The believer . . . is still living through the pangs of the Messiah, free
> because he has been called once for all into sonship but menaced by
> the last enemy which is death and therefore by the cosmic principali-
> ties; these are continually striving to wrench him away from sonship
> and freedom, and so he is compelled continually to be reestablished in
> the *nova oboedientia* [new obedience].[10]

Käsemann has been criticized for placing too much emphasis on
the "expectation of the imminent Parousia" as the defining feature of
apocalyptic, but a review of his essays in Pauline theology suggests
more nuance. There he maintains the provisional character of the
revelation in Christ—the believer is still "menaced by the cosmic principalities," and even the lordship of Christ is destined to give way to

---

7. See Richard E. Sturm, "An Exegetical Study of the Apostle Paul's Use of the
Words APOKALYPTŌ/APOKALYPSIS: The Gospel as God's Apocalypse" (Ph.D. diss.,
Union Theological Seminary, 1983), 32–34.
8. Ernst Käsemann, "On the Subject of Primitive Christian Apocalyptic," in *New
Testament Questions of Today*, trans. W. J. Montague (Philadelphia: Fortress Press;
London: SCM Press, 1969), 134.
9. Käsemann, "Primitive Christian Apocalyptic," 134.
10. Käsemann, "Primitive Christian Apocalyptic," 136.

the lordship of God. At the same time, Käsemann emphasizes, there is the certainty that "the day of the End time has already broken" in the death and resurrection of Christ and that the realm of power defined by that revelation is signaled in the present by obedience. It is first through identification with Christ's death that one is enabled to participate in the *nova oboedientia*. But in Käsemann's reading of Paul, there is always a tension between the death on the one hand and the parousia on the other. The confrontation of the powers continues, demanding an answer to the question, "Who is Lord?"

> Man for Paul is never just on his own. He is always a specific piece of world and therefore becomes what in the last resort he is by determination from outside, i.e. by the power which takes possession of him and the lordship to which he surrenders himself.[11]

The confrontation, Käsemann is careful to say, involves more than human allegiances. The coming Day of the Lord will reveal God's sovereignty not only in the subjective experience of the believer but in the whole creation. The parousia, then, keeps Paul's gospel from a one-sided emphasis on salvation as a subjective human experience at the expense of its universal, cosmological scope. God's saving activity has to do with more than human beings here and now. It has also to do with the future redemption of God's whole creation.

The polemical edge of Käsemann's thesis reflects a division in Protestant theology created by Rudolf Bultmann's "demythologizing" of the New Testament. Bultmann recognized the apocalyptic tenor of early Christian texts, including Paul's, but declared the apocalyptic worldview obsolete, an impediment to the proclamation of the gospel in the modern world. To address the offense of apocalyptic, he rendered the questionable motifs in terms more acceptable to the modern mind. Eschatology was now translated into existential self-concern; both Jesus' and Paul's eschatological sayings were interpreted to mean that every hour is the "last hour," that is, the hour that demands human decision for authentic life in the present.

Käsemann, among others, engaged in a vigorous refutation of (his teacher) Bultmann's existentialist premises. For Käsemann, the transfer of emphasis from God's sovereign power (understood apocalyptically) to human decision (understood existentially) represented a fatal theological error which could be corrected only by the rediscovery of primitive apocalyptic itself.

---

11. Käsemann, "Primitive Christian Apocalyptic," 136.

In two bold propositions, Käsemann announced a direct connection between apocalyptic and the theology of the cross. The first is that "apocalyptic . . . [is] the mother of Christian theology,"[12] the second, that the heart of Paul's thinking is the "righteousness by faith" which is guaranteed by Jesus' death for the ungodly. Whoever enters into the apocalyptic realm of the *nova oboedientia* (new obedience) enters by way of the cross:

> For his [Paul's] teaching speaks of God only being "for us" when he destroys our illusions and delineates the new obedience of the man who surrenders his autonomy in order to await his salvation from God alone. . . . The dying Christ becomes creator of the new mankind by freeing us from the temptation to follow the way of the law on the one hand and from the rebel's despair on the other. He is the ground and sphere of reality of the justified.[13]

In a similar connection, Käsemann writes,

> The token which distinguishes his [Christ's] lordship from the lordship of other religious founders is undoubtedly the cross and the cross alone. . . . Following Jesus means, uniquely and unmistakably, becoming a disciple of the one who was crucified.[14]

To whom, then, does the sovereignty of the world belong? It belongs to the Crucified who became Lord by virtue of his death for the sake of the ungodly, thus ending the power of sin and freeing humanity for the *nova oboedientia*.

In his insistence on the primacy of apocalyptic in Paul's theology, its rootedness in the question of lordship, and in his emphasis on the imminent expectation of the parousia, Käsemann has set strong alternatives to Bultmann's existentialist reading of Paul. Although Käsemann, no less than Bultmann, credits Paul with the development of a new anthropology,[15] namely, a new understanding of humanity in light of apocalyptic, he does not allow that anthropology to be interpreted apart from its cosmological, apocalyptic context.

J. Christiaan Beker. In his major book on Paul, *Paul the Apostle: The Triumph of God in Life and Thought,* and in several other works, Beker has argued that apocalyptic constitutes the "coherent center" of

---

12. Käsemann, "Primitive Christian Apocalyptic," 137.
13. Ernst Käsemann, "The Saving Significance of the Death of Jesus in Paul," in *Perspectives on Paul,* trans. Margaret Kohl (Philadelphia: Fortress Press, 1969), 42.
14. Käsemann, "The Saving Significance of the Death of Jesus," 54.
15. Käsemann, "Primitive Christian Apocalyptic," 131.

Pauline theology. In its principal features, Beker's definition of apocalyptic is very like Käsemann's. For both, the apostle's expectation of an imminent parousia necessarily qualifies present eschatology and balances the existential dimensions of Paul's anthropology. But Beker sees different implications in the cosmological scope of Paul's "temporal apocalyptic mooring." For Beker, the emphasis in Paul's apocalyptic lies on God's imminent triumph, which will bring Christ's resurrection into focus as the beginning of the general resurrection of the dead, the signal of God's liberation of the entire created order (i.e., not just human beings). Beker agrees with Käsemann that neglect of the cosmic-temporal theme of Paul's thought leads to serious misconstruing of Paul's anthropology and understanding of the church. But he calls into question Käsemann's distinction between the reign of Christ (coterminous with the church) and the reign of God (set to redeem all creation).[16]

> Paul's church is not an aggregate of justified sinners or a sacramental institute or a means for private self-sanctification but the avant-garde of the new creation in a hostile world, creating beachheads in this world of God's dawning new world and yearning for the day of God's visible lordship over his creation, the general resurrection of the dead.[17]

Both person and church, already in fact incorporate in the created order, now through the resurrection of Christ come into solidarity with God's cosmic redeeming work. For Beker, as for Käsemann, the present time demands obedience from those who are claimed by God's gift and power. For Beker too, the existentialist reading of obedience as the "actualizing" of what Christ makes "*possible*" overemphasizes the human will and compromises the sovereignty of God. Beker's unique contribution is to work out the implications of this demand for Christian ethics. He writes,

> The imperative [of Christian obedience] is meaningful only in a world where death is still "the last enemy" and where hostile powers still threaten Christian existence. Moreover, the world's need for redemption inspires both the sighing of Christians and the imperative of their redemptive activity in the world. It stamps Christian life as both redemptively active and yet actively waiting for the Parousia of Christ.[18]

---

16. J. Christiaan Beker, *Paul the Apostle: The Triumph of God in Life and Thought* (Philadelphia: Fortress Press, 1980; paperback edition, 1984), 17.

17. Beker, *Paul the Apostle*, 155.

18. Beker, *Paul the Apostle*, 277.

In part because of his strong ethical focus, Beker questions Käse-mann's designation of the theme of "righteousness by faith" as the center of Paul's apocalyptic thought. Rather, he says, this theme should be considered as one symbol among others in Paul's "sym-bolic apocalyptic field."[19] Exclusive concentration on this symbol, Beker argues, confuses the gospel's "deep structure" with its "surface structure" and fails to recognize the contingencies of particular situa-tions in which Paul preached. "The symbol of 'righteousness' . . . is proper for the situation in Galatia and Rome, but it does not meet the needs in Corinth, where 'wisdom' is employed."[20]

Such a bold qualification of Lutheran theological presuppositions sets Beker's work apart not only from Käsemann[21] but from the ma-jority of Pauline interpreters who have viewed Paul through Refor-mation lenses. He poses a direct challenge for reading 1 Corinthians, too, when he claims that the "symbol" of "justification by faith" is nei-ther applicable to the community behind 1 Corinthians nor present in Paul's letter. We will take up this challenge along with its counter-part—Beker's argument for a concrete, participatory apocalyptic ethic—in our analysis of that letter's first two chapters.

J. Louis Martyn. Martyn too has built upon Käsemann's basic premises, and, like Beker, he has added his own emphases and alter-natives to them. But whereas Beker has pressed for more depth and clarity on apocalyptic ethics, that is, the relation between God's will to redeem the creation and how human beings participate in that will, Martyn focuses on the often disjunctive relation between what God has done/is doing and what people actually *perceive* or *know* God to be doing. Paul's own "apocalypse of Jesus Christ," Martyn notes, was a rev-elatory event with profound epistemological consequences. What he "saw" when Christ was "apocalypsed" to him forever changed the way he perceived all things. In several essays on Paul's letters to Galatia and Corinth, Martyn defines apocalyptic primarily as an epistemologi-cal category and explores, in ways that both amend and strengthen Käsemann's conclusions, how the revelation of Christ leads Paul to ar-ticulate an apocalyptic epistemology. In an essay that argues that Gala-

---

19. Beker, *Paul the Apostle*, xx.
20. Beker, *Paul the Apostle*, 18.
21. Käsemann ("The Saving Significance of the Death of Jesus," 32–33) makes the Reformation insight central to interpreting the cross in Paul.

tians is "thoroughly apocalyptic," Martyn defends his reliance on epistemological categories:

> Epistemology is a central concern in all apocalyptic, because the genesis of apocalyptic involves a) developments that have rendered the human story hopelessly enigmatic, when perceived in human terms, b) the conviction that God has now given to the elect true perception both of present developments (the real world) and of a wondrous transformation in the near future, c) the birth of a new way of knowing both present and future, and d) the certainty that neither the future transformation, nor the new way of seeing both it and present developments, can be thought to grow out of conditions in the human scene.[22]

One consequence of Martyn's definition is the recognition of some texts as apocalyptic that demonstrate few of the features commonly associated with that term. Indeed, a text like Galatians, although never before classified as apocalyptic,[23] shows us, according to Martyn, "precisely what the nature of Paul's apocalyptic was."[24] Of what he calls the letter's "cosmic announcements" in Gal 6:13 (i.e., Paul's testimony that he was crucified to the world and the world to him), Martyn writes,

> Here, Paul speaks of two different worlds. He speaks of an old world, from which he has been painfully separated by Christ's death, by the death of that world and by his own death; and he speaks of a new world, which he grasps under the arresting expression, New Creation.[25]

In Galatians, the perception of New Creation is linked primarily with the perception of Jesus' death. One who sees this link sees the dissolution of the old world and the initiation of the new already taking place.

Thus, for Martyn, the new way of knowing that characterizes Paul's epistemology is "knowing according to the cross (*kata stauron*)."[26] That Paul sees the cross as the center of the new perception is demonstrated in what is perhaps his most explicit epistemological statement:

---

22. Martyn, "Antinomies," 424 n. 28.
23. But see Martyn's observation ("Antinomies, " 421 n. 4) that Käsemann himself found apocalyptic theology everywhere in the Pauline epistles." Martyn cites Käsemann, "Primitive Christian Apocalyptic," 131.
24. Martyn, "Antinomies," 412.
25. Martyn, "Antinomies," 412.
26. J. Louis Martyn, "Epistemology at the Turn of the Ages: 2 Corinthians 5:16," in *Christian History and Interpretation: Studies Presented to John Knox*, ed. W. R. Farmer, C. F. D. Moule, and R. R. Niebuhr (Cambridge: Cambridge University Press, 1967), 264.

> From now on, therefore, we regard no one from a human point of view; even though we once regarded Christ from a human point of view, we regard him thus no longer. Therefore, if any one is in Christ, that one is a new creation; the old has passed away, behold, the new has come. (2 Cor 5:16-17)

The context of these verses demonstrates to Martyn that the turning point between the old and the new (the "once" and the "no longer") is none other than the death of Jesus; v. 15 makes it explicit: "And he died for all, that those who live might live *no longer* for themselves, but for him who for their own sake died" (2 Cor 5:15). Hence, in Martyn's view, Paul's principal contribution to apocalyptic, and the perception that drives his own mission, is that the cross has brought about the turning of the ages and, for those who can see it, the new and apocalyptic perception appropriate to the juncture between old and new.

Martyn's attention to the cross as the center of Paul's apocalyptic perception is occasionally balanced by mention of the parousia, but this future event does not have nearly the power to shape perception and behavior in Martyn's analysis as it has in both Käsemann's and Beker's analyses. About the relative weight Paul gives to the two events in Galatians, Martyn writes,

> The motif of the triple crucifixion—that of Christ, that of the cosmos, that of Paul—reflects the fact that through the whole of Galatians the focus of Paul's apocalyptic lies not on Christ's parousia, but rather on his death. There are references to the future triumph of God (5:5, 24; 6:8), but the accent lies on the central fact of the advent of Christ and his Spirit, and especially on the central fact of the advent: the crucifixion of Christ, the event that has caused the time to be what it is by snatching us out of the grasp of the present evil age (cf. 1 Cor 2:8).[27]

The impetus for Christian obedience in solidarity with God's redemptive plan, which Beker derives from Paul's expectation of the imminent triumph of God, is muted in Martyn's focus on what is already accomplished in the cross. While the perception of the turning of the ages is always a perception of battle between the powers of the Flesh and the powers of the Spirit (Gal 5:13, 16-17), the cosmic warfare that Martyn describes is never explicitly associated with human participation. Although "the space in which human beings now live is a newly invaded space, and that means its structures cannot remain

---

27. Martyn, "Antinomies," 420–21.

unchanged," Martyn is careful never to attach the perception of the "new space" to the notion of human possibility. The structures are changed or unchanged by a Power beyond human decision. A qualitative distinction between God and the human being prevails such that all language of ethics as the realm of human decision falls away.

Martyn's reticence to discuss the human response to the perception God grants in the cross has not prevented a number of attempts to move from his insights on Paul's apocalyptic epistemology to consideration of "applied apocalyptic."[28] John Koenig, for example, has argued perceptively from Martyn's conclusions on 2 Cor 5:16 that the chief consequence of knowing according to the cross, a consequence "more important even than the Corinthians' rededication to Paul and the truth of his gospel, is their fuller participation in God's cosmic reconciling activity."[29] Koenig takes Martyn's focal text in the essay "Epistemology at the Turn of the Ages," 2 Cor 5:16-21, to be a part of a larger discourse on the theme of knowing the "glory of God." In context, he argues, Paul is saying that "anyone who beholds the glory of the Lord, who walks by faith rather than by conventional sight, . . . as a result, both perceives and joins up with God's renewal of the cosmos."[30]

Other interpreters of Paul searching for applications of Martyn's apocalyptic have stayed closer to his own language (and Käsemann's). Katherine Grieb, for example, seeks to make the reconciling activity of the believer a function of being drawn involuntarily into Christ's realm of power. Grieb writes,

This power is never our own; we merely become witnesses to the power of the gospel in and over its servants.[31]

Similarly, Nancy Duff, drawing on both Käsemann and Martyn, writes,

There are no human actions apart from the powers that rule us. This does not mean that human beings are reduced to marionettes with no will of their own. It does mean that the self always acts in relation to a

---

28. The expression "applied apocalyptic" is used by Katherine Grieb in "Sacrifice at the Turn of the Ages: Applied Apocalyptic, or Paul's Use of Cultic Metaphor in Romans 12:2" (Paper presented at the Annual Meeting of the Society of Biblical Literature, San Francisco, November, 1992) 1.

29. John T. Koenig, "The Knowing of Glory and Its Consequences (2 Corinthians 3-5)," in *The Conversation Continues: Studies in Paul and John in Honor of J. Louis Martyn* (Nashville: Abingdon Press, 1990), 159.

30. Koenig, "Knowing of Glory," 164.

31. Grieb, "Sacrifice," 5.

power beyond itself. . . . Ethics is not centered in knowing what is the good, but in knowing who is our Lord.

Duff continues,

Christ is not a static ideal or principle. Christ is the living Lord who draws us into a new orbit of power.[32]

These discussions are not, of course, satisfying to everyone. The apocalyptic idiom that replaces human choice with irresistible "orbs of power" is simply too abstract for many to accept. And despite the disclaimer, "human beings are not reduced to marionettes," the reductionist charge lingers.

CONCLUSION

By now it is clear that even where there is consensus on the definition of apocalyptic as a theological category, there remains considerable disagreement on apocalyptic hermeneutics. First Corinthians gives us opportunity to explore the thorniest of the problems of "applied apocalyptic" unearthed and debated by Käsemann, Beker, and Martyn. Here we encounter a text that is fundamentally concerned to promote a new way of *being* in the world, namely, a way characterized by unity and reconciliation, by eliciting a new way of *knowing* "according to the cross."

In 1 Corinthians, we will see, the epistemological issues of the early chapters prepare for the explicitly ethical issues of later ones. The change of mind called for in 1 Corinthians 1–2 is inseparable from the description of embodied love and service outlined in chapters 3–14 and from the doctrine of the resurrected (and transfigured) body in chapter 15. Finally, the letter stands as a sustained argument for the cruciform unity of mind and body. To have the "mind of (the crucified) Christ" is also to be transformed in the body by Christ's self-giving and sovereign love and therefore to be "joined up with" God's reconciling action in Christ. In 1 Corinthians, Beker's concerns and Martyn's meet. And Paul blesses their union.

---

32. Nancy Duff, "Pauline Apocalyptic and Theological Ethics," in Marcus and Soards, *Apocalyptic and the New Testament*, 283 and 291.

2

The Word of the Cross as
Apocalyptic Disclosure

Paul's language about the cross is a specific kind of apocalyptic language. Without using the apocalypse genre, Paul adopts and adapts the essential theological perspective of that genre, namely, the perspective characterized by expectation of a future reign of God, confirmed by present revelatory experience.[1]

It is relatively easy to demonstrate that Paul typically articulates his understanding of the Christ-event in ideas and images drawn from Jewish apocalyptic thought, shaping these ideas to conform to the new historical circumstances articulated in the kerygma. He is as apt to use apocalyptic motifs in proclaiming what has *already happened* in the Christ-event as he is in speculating on future events (e.g., the return of Jesus at the parousia; see 1 Thess 4:13—5:12). For Paul, the new creation does not simply await the parousia but is already present in the transformed life of the believer and indeed, in a hidden way, throughout the cosmos (1 Cor 7:31; 2 Cor 5:16).

Corollary to Paul's belief that the new creation is present is his conviction that the forms of this world are passing away (1 Cor 7:31) and that the believer lives at a unique vantage point (2 Cor 5:16) from which to see both the dissolving of the old order and the emerging new cosmos.[2] Indeed, certain of Paul's rhetorical

---

1. That Paul expects a future end is obvious throughout his writings. Paul modifies apocalyptic themes, however, when he argues implicitly that, in the death and resurrection of Jesus, the reign of God is already breaking into the present. See 1 Cor 4:20; 7:31; 15:20-27; 2 Cor 5:16-17; 6:2.

2. In his treatment of 2 Cor 2:14—6:10, J. Louis Martyn has argued that what Paul advocates here is a way of knowing *kata stauron* ("according to the cross") that properly characterizes "epistemology at the turn of the ages." See J. Louis Martyn, "Epistemology at the Turn of the Ages: 2 Corinthians 5:16," in *Christian History and Interpretation: Studies Presented to John Knox*, ed. W. R. Farmer, C. F. D. Moule, and R. R. Niebuhr (Cambridge: Cambridge University Press, 1967), 269–87.

strategies seem designed primarily to make his hearers aware of their precarious stance between the ages. Among these strategies is his juxtaposition of the "already" with the "not yet" as in 2 Cor 5:16—6:2 and especially his unconventional treatment of conventional paradigms, for example, "In Christ there is no male or female, slave or free, Jew or Greek" (Gal 3:28), or "Let those who rejoice live as though not rejoicing, . . . for the form of this world is passing away" (1 Cor 7:29-31).

Careful observation of Paul's language about the emergence of the new creation within the structures of the old world reveals that his perceptual transformation begins with the image of the cross of Christ as the turning point between the ages.[3] Often when the cross appears in his letters, it is surrounded by apocalyptic and perceptual images that call for a new orientation to the old world. From the vantage point of the cross, Paul is able to proclaim God's victory over the powers of the old world while yet living provisionally in that world. Because for Paul the cross is the pivot between the ages (2 Cor 5:17-21), however, it is apt to generate misunderstanding before it generates new insight. From the conventional perspective of the old world, it is the symbol of suffering, weakness, folly, and death. But from the perspective of the new creation, it is the transforming symbol of power and life. The movement of his audience from the one perspective to the other through the re-presentation of the cross in preaching (the repetition of the kerygma) is Paul's persisting apocalyptic objective, not only in 1 Corinthians but throughout his writings. It is precisely this cross-inspired movement that we seek to understand.

SPEECH ACT THEORY AND 1 CORINTHIANS 1–2

One way to talk about the effects of Paul's Word of the Cross is to use his own language, the time-honored language of apocalyptic that is

---

3. J. Louis Martyn has coined the expression "bi-focal vision" to describe Paul's perception at the turn of the ages. He writes, "If we are to converse with Paul, we are required to speak of bi-focal vision, an expression not found, of course, in Paul's letters, but one which may help us to understand his letters. The dictionary defines 'bi-focal,' as regards eyeglasses, as a lens having two portions, one for near vision, one for far vision. In order to find a metaphor helpful to our interpretation of Paul, we will have to imagine looking simultaneously through both of these lenses. Looking in that manner would cause you to see everything in another perspective." See J. Louis Martyn, "From Paul to Flannery O'Connor with the Power of Grace," *Katallagete* 6 (1981): 12.

sounded whenever despair of the present order meets the hope of a new beginning. In these times, apocalyptic language may work not only to predict destruction but to elicit hope, to create new forms, to inspire new vision. In these times, apocalyptic language not only says something but does something in the saying. It does not merely describe a state of affairs, it produces hope.

Modern philosophers and literary critics have found other ways of talking about the power of words to effect conditions. The work of analytic philosopher J. L. Austin on what he called the "performative force" of certain utterances has inspired an array of inquiries from diverse quarters into how words "work." Not least among Austin's admirers is a growing number of biblical scholars who appreciate, among other things, the functional nature of his method and the freedom it offers the interpreter from both formalist and metaphysical preoccupations of other methodologies.[4] In addition to its place in the systematic application of Austin to biblical texts, the term "performative" has come to be used much as "word-event" language was used a few decades ago by interpreters like Ernst Fuchs and Gerhard Ebeling. To my knowledge, J. Louis Martyn was the first to apply the term in this way to 1 Corinthians when he wrote of the Word of the Cross as a "performative word."[5] But Martyn's use of "performative" is merely suggestive; he does not develop what he means by the term, or how, precisely, the Word of the Cross may be said to "perform" in 1 Cor 1:18.

My own efforts to evaluate the function of the Word of the Cross in Paul's discourse have been stimulated first by Martyn's "performative" suggestion. But because I was not satisfied with this merely suggestive use of the term, and because I am concerned to develop the *function* of Paul's preaching on the cross, I have undertaken a closer

---

4. Hugh C. White describes the attraction of literary critics to Austin's theory: "Literary critics have been attracted to speech act theory for two primary reasons. First the theory has opened the possibility of a functional approach to literature which is less encumbered with metaphysical presuppositions than previous theories of criticism. . . . Secondly, speech act theory offers the means to orient the reader away from various formalisms which detach the text from its historical and social matrix, toward its concrete context, without engulfing it once again in the psychological, social and historical conditions of its production" (Hugh C. White, "Introduction: Speech Act Theory and Literary Criticism," *Semeia* 41 [1988]: 2). In my own use of the theory, I wish to deny neither metaphysical implications of the text nor the importance of the historical conditions of its production. Speech act theory is certainly not "engulfed" by these concerns, but neither are they necessarily precluded by the methods that speech act theory engenders.

5. J. Louis Martyn, "Paul and His Jewish-Christian Interpreters," *USQR* 42 (1988): 1–15.

examination of Austin's work to determine just how his concept "performative" might apply to our text. Although I borrow from Austin's work very selectively, attending primarily to his insights about the conventions of language that enable it to function, I see enough parallels between Austin's performatives and Paul's apocalyptic presentation of the cross to make a formal comparison that I hope will enhance our understanding of how Paul's Word of the Cross works in a particular social and linguistic context.

Paul's proclamation of Jesus' death, I will argue, has what Austin calls "performative force" to effect in the minds of its hearers the transformation it narrates. While I claim only a modest usefulness for the application of Austin's ideas, I believe the theory does have value for enhancing our understanding of the Word of the Cross as a functional, indeed transforming, agent of the discourse as a whole.

In what follows, I will briefly review features of Austin's theory that are relevant to my interpretation. Then, with Austin's insights in mind, I will turn to the text itself to suggest how the performance of the Word of the Cross takes place.

Austin's Discovery: The "Performative Utterance"

Austin's most celebrated contribution to analytic philosophy is his division of spoken utterances into two classes that he took at first to be absolutely distinct. Constatives, he said, are utterances that state or describe something; their aim is to represent reality. "The cat is on the mat" is his best-known example of a constative. Other utterances, which he called "performatives," do more than describe reality; they aim to *do* something. Some performatives he called "illocutionary acts." These are utterances that *do* what they *say* in the saying, such as warnings, promises, and bets. Others, called "perlocutionary acts," bring about an effect in the hearer *by* the saying, such as when a speaker convinces, persuades, or intimidates someone. The perlocutionary act, Austin reasons, is the achieving of certain effects *by* saying something, while the illocutionary act has a certain (conventional) force *in* saying something.[6]

Austin thought it important to distinguish between these two kinds of performance. The difference turns on whether the utterance acts

---

6. J. L. Austin, *How to Do Things with Words* (Cambridge: Harvard University Press, 1962), 108–109.

in the saying or acts *by* the saying. The illocutionary capacity of an utterance to act *in* the saying depends entirely on the presence of conventions recognized and accepted by both speaker and hearer. The conventions that define marriage, for example, make it possible for the words "I do" to actually accomplish the joining of two people in marriage. Perlocutions, he thought at first, were nonconventional, although he admitted a certain tentativeness about defining conventions. "It is difficult to say," he admitted, "where conventions begin and end."[7]

As Austin's argument progresses in *How to Do Things with Words*, the sort of hedging he does on the precise definition of conventions extends more generally to the distinction between illocution and perlocution and finally even to the distinction between constatives and performatives. In fact, as he elaborates on this principal distinction, he begins to demonstrate the difficulty of holding to it absolutely and to show that many statements that appear to be constatives actually *function* as performatives. What appears to him first as the exceptional class, performatives, finally swallows the general class, constatives. One of Austin's most appreciative critics, Sandy Petrey, has captured this development in a particularly memorable way:

> Say John has a large piece of bright green vegetable matter stuck between his front teeth, while you, John, and a group of comparative strangers whom John wants to impress are discussing the federal budget deficit. If you interrupt the discussion to announce what you see to John and the others present, you have provided a description meeting all possible criteria of truth and accuracy. But it would be fallacious beyond belief to pretend that providing a description was the only thing you had done. Saying what is can effect a set of circumstances with every bit of transformational impact that Austin first invoked to show that words do things other than what they say.[8]

The surprising result of Austin's labors, then, is the demonstration that *all* language is potentially performative. Even statements of fact turn out to be acts of informing someone of something and the stating of a fact may have any number of effects on the one who is informed. Everything depends, he says finally, on the total speech act in the total speech situation:

---

7. Austin, *Words*, 118.
8. Sandy Petrey, *Speech Acts and Literary Theory* (London: Rutledge & Kegan Paul, 1990), 27.

In order to explain what can go wrong with statements we cannot just concentrate on the proposition involved (whatever that is) as has been done traditionally. We must consider the total situation in which the utterance is issued—the total speech-act—if we are to see the parallel between statements and performative utterances, and how each can go wrong.[9]

Despite his discovery of the performative potential of all normal speech, Austin insisted that *literary* language is by definition devoid of real illocutionary force:

A performative utterance will, for example, be in a peculiar way hollow or void if said by an actor on the stage, or if introduced in a poem, or spoken in soliloquy. This applies in a similar manner to any and every utterance—a sea-change in special circumstances. Language in such circumstances is in special ways—intelligibly—used not seriously, but in ways parasitic upon its normal use—ways which fall under the doctrine of the etiolations of language. All this we are excluding from consideration.[10]

Literary critics naturally question this exclusion of literary language from the category of true performatives. To Austin's example that "Walt Whitman does not seriously incite the eagle of liberty to soar," for example, Sandy Petrey responds,

Even if Walt Whitman doesn't "seriously" incite the eagle of liberty to soar, the influence of Whitman's poetry in the history of American discourse on liberty is a very serious matter indeed, as is the capacity of that discourse to do things with substantive impact on the reality of American life.[11]

Biblical critics have even more reason to object to Austin's exclusion, since, as sacred scripture, the Bible often operates in ways not simply mimetic or "parasitic" on real speech but as real world speech act.[12] Petrey suggests that Austin betrays his own best insights when he limits the realm of illocution to "normal" face-to-face oral speech and calls for an extension of the theory in line with Austin's own assimilation of constatives to performatives:

While Austin never did for the literary what he did for the constative— proclaim the speech-act character of what was originally excluded

---

9. Austin, *Words*, 52.
10. Austin, *Words*, 22.
11. Petrey, *Speech Acts*, 52.
12. Hence, the observation of Hugh C. White that "speech acts such as the promise of land, or the Sinai covenant, claim to be real world speech acts, in some sense, and not parasitic" (Hugh C. White, "Introduction: Speech Act Theory," 5).

from speech-act theory—those of us who have ignored his strictures about literature are respecting the spirit of his writings as we ignore the letter.[13]

Paul as "Speech-act"ivist

It is in this spirit, and recognizing the special claim of biblical literature to function as real world speech act, that I propose parallels between Austin's speech acts and the work of Paul's epistolary utterances, especially that extended utterance in 1 Cor 1:18—2:16 whose subject is "the Word of the Cross." Clearly, Paul uses the discourse on the cross to bring about effects in his hearers, the most obvious being the effect of reconciliation. Here and throughout his writings he seems to operate in the shadowy area between the two kinds of saying that Austin labeled "performative."

On the one hand, Paul's writing is filled with expressions that *do*, within certain conventions, carry the force of acts. "I . . . remind you . . . in what terms I preached to you" (1 Cor 15:1), for example, is an utterance that constitutes an act. Here Paul does more than report a fact; in saying, "I remind you," he actually does remind, provided his utterance invokes the conventions that allow the expression "I remind you" to function as a reminder in a given setting. Indeed, the very process of writing may be said to have illocutionary force. It is generally recognized, for example, that 1 Thessalonians functions largely as parenesis. Here Paul's writing *in order to instruct* itself *does* the instruction, and does so within shared conventions that define his speech act as parenesis.

On the other hand, Paul's letters often function as persuasive argumentation designed to achieve "certain effects by saying something," that is, Austin's perlocutionary act.[14] When Paul writes, for example, to the Thessalonians, "For I was gentle as a nurse" he uses a rhetorical figure to persuade the Thessalonians of his good intentions and of their own security in his care.[15] The expression itself does not do what it says, as the expression "I comfort you" might, and yet it may have the effect (among others, depending on the circumstances and conventions of the audience) of comforting.

---

13. Petrey, *Speech Acts,* 53.
14. Austin, *Words,* 121.
15. On this parenetic element in 1 Thessalonians, see Abraham J. Malherbe, "'Gentle as a Nurse': The Cynic Background to 1 Thess 2," *NovT* (1970): 203–17.

It is not easy, and perhaps not possible, to determine exactly what role Austin allows convention in perlocutionary acts once he begins to collapse the distinction between illocution and perlocution. Surely the conventions that define parenesis in 1 Thessalonians are distinct from institutional conventions that make the words "I do" work in a marriage ceremony. Yet, in both cases, the performance of the words spoken depends on rather specialized social and linguistic conventions.

When Paul writes letters that state astonishment or concern, affection or anger, he relies on conventions he shares with his audience to make his words meaningful. In a different but no less conventional manner in 1 Corinthians, he relies on agreement about certain conventionally paired opposites—for example, wisdom and folly—to show (and by showing, make effective) the end of the world conventionally described by those opposites.[16] As I will demonstrate in my treatment of 1 Corinthians 1–2, he uses convention to go *beyond* convention. Here, no less than in Austin's strictest illocution, the world after the performative utterance is not the same as it was before. By stating what the cross *is*, using conventional language unconventionally, Paul "speaks" the conditions of the new world.

My reading of 1 Corinthians 1–2 will be attentive to Paul's play on conventions of language defined more broadly than the strict institutional conventions that limit Austin's illocutionary acts. Finally, it is Austin's sensitivity to the transformative interaction of language with society, his recognition that words have power to *do* things within certain conventions, and not his minute distinctions among types of conventions that will be most useful for interpreting Paul's Word of the Cross as an apocalyptic speech act.

THE "TOTAL SPEECH SITUATION" AT CORINTH

Austin's attention to the "total speech situation" mirrors concerns for describing social setting and contextual meaning in biblical exegesis. If we are to see how Paul's message to the Corinthians depends on the potential of the Word he preaches to bring about perceptual

---

16. On the thought in antiquity that the structure of the cosmos lies in pairs of opposites and that Paul both presupposes and disrupts this conventional epistemology when he writes Galatians, see J. Louis Martyn, "Apocalyptic Antinomies in Paul's Letter to the Galatians," *NTS* 31, no. 3 (1985): 410–24, esp. 414 n. 12 and n. 13.

and behavioral transformation, it is necessary to set that Word, as nearly as possible, into the context of its original use.[17]

The Literary Context

I assume, first of all, that 1 Corinthians 1–2 functions as a unit devoted to the task of perceptual shift within the larger unit, 1 Corinthians 1–4.[18] This judgment is based in part on the movement of the discourse from the noetic division Paul notes in 1:10, "I appeal to you, . . . be united in the same *mind (en tō autō noi)*," to its opposite, the noetic denouement in 2:16, "But we have the *mind* of Christ (*nous tou Christou*)." Between these noetic markers, I suggest, Paul provides a strategy to facilitate the shift from the alienated and divided *nous* to the unified and reconciling *nous tou Christou*. While chapters 3–4 extend the experiential implications of the noetic shift and thus function within the same realm of discourse, *the shift itself* is the focus of chapters 1–2.

The Rhetorical Context

I take 1 Corinthians to be a unified composition[19] that arises apparently from a conflict between Paul and certain church members in Corinth in large part over what it means to be a *pneumatikos,* or "spiritual person." The presenting problem is disunity, news of which has reached Paul by the emissaries of Chloe. His response in chapter 1 suggests that the problem is related on the surface to issues of apostolic authority and baptism. Already in 1:12, we hear in the slogans, "I am of Paul," "I am of Cephas," "I am of Christ," that some in Corinth are boasting of their allegiance to one or another apostle or to Christ.

Paul's initial response to these claims comes in a series of rhetorical questions that function to discredit the claims themselves (1:13).

---

17. This is not the place to review the literature on the social-historical setting of 1 Corinthians. The brief summary offered here represents widely accepted views on the situation of the letter.
18. The larger unit is framed by the two appeals (*parakalō*) in 1:10 and 4:16. It is worth noting that the discourse on the cross between 1:18 and 2:16 is marked by the use of the first person plural.
19. For a summary of the arguments for the integrity of 1 Corinthians, see Werner G. Kümmel, *Introduction to the New Testament,* rev. ed. (Nashville: Abingdon Press, 1975), 269–79.

"Is Christ divided?" "Was Paul crucified for you?" "Were you baptized in the name of Paul?" In these questions, the grouping of references to division, crucifixion, and apostolic authority ("in the name of Paul") mirrors the concerns of the larger unit (1 Corinthians 1–4) where both the disunity born of boasting and apostolic authority are evaluated in light of the cross.

Verse 13 indicates that baptism, especially, had bred boasting among the congregants. There is scholarly speculation that the Corinthians were influenced by Hellenistic mystery cults or mystical traditions of Judaism that led them to elevate their baptizers to the position of mystagogues whose role was to teach them esoteric wisdom. All that is certain is that for *some* reason, Paul is careful to define his apostolic call as an exclusive call to *preach the gospel* and *not to baptize.*

Elsewhere in the letter, Paul seems to find the deeper cause for the Corinthian boasting in their excess of spiritual enthusiasm. In his own rhetoric, we hear overtones of theirs—for example, the catchwords he attributes to them: *sophia* ("wisdom"), *pneuma* ("spirit"), and *gnōsis* ("knowledge"). Claiming both superior knowledge (*gnōsis*) of God (8:1-2) and perfection (*teleios*) in the Spirit (2:6), Paul suggests, they separate themselves as an intellectual and spiritual elite (8:10-13), quarrel among themselves about the sources of their spiritual powers (1:10-16), and demonstrate their freedom in the Spirit by acting immorally (5:1-5) and disregarding the weak and the poor in the community (8:10-13; 11:17-22).

The Religious Context

There is evidence in the letter that the Corinthians appeal to certain combinations of pagan, Jewish, and Christian ideas favoring spiritual over bodily realities to provide the rationale for their ideology and behavior. While the precise contours of these parallel traditions will not be my focus, I assume that Paul's argument is designed with pointed references to them that would not be missed by his hearers. As we have already suggested, Paul punctuates his discourse with what appear to be the Corinthians' key terms and slogans, now turned ironically toward his own rhetorical purposes—for example, in 4:8: "Already you are filled! Already you have become rich. Without us you have kings!" and in 8:1: "We know that 'all of us possess knowledge.'" I take these slogans to indicate (at least) a Corinthian preoccupation with knowledge (*gnōsis*) as a spiritual endowment that separates some Christians (the *teleioi*) from others.

Over against the Corinthian preoccupation with an exalted spiritual *gnōsis*, Paul demonstrates another way of knowing that takes its bearings from the cross of Christ—"For I decided to know nothing among you except Jesus Christ and him crucified" (1 Cor 2:2)—construed as an event of apocalyptic import—"For the word of the cross is folly to those who are perishing, but to us who are being saved it is the power of God" (1 Cor 1:18).

As the Corinthians' perception is articulated in wisdom terminology, so is Paul's own way of knowing shaped and expressed by the language of apocalyptic. Because I take Paul's joining of apocalyptic language with the cross to be central to the performative function of his discourse, it is important to show where and how the association is made in his letters and to explore exactly what sort of apocalyptic language Paul employs.[20]

The Cross and Apocalyptic Motifs in 1 Corinthians 1–2

A survey of the cross (*stauros*) terminology in Paul's seven undisputed letters reveals that he often places the cross in an apocalyptic frame of reference.[21] While it is more concentrated in our letter than

---

20. Long before Paul's time, the motifs of perceptual transformation and apocalyptic were joined in Jewish literature. In Jewish apocalyptic texts, the visionary's perception of what is "really real" shifts before there is any change in the actual conditions of life. Because of what has been revealed, the seer is able to see and to proclaim the coming end of present worldly conditions and to encourage hope in a new world order (the "real world") to come. The new world the visionary announces is perceived, even experienced, before it is actual. See, e.g., 4 Ezra where complaint turns to praise (4 Ezra 13:48), and 2 Baruch's perceptual shift in 83:15. Paul follows in the tradition of his apocalyptic forbears when he proclaims, on the basis of a revelatory experience, the end of one world and the advent of a new creation. But for him, it is a historical event, the cross of Jesus Christ, that reveals the separation of old from new and marks the transition from one to the other. Thus, when Paul speaks in Galatians of his own transformation, he uses explicitly apocalyptic images, combined with a personalized language of the cross; the result of God's "apocalypse" of Jesus Christ to Paul is Paul's own death to the world (described as crucifixion) and his entry into the "new creation" (Gal 1:16; 6:14-15). Paul's experience of the Christ-event as apocalypse draws upon a Jewish apocalyptic worldview even as it extends the boundaries of the classical apocalyptic vision. What is now revealed and proclaimed is not only that the turning of the ages is at hand but that in God's action at the cross it has already decisively begun.

21. I have provided a more complete survey of the use of *stauros* in the Pauline corpus in my dissertation, Alexandra R. Brown, "Paul's Apocalyptic Word of the Cross: Perception and Transformation in 1 Corinthians 1–2" (Ph.D. diss., Columbia University, 1990), 44–62.

in others, the apocalyptic and perceptual context of *stauros* terminology in 1 Corinthians is consistent with what we find in other letters. Apocalyptic associations, for example, are most obvious (and familiar) in 1:18 and 2:8. In the first instance (1:18), end-time apocalyptic judgment is clearly in view as Paul shows the cross (or, more precisely, the *Word* of the Cross) to be the divider of humanity into two groups, the "ones being saved" and "the ones perishing." In the second instance (2:8), apocalyptic significance attaches in a more obvious way to the term "rulers of this age." A third apocalyptic motif in 2:8 is the reference to the *present* age (*aiōnos toutou*) which implies *another* age (opposite the ruler's age), and thus the two-age schema typical of apocalyptic thought (cf. Gal 1:4; 1 Cor 1:12; 2:6; 3:18; and 2 Cor 4:4).

The remaining references to the cross or crucifixion in 1 Corinthians imply apocalyptic significance in that they concern the true or false perception that arises from the cross as revelatory event. In 1:13, Paul protests the schismatic and misdirected allegiance of some he had baptized with the disclaimer, "Was Paul crucified for you?" thereby placing the cross of Jesus against all other systems of allegiance. Again, in 1:17, he places the cross at the center of his preaching in claiming that it is *solely* the cross of Christ, not baptism by any apostle (or baptism at all), that is the operative "power" in the experience of salvation. In 1:23 we find an echo of the cross as apocalyptic divider seen earlier in 1:18: "But we preach Christ crucified, a stumbling block to Jews and folly to Gentiles." Here, the ones separated by their misunderstanding are the Jews and the Greeks (i.e., the whole world) whenever what they seek (signs or wisdom) is not satisfied by the preaching of the cross. Finally, in 2:2, Paul makes a pointed autobiographical statement about the connection of the cross to *knowledge:* "I decided to know nothing among you except Jesus Christ and him crucified (*estaurōmenon*)."

The emphasis Paul places on the perceptual or epistemological effects of the cross in 1 Corinthians reflects not only the apocalyptic character of his own vision but also the special vulnerability of the gospel in the Corinthian context to perceptual error.[22] Indeed, Paul

---

22. The perceptual terminology in 1 Corinthians 1–2 is remarkably extensive. Below, I list what I take to be the operative vocabulary of perception in this text.

Greek	Translation	Text
aiteō	seek; ask	1:22
anakrinō	question; examine; discern	2:15
apodeixis	proof; demonstration	2:4

seems to locate the Corinthian error in an insufficient comprehension and experience of the cross. Thus, he adamantly emphasizes his role to "preach the gospel . . . lest the cross . . . be emptied" (1:17) and, over against their *gnōsis,* decides to "know *nothing* among [them] except Jesus Christ and him crucified" (2:2). As we focus more closely on 1 Corinthians 1–2, we will observe a rhetorical strategy custom-fitted to the vulnerabilities of this particular community and yet, by virtue of its enduring linguistic innovations, able to facilitate the apocalyptic performance of the Word even beyond this first-century context.

PAUL'S PERFORMATIVE STRATEGY

Paul's letters demonstrate that he often faces two kinds of challenge in any given "speech act situation." The first is the overt difference of opinion or perspective between himself and his audience which elicits the letter in the first place.[23] The second challenge involves the ambiguity of language; persuasive speech may convert an audience to another point of view which is yet not the point of view he intended. Paul's letters are full of instances in which he has preached

apokalypsis	unveil; reveal	1:7; 2:10
apokryptō	hide; keep secret	2:7
blepete	see	1:26
dexomai	accept; approve	2:14
didaktos	instructed	2:13
eidon	see; perceive	1:16; 2:2,11
eraunaō	search; examine	2:10
ginōskō	know	1:21; 2:8,14,16
gnōmē	intention; mind	1:10
gnōsis	knowledge	1:5
krinō	judge; consider; decide	2:1
mōrainō	make foolish	1:20
mystērion	mystery	2:1
nous	mind	1:10; 2:16
oida	know	2:12; 3:16
peithō	convince	2:4
phronimos	thoughtful; sensible	4:10
prooraō	foreknow	2:7
sophia	wisdom	1:17, etc.
sygkrinō	combine; compare	2:13
symbibazō	unite; conclude; instruct	2:16
synēsis	comprehension	1:19
zēteō	seek; consider	1:22

23. Elisabeth Schüssler Fiorenza, "Rhetorical Situation and Historical Reconstruction in 1 Corinthians," *NTS* 33 (1987): 386–403, esp. 393–94.

the gospel to an audience who is persuaded by it and yet suffer serious misperceptions about its meaning.[24]

Both types of challenge face Paul at Corinth. The overt challenge is dissension in the community. The more subtle challenge, which I believe is recognized by Paul, is that the Corinthians have assigned values different from Paul's own to certain key terms of the basic gospel message. For example, Paul's "word" (*logos*) reflects a specific content, that is, the cross event and its consequences, and a specific activity, that is, God's act of revelation.[25] The Corinthians' "word" (*logos*), on the other hand, is attached to some ideas about wisdom evidently not shared by Paul, given his sharp polemic against "wisdom of word" (*sophia logou*).

The juxtaposition of these two *logos* interpretations constitutes a subtle linguistic challenge. If the Corinthians were predisposed by their Hellenistic Jewish surroundings to associate wisdom with *logos*, it is possible that Paul has opened the door for the mishearing of his gospel by using the word *logos* in his initial preaching without clarifying his terms. Has he made the same mistake twice by using it again here in his opening argument (1:18) where he might have used "gospel" (*euangellion*) or *kērygma* to express the same concept? It is my opinion that Paul deliberately takes this risk in order (*a*) to draw the Corinthians' *logos* into the service of his theology of the cross and (*b*) thereby to effect the transformation of the Corinthians' own use of the term. But Paul is concerned with more than mere linguistic transformation. As the argument proceeds from 1:18, it becomes clear that he intends to make way for the Word's transformation of human consciousness which was the hallmark of his own apocalyptic experience (Gal 1:16; 2 Cor 5:17).

---

24. See in particular Paul's correspondence with the Galatians. For a skillful and persuasive treatment of 1 Corinthians as deliberative rhetoric accomplished through "comparison with the conventions for the invention and arrangements of arguments in rhetorical conventions in Greco-Roman antiquity," see Margaret M. Mitchell, *Paul and the Rhetoric of Reconciliation: An Exegetical Investigation of the Language and Composition of 1 Corinthians* (Louisville: Westminster/John Knox Press, 1991), 6.

25. A survey of Paul's use of the term *logos* reveals that in nearly every case where he uses it substantively, it is the equivalent of the term "gospel." Thus we see that the content of *logos* is the death and resurrection of Jesus and/or the saving effects of these events (see 1 Thess 1:5; 2:13; 4:15; Phil 1:14; 2:16; 2 Cor 2:17; 8:7; 10:10; 11:6; Gal 5:14; 6:6; Rom 9:6, 9, 28; 13:9; 14:12; 15:18). Moreover, the *logos* is, for Paul, an active agent. It "sounds forth" (1 Thess 1:8), "works among believers" (1 Thess 2:13), calls the church to unity of mind (Phil 2:5-11), gives life (Phil 2:16), acts as God's agent for reconciliation (2 Cor 5:19), and judges by continually electing and rejecting (Rom 9:28). In all of its attributes, the *logos* reveals divine power to save, to unify, to reconcile through its proclamation of the cross and resurrection.

The Strategy of Oddly Paired Opposites

In the first seventeen verses of 1 Corinthians 1, Paul introduces nearly every major theme of the letter,[26] including the themes of perception (1:5, 10), apocalypse (1:7), the cross (1:13), and spiritual gifts (1:7). Already in these verses he begins the play of opposites and ironies that dominates the discourse. Then, in v 17, he states the central polemic:

> For Christ did not send me to *baptize* but to *preach* . . . , and not with *eloquent wisdom*, lest the cross of Christ be *emptied*.

In his arrangement of the two pairs of terms, on the one hand, "baptize/preach" and on the other, "wisdom/emptiness," Paul anticipates both the strategy and the content of his message. In each paired opposite he sets something exalted by the Corinthians against something not exalted by them. Thus, *baptism* and *wisdom*, both elevated by the Corinthians, are opposed to *kerygma* and *cross emptiness*. Simultaneously, we find a subtle and subversive *equation* of "wise words" (*sophia logoi*) (again something exalted in the Corinthians' world) with emptiness (*kenos*). Paul's performative strategy is anticipated in his play on conventional opposites and especially his subversion of the catchwords "baptism" and "wisdom." The world in which these terms play second to the cross is a world dramatically restructured. While the exact *content* of his "preaching" is left unstated, its subject is clear—he is sent to preach "lest the cross of Christ be emptied."

The strange pair of opposites introduced in 1:17, empty "wise words" (*sophia logoi*) versus the "not emptied cross" ("*hina mē kenōthē ho stauros*"), becomes the governing motif of the discourse that runs from 1:18 to 2:16. I am in agreement with the now widely held opinion that Paul's use of the terms *sophia, logos,* and *gnōsis* in the text reflects his polemic against a type of wisdom theology that was influential in Corinth.[27] I am further inclined to agree with those who describe the Corinthian wisdom theology as "protognostic," that is, not yet reflecting a fully developed gnosticism, but already emphasizing the soteriological powers of *gnōsis*. This would explain the urgency of Paul's appeals to perception; he opposes a tradition that not only prides itself on having already attained the perfect *gnōsis* of God and,

---

26. Notably absent in the thanksgiving section (1:4-9) is reference to *sophia*, one of the gifts evidently being claimed by the Corinthians.

27. Numerous studies have attempted to describe this wisdom theology. There is general consensus that it was "pregnostic" or "protognostic."

hence, having already realized the resurrection in the present, but one that is gaining considerable territory in the Christian mission.

Whatever the exact contours of the Corinthian wisdom, my focus here is on how Paul addresses the ideology he encounters at Corinth. In what I take to be a deliberate rhetorical strategy, he allows the Word he preaches to make its first inroads into the consciousness of his hearers by disrupting standard expectations about the structure of language and, hence, the world. Then, in a related but different strategy, most evident in 2:6-16, having once disrupted the received linguistic paradigm, he goes on to subvert particular terms within the old paradigm toward the service of a new perceptual model. Using convention to go beyond convention, he prepares his hearers for transformation.

The Performance as a Drama in Two Acts

What makes Paul's Word of the Cross an event that accomplishes "salvation" or "destruction" is not merely the shared knowledge of speaker and hearer about how the language works (its conventions), nor merely the necessary agreement about how the utterance is to be understood, but what the Word actually *says*. The Word of the Cross, like Austin's performatives, is effective in more than the pragmatic sense of activating the conventions shared by speaker and hearer; it does something more to the perception of the hearer. It points the hearer toward another reality, governed by a new image of who God is, namely, the One who is present in the cross event.[28]

The two functions of Paul's message—the destructive function, accomplished through his unconventional use of standard conven-

---

28. In recent essays on the theology of 1 Corinthians, both Gordon Fee and Victor Paul Furnish have emphasized the element of divine self-disclosure in the cross. Fee writes, "Thus in his crucifixion Christ not only effected salvation for the called, but ultimately revealed the essential character of God, which is revealed further in the servant character by Paul's apostleship (3:5; 4:1-2, 9-13)." Gordon Fee, "Toward a Theology of 1 Corinthians" (Revised version of paper delivered at the One Hundred Twenty-seventh Annual Meeting of the Society of Biblical Literature, 1991), 5. See the similar emphasis in Furnish: "Paul is not interpreting Jesus' death on the cross as an act of atonement for sins, even though such an idea surfaces elsewhere in the letter (15:3; cf. 8:11; 11:24). Rather, his point is that specifically the crucified Christ discloses the nature of God's power and wisdom. The cross is thus definitive for a properly Christian understanding of God." Victor Paul Furnish (Revised version of paper delivered at the One Hundred Twenty-seventh Annual Meeting of the Society of Biblical Literature, 1991), 11. Both essays are included in *Pauline Theology, Volume 2: 1 and 2 Corinthians*, ed. David M. Hay (Minneapolis: Fortress Press, 1993).

tions, and the constructive function, the construction of the new mind—may be understood as two "acts" in the dramatic performance of the text. In act 1, the Word of the Cross works to expose and "de-center" the perceptions of the hearer. This de-centering is the first step in its powerful and transformative play against what Paul calls the "wisdom of the world." At the next level of the discourse, the burden of Paul's rhetoric is to clear a path through the rubble of his hearers' now-deconstructed language, building a new framework for perception. Act 2 of the drama brings the completion of the new structure—in our text, Paul's refiguring of the terms wisdom and folly, power and emptiness, psyche and spirit—and invokes the power of the Spirit, already at work throughout act 1, to bring the hearer into the transformed mind. In act 2, the one who was seized by the cross in the first act now grasps what seized him.[29] Now in possession of the "mind of Christ," this one embodies the power of the cross to work toward salvation.

The whole progression has the quality of incitement and persuasion. I do not mean to suggest a "magic" moment of transformation that happens literally just as the hearer arrives at the final verse, "But we have the mind of Christ." Nor do I see the two acts as defining "an actual shift from text to Spirit as the effective agent of change."[30] Both text and Spirit are at work thoughout the discourse. What I mean to suggest, rather, is that Paul, like Walt Whitman inciting the eagle to fly, incites the Corinthian hearer to "have the mind of Christ" and by his arrangement of words and images provides the deconstructive apparatus that frees the "eagle," that is, the liberating message of the cross, from captivity to the world.

Performance as Repetition: Paul's Earlier Preaching in Corinth

The total speech situation in Corinth, it must be said, includes Paul's first preaching there and his founding of the church whose members he calls "saints" in 1:2 and whose endowment with spiritual gifts he

---

29. This way of expressing what happens in 1 Cor 2:6-16 comes from Gerd Theissen, *Psychological Aspects of Pauline Theology* (Göttingen: Vandenhoeck & Ruprecht, 1983; Philadelphia: Fortress Press, 1987), 352. The expression "They grasp what seized them" says (and does?) more in German—"Sie begreifen, was sie ergriffen hat"—where the verb *ergreifen* connotes not only arrest, seizure, but also to be moved by feeling, altered, changed.

30. From Jouette Bassler's unpublished response to my paper, "Seized by the Cross: The Death of Jesus in Paul's Transformative Discourse" (SBLASP; Atlanta: Scholars Press, 1993), 3.

recognizes (1:5-7).[31] For this congregation, then, *a transformation of consciousness has already occurred.* Yet, the transformation has been incomplete, as their quarreling and divisions now demonstrate. The disjuncture between their being called (1:1, 24) and their *appropriation* (perceptually and ethically) of that calling is what Paul brings into bold relief and what gives power to his unconventional and destabilizing pairings of opposites. To those who have accommodated the gospel to worldly preferences, who have made it into a message of exalted knowledge and spiritual power and by so doing have failed to embody the very different power of downward moving, suffering love exemplified in the cross, Paul presents a disturbing equation: the folly of the cross is the power of God. Whoever believes that their calling is otherwise constructed has rested faith in the wisdom of human beings and not in the power of God (2:5). In Corinth, Paul encounters the faith he founded gone astray, captured by the world. Now he attempts the most difficult sort of transformative discourse, the correction of a prior speech act that has misfired. To those who think they already "have it," the gospel must be preached again in such a way as to bring to light the misfire and to put the Word of the Cross back on target in perception and action.

In the next chapter we will follow Austin's insight that language performs or does not in particular linguistic settings and under special conditions that determine both the meaning and the power of what is being said. We have seen that the Corinthians operate in a language world that gives preeminence to the terminology of "wisdom" and "knowledge." Paul, too, comes from a cultural and religious setting that values the wisdom tradition and the ways of knowing this tradition promotes. His response to the Corinthian "wisdom" reflects his knowledge of Hellenistic Jewish wisdom traditions popular in his day no less than it reflects his apocalyptic heritage. These two streams of tradition, wisdom and apocalyptic, are at some points in concert and at others in conflict, a fact Paul exploits for the articulation of his own apocalyptic wisdom of the cross.

In order to understand the exchange between the Corinthian "wise" and Paul—to get at what Austin calls the "total speech situation" represented by our text—we must investigate the complex of wisdom and apocalyptic traditions that have informed their respective positions.

---

31. Jouette Bassler has pointed out to me the increased complexity of the speech situation in 1 Corinthians due to the fact that Paul has already preached a transformative (and at least partly successful) word among the Corinthians. Brown, "Seized by the Cross," 2.

3

"What the Cook Draws from the Larder": The Context of the Performative Word in Corinth

Time and again in Paul's missionary journeys he meets and collides with the old world. Often this world appears in the forms of religious traditions that, in his view, cannot be accommodated to the gospel of the cross. Both Paul and his hearers are indebted to Jewish and Greek traditions; even the "new creation" remains *in* the world, if not *of* it. But Paul's experience has made him acutely sensitive to the interpretation of those traditions, especially when he thinks a particular interpretation compromises the gospel. This is sharply evident, for example, in Galatians where Jewish traditions about circumcision are being prescribed for Christians. On the premise that the Christ-event has made the law of circumcision obsolete, Paul opposes such interpretations vigorously. On the other hand, the apocalyptic theology of his Jewish heritage is still usable for Paul, although it is now reassessed in the light of what to him is the decisive apocalyptic event—the life, death, and resurrection of Jesus Christ.

First Corinthians gives evidence of at least one tradition-based interpretation which, like Christian law observance in Galatians, collides with Paul's gospel. The identification of this other tradition has long occupied interpreters of 1 Corinthians and remains in question. It is safe to say, however, that whatever its precise contours, this tradition placed a high value on wisdom and evaluated human beings according to the measure of wisdom they possessed.

A possible source (although probably not the only source) of this wisdom theology at Corinth—especially if Luke-Acts is correct that certain members of the church were former leaders of the synagogue—is the Jewish wisdom tradition. There is ample indication in our text that both the Corinthians and Paul are at least indirectly influenced by a hellenized form of Jewish wisdom theology. Yet, one must note, in 1 Corinthians and in other literature of the period, this tradition is not present in isolation from others. In our text, wisdom is quite clearly joined to apocalyptic and perhaps to certain other Hellenistic philosophical or mystical traditions. But it is unclear on the surface of the text what the function of such joinings may be for Paul or for his audience. One possibility is that the joining of wisdom and apocalyptic traditions functions in one way for Paul and in a very different way for the Corinthians and that the difference has to do with the role of the cross in their respective Christologies.[1] For both, certainly, traditional language is put in the service of interpreting Christ. But their differing views on the content and consequences of knowing Christ—and knowledge is the clear focus of our passage—reflect not only conflicting Christologies but very different ways of construing both tradition and present reality.

SPEECH ACTS IN CONTEXT

Although it is not possible to meet all of Austin's criteria for determining the "total speech situation" of Paul's discourse at Corinth, we may gather clues from our text and from other texts of the period that enable us to make informed and productive judgments about how Paul's word may have "performed" in its context. We discover in the process that despite the clear influence of both wisdom and apocalyptic traditions in 1 Corinthians 1–2, the task of interpreting exactly what ideas or movements influenced the Corinthians, and in what configurations, is very difficult. This is due in part to the great diversity of religious movements that found their way to first-century Corinth[2] and in part to the tendency of modern interpreters to read our own cultural values into the text. Exegesis of 1 Corinthians, because of its place in Reformation history, often reflects, sometimes

---

1. For a helpful analysis of the joining of wisdom and apocalyptic traditions in Paul, see Elizabeth Johnson on Romans 9–11, "The Function of Apocalyptic and Wisdom Traditions in Romans 9–11" (Ph.D. diss., Princeton Theological Seminary, 1987).

2. J. Murphy-O'Connor has recently compiled ancient texts about Corinth that testify to the religious pluralism that characterized Corinth in the Hellenistic period. Philo, writing in the first century, makes reference to Corinth as the home of a Jewish community. Pausanius sometime later (160–185 C.E.) makes frequent reference to Greek religious sites and to the myths and practices that accompany them. Temples and statues to Aphrodite, Artemis, Athena, Nike, Dionysus, Tyche, Hermes, Apollo, and Zeus are described, as are various indicators of the imperial cult. See J. Murphy-O'Connor, *St. Paul's Corinth: Texts and Archeology* (Good News Studies 6; Wilmington, Del.: Michael Glazier, 1983).

inadvertently, Reformation doctrine. Similarly, the monumental discovery of the Coptic library at Nag Hammadi in our century has inspired a generation of scholars to seek Gnosticism at the heart of early Christianity and its controversies and to find a significant proof text in 1 Corinthians.

Although we are concerned principally with the ancient contexts of the debate in Corinth that shaped what Paul said and what his hearers heard, we will proceed with awareness of and occasional references to the twentieth-century contexts that shape what we hear. In modern interpretations of Paul, no less than in Paul's interpretations of *his own* inherited traditions, we find the constant shaping of words and their meanings by the linguistic contexts into which they fall.

Cultural Influences in Corinthian Christianity

The vocabulary of 1 Cor 1:17—2:16 confirms that the Corinthians' ways of knowing Christ were at least partially expressed in their claims to *sophia* (wisdom). Whether this *sophia* reflected more the personified wisdom figure of Wisdom of Solomon and Sirach or the speculative or rationalist philosophy of the Greco-Roman world is impossible to discern from our text which allows *sophia* a wide range of meanings. Paul's language suggests ambiguity even in his own understanding of wisdom. On the one hand, he can deny "speaking wise and persuasive words" (1 Cor 2:4), as if he meant to avoid the rhetorical traditions of Greek philosophy. On the other hand, when he speaks of Christ as "the wisdom of God," he recalls the personified wisdom in Jewish literature; like a philospher or sage, he claims to impart a certain wisdom among the mature, but immediately he qualifies that wisdom as the "secret and hidden wisdom of God," available only through the mediation of the Spirit.

Similar ambiguity attends Jewish texts of the Hellenistic period, where contact between Greeks and Jews has encouraged the development of apologetic literature comparing Jewish wisdom (and Torah) to the highest philosophical wisdom of the Greeks. It is likely, then, that the wisdom "theology" at Corinth, whether expressed by Paul or by those with whom he disagrees, is heir to both Jewish and Greek ideas about *sophia*.

The other stream of tradition standing prominently in the background of 1 Corinthians is Jewish apocalyptic. In 1:7, Paul anticipates the *"apokalypsis* (revelation) of our Lord Jesus Christ"; in 1:10 and

5:5, 13, he uses the eschatological concept, the "day of the Lord"; in 1:18, he depicts the Word of the Cross as apocalyptic divider of the saved from the perishing; in 7:26, he makes reference to the eschatological "distress" (*anankē*) typical of apocalyptic scenarios; and in chapter 15, he relies on apocalyptic motifs to articulate his teaching on the resurrection of the dead.

The presence and the prominence of these apocalyptic images make one wonder how the mixed audience of Jews and Gentiles at Corinth would have heard Paul's message. Would the non-Jews among them have had any preparation for an apocalyptic discourse? While it seems unlikely that Paul's language would be intelligible to them without some acquaintance with, perhaps even *acceptance of*, certain apocalyptic presuppositions, the letter suggests that some had views on ultimate matters that differed substantially from Paul's apocalyptic perspective. Opposing his firm insistence on the not-yet-completed aspect of God's intervention in the present age (e.g., 1:7; 7:31), some boasted already of possessing "wisdom in this age" (3:18), and some claimed "already" to be "filled" (4:8). Some evidently used the slogan, "All of us possess knowledge" (*gnōsis*) (8:1), and some denied the future (bodily) resurrection of the dead (15:12).

Perhaps the formulators of these ideas were Christians for whom Paul's apocalyptic images found little resonance from the time of his first preaching in Corinth. For these, a felicitous "speech situation" may have required a more nuanced presentation of apocalyptic themes, particularly as they relate to the cross, than Paul had at first offered. Perhaps the hellenized Corinthians, steeped in the world-transcending philosophies of their age, tended to translate apocalyptic ideas, which in Judaism never ceased to be historical, into antihistorical terms, thereby diminishing the historical Christ, and especially his crucifixion.

Wisdom and Apocalyptic as Ways of Knowing

Our primary interest is in one question shared by wisdom and apocalyptic thinkers long before Gnosticism arrived on the scene: "What can human beings know (or perceive) about God and God's ways with the world?" The Corinthians were keenly interested in this epistemological question, and it is reasonable to imagine that wisdom and apocalyptic traditions enter Paul's discourse in response to particular forms of the question being raised in Corinth. Note, for example, how Paul punctuates his argument with pointed references to epistemological terms and slogans current in Corinth now turned ironically to his own purposes, for example, in 8:1-3, "We know that 'all of us possess knowledge,'" to which Paul replies, "Knowledge puffs up, but love builds up. Anyone who claims to know something does not yet have the necessary knowledge; but anyone who loves God is known by [God]" (NRSV). No other Pauline letter displays such interest in *what* and *how* one "knows," and none other brings so prominently and polemically into play the epistemologies of the wisdom and apocalyptic traditions. In his effort to effect a perceptual reorientation at Corinth, Paul must take account of those conventional structures of knowing that will determine how his Word of the Cross is heard and appropriated.

It is a commonplace that conventional ways of knowing sometimes give way to new ways of knowing that would have been unimaginable before some event or perception necessitates a change. Many of us have experienced the sort of crisis that forever changes our ways of viewing the world. More commonly, our shifts from one world to another occur gradually over time. One day we realize that on this issue or that, or perhaps on a whole set of issues, our minds have changed.[3]

The two bodies of literature that we will explore here give us glimpses of two ways in which Israel managed the epistemological question—one called wisdom and the other apocalyptic—and how these ways of knowing came to be variously amended and combined as national crises or more subtle changes imposed the collective changes of mind now inscribed in each tradition's literature. Both traditions are self-consciously concerned with epistemology, that is, with questions of how one knows God, self, and world, and especially with the value of knowledge for salvation. Both, therefore, are characterized by a vocabulary rich in the language of perception, a feature that, not coincidentally, also characterizes 1 Corinthians.

Four general questions about the content and accessibility of knowledge will guide our inquiry into each of the traditions:

---

3. For helpful discussions of perception change in sociological perspective by which my own ideas have been informed, see Peter L. Berger and Thomas Luckman, *The Social Construction of Reality: A Treatise in the Sociology of Knowledge* (Garden City, N.Y.: Doubleday & Co., 1966). For a good application of sociology of knowledge to Christian theology, see C. Daniel Batson, J. Christiaan Beker, and W. Malcolm Clark, *Commitment without Ideology* (Philadelphia: United Church Press, 1973).

1. What can/do human beings know or perceive about God and God's way with the world?[4]
2. How is this knowledge communicated?
3. Who may receive or comprehend this knowledge?
4. Why is such knowledge desired or sought?

THE WISDOM TRADITION AND THE SEARCH FOR KNOWLEDGE

In the early wisdom tradition (e.g., Proverbs) the content of wisdom is generally associated with observable phenomena in nature and human relations or, if hidden, with a divine initiative toward self-revelation. In both cases, Wisdom wants to be known and seeks out her knowers. When Job and Qoheleth face the distance or even the loss of an organizing order that they associate with Wisdom, their voices sound nevertheless within the boundaries of conventional understandings of Wisdom's manifestation and hiddenness. In short, in none of the early wisdom texts is Wisdom finally hidden. Wisdom is always in the process of making herself known (e.g., Proverbs 8).

By the late Second Temple period, the wisdom texts of Sirach, Baruch and Wisdom of Solomon present Wisdom's hiddenness in contexts similar to those of earlier tradition (compare Sirach 24 to Proverbs 8), but now we see a subtle change—hiddenness is more the rule than the exception. In these texts we are impressed by the presence of a new vocabulary; "mystery," "secrets," and "revelations" become standard features of wisdom speculation.

The development of the language of mystery arises within a larger effort to define Jewish wisdom in a new and more cosmopolitan intellectual milieu. Despite (or perhaps because of) the cultural and intellectual challenges they face, the wisdom writers of this new age do not succumb to the pessimism that had threatened the wisdom theologies of Qoheleth and Job. Rather, in the struggle to say just what this hidden wisdom *is* and to explain its hiddenness, these writers develop a revelation theology that finds wisdom both within and (more often) outside the human realm and yet affirms wisdom's availability to human beings through various modes of divine revelation. Again, in this development, older wisdom themes are taken over, but they

---

4. In the wisdom corpus, this question often is couched in wisdom language, i.e., "What is wisdom?"

are amended, enhanced. That wisdom is revealed and/or self-revealing, then, is a typical feature of this literature. But exactly what is that wisdom? *How, to whom,* and for *what purpose* is wisdom revealed? To these questions, late Second Temple period texts offer several diverse but related answers.

Sirach

As in the earlier literature, wisdom in Sirach is generally synonymous with divine order. One who seeks to understand the cosmic and moral structure of the world and the human role in that structure pursues wisdom, and in that pursuit perceptively observes the natural world. Two new elements appear in Sirach's wisdom profile, however. One is the linking of wisdom's ordering function explicitly with the Torah; the other is the related development of the sage as one who is uniquely inspired by God to receive and interpret the mysteries of Torah (e.g., Sir 39:6 and 51:1-30).

The linking of wisdom with Torah occurs at several levels in the text. At some points, the connection is made directly; in Sir 6:24, wisdom is described as a yoke, a term that here and in 51:25-26 serves as a double reference to both wisdom study and Torah observance. The two activities are virtually equated in Sirach 6:

> Reflect on the *statutes of the Lord,*
> and meditate at all times on his *commandments.*
> It is he who will give insight to your mind,
> and your desire for *wisdom* will be granted. (Sir 6:37)

Similarly direct equations of wisdom and Torah are made in Sir 1:26; 19:20; 24:25-26; and 39:1. What is perhaps the pivotal text for this equation is 24:1-34, where Wisdom's descent to earth is described. Displaying characteristics that recall the descending Wisdom of Proverbs and Job (compare Sir 24:5 to Job 38:16), Wisdom now does something radically new—after vainly seeking a dwelling among others, she finds a resting place in Zion where she now appears as Torah (24:23).[5]

Like Woman Wisdom in Proverbs 8 (where wisdom is not associated with Torah), Sirach's Wisdom is a wooer of humanity, rushing out to meet disciples on the way, turning aggressively to them as

---

5. Cf. 1 Enoch 42:1, where we find wisdom's rejection on earth and relocation in heaven.

eager lover or solicitous mother (Sir 15:2-8; 24:19-22). While it is her association with Torah that defines her resting place as Zion (2:7-12), she yet retains her universal identification with the created order (1:4, 9). Wisdom is named the "first" of God's creations; she is "poured out upon *all* God's works" (1:9). In images that recall the Genesis creation account and particularly the role of the *ruah* ("wind" or "spirit") in that account, Wisdom in Sirach covers "the earth like a mist" (24:3). Wisdom is, in short, manifested supremely in creation (42:15-25; 43:1-33).

Ben Sira's conviction that wisdom is at once universal in creation and particularly situated in Torah determines his approach to the persistence of life's moral ambiguities. He begins with cosmic structures; God has structured the world, including the parts of the human soul, in pairs of opposites (33:15). As one consequence of this structure, the human being is possessed of two "inclinations," the good and the evil. These inclinations war against each other, leaving the human being in the tension of life's moral opposition, constantly challenged to choose between two ways (5:2; 5:14 and 8:7-8; 33:20-23). Yet, as is fitting in a creation so ordered, there is an "opposite" even to this confusion. There is Torah and there is the sage who is gifted by God to seek out Torah's hidden meanings and to "pour forth words of wisdom" (39:6). The sage is a guide to the perplexed, an interpreter of the letter of the law and of its deep mysteries (39:1-4). To the sage alone is Wisdom manifested in her fullness (6:22).

In effect, then, Sirach reveals a type of epistemological hierarchy. At the lower ranks of society, among the simple, Wisdom is known in the created order, but there she is known only in part. In the face of spiritual and moral ambiguities, people must rely on the knowledge of the sage for guidance. This wise interpreter of Torah's mysteries (43:33), along with students who are "willing to be taught" (6:32), becomes the arbiter of knowledge for all. His is the authoritative model of the divine order—the "way of Yahweh" (51:27). It is only the ungodly who cannot know something of the divine, cosmic order; this is their curse (41:8).

Sirach answers all four of our questions at least indirectly. *What* can be known is the divine order of creation and the Torah as the authoritative guide to that order. Such knowledge or wisdom is necessary for a meaningful and godly life (*Why*). Although this knowledge is poured out on all creation, in its fullness it is reserved for the sage who seeks it through diligent study of Torah. But the uneducated one is not lost. The sage is a guide to the perplexed, an interpreter of the law and of its deep mysteries (39:1-4) (*How* and *Who*).[6]

The shifts in wisdom perspective at this point are subtle. The development of the sage as interpreter of the increasingly opaque and increasingly elevated Torah, however, hints at changing circumstances in Israel, circumstances that suggest the encounter of new realities, perhaps the social and cultural dislocations of Hellenism, that challenge the simpler equations of conventional wisdom.

Baruch

Embedded in Baruch is a wisdom psalm that shares certain themes of Sirach 24, notably, the idea of Wisdom's hiddenness from all but Israel, to whom she is revealed as Torah.[7] The description of Wisdom in the poem in Bar 3:9—4:4 identifies Wisdom's content again, as does Sirach, with Torah: "She [Wisdom] is the book of the commandments of God, and the Torah" (4:1); she is the "way of God" (3:13). In her identity as law, Wisdom is no less than the guarantor of eternal life for her adherents and of death for her forsakers (4:1).[8] Yet despite these high stakes, Wisdom is not readily available to all. Many are the alien nations from whom she is hidden (3:15-23, 29-31); indeed, "he who knows all things" (i.e., God) has found "the whole way to knowledge" and revealed it to Israel alone in Torah. The universalizing tendency in Sirach's treatment of wisdom disappears in Baruch, where Israel is exhorted not to give the glory (*doxa*) of wisdom to the alien people (4:2).

Such exclusivism must be understood in the larger context of Baruch's poem, which reflects upon Israel's own experience of alienation in exile (3:8). Although Israel's own suffering is attributed to forsaking wisdom (i.e., Torah), there is yet time to return to Wisdom,

---

6. The reader should note that while Torah observance does not emerge as an issue in the wisdom debates in Corinth, there is in Corinth an analogous interest in certain prerequisites to knowledge, e.g., reason, and in the elevation of the one who demonstrates these prerequisites.

7. Robert H. Pfieffer, *History of New Testament Times* (New York: Harper and Brothers, 1949) 417-18. The psalm was probably written originally in Hebrew and reflects older tradition than that of the final redactor, who wrote in Greek between 150 and 60 B.C.E.

8. Cf. 1 Cor 1:18.

who yet dwells in Israel offering light and life to all who "hold her fast" (4:1).

Wisdom in Baruch is thus both hidden and revealed. But while her hiddenness to those outside Israel is by God's design, her hiddenness to Israel is due to Israel's folly (3:12-13). Because of this folly, the people have been taken captive, but by learning again where Wisdom is, that is, by "walking in the way of God" (=Torah), Israel will again find strength, understanding, length of days, light and peace (3:14)—in short, all the gifts of wisdom. The crisis of knowledge that Israel suffers in exile, therefore, finds both its cause and its cure in the law. As the wisdom of God that has come down to dwell in one nation, the law both defines Israel's unique identity among foreigners and promises to those who obey a way home.

As in Sirach, the *content* of saving knowledge is revealed in Torah (*What*). Torah observance is therefore the way to knowledge and wisdom; who would be wise must "hold her fast" (Bar 4:1) (*How*). We notice here less emphasis on the role of the sage than in Sirach and much more on the collective Israel as representative of the law (*Who*). Because Baruch reflects on the loss of land and temple in Israel's exile, there is an almost apocalyptic interest in wisdom as the guarantor of both salvation for Israel and destruction for Israel's foes (*Why*).

Wisdom of Solomon

The pseudonymous Wisdom of Solomon (ca. 100 B.C.E.) comes from Hellenistic Jewish circles in Egypt. In this remarkable text, we see a major expansion of the concept wisdom which, in contrast to wisdom's more nationalistic role in Sirach and Baruch, presses beyond the particular setting of wisdom (=Torah) in Israel, "to embrace the whole of the world, visible and invisible."[9]

As in older wisdom texts, wisdom in Wisdom of Solomon is associated with law observance (6:4, 18), personified as a woman (e.g., 6:12-16; 8:1-21) and as the preexistent architect of the universe (7:21-22). But wisdom is also, now in language more typical of Hellenistic philosophical or mystical traditions, the "unerring knowl-

---

9. Martin Hengel, *Judaism and Hellenism* (Philadelphia: Fortress Press, 1974), 130.

edge of what exists," the "initiate in the knowledge of God" (8:4), the "pure emanation" of God's glory (7:25), the "reflection of eternal light" (7:26),[10] and the being that "pervades and penetrates all things" (7:24-26).[11]

Along with wisdom's new and mystical content comes, not surprisingly, a new understanding of how wisdom is attained. As in earlier tradition, only the righteous who seek it receive wisdom (6:16). But now Greek ideas about the separation of body (*sōma*) and soul (*psychē*) enter the wisdom formulae. To be enlightened by wisdom, "God's pure emanation," is to be liberated from the material world. To be "saved by wisdom" (9:18) is to be freed from the "perishable body" (*sōma*) that "weighs down the soul" (*psychē*) and from the "earthy tent" that "burdens the thoughtful mind (*nous*)" (9:15). The soul thus freed reaches wisdom's new goal, namely, immortality in the presence (kingdom) of God (1:15; 2:23; 3:4, 14; 5:15; 6:19; 10:10; chap. 14). Wisdom is now quite remarkably detached from human will and reason ("for the reasoning of mortals is worthless," 9:13-14); rather, it is a gift from God, preexistent (9:9) and "sent by the Holy Spirit (*pneuma*) from on high." To one who prays, "the spirit of wisdom" comes (7:7).[12]

While Wisdom of Solomon emphasizes that all are mortal, sharing a "common entrance into life and a common departure" (7:6), the author nonetheless elevates the sage whose seeking after wisdom leads to perfection (*teleios*) (4:13, 16-20; 9:6).[13] Unlike his counterpart in Sirach, however, the ideal sage here is characterized by suffering. Indeed, the possession of wisdom seems to predispose this person to severe testing and oppression by the wicked

---

10. On the conjunction of wisdom and primal light, see Hengel, *Judaism*, 169–70, who finds the idea in Aristobulus, Philo, Tannaitic literature, and apocalyptic literature.

11. In this last attribute particularly, Wisdom's Stoic features are sharply pronounced: the terms "pervade" and "penetrate" are technical terms in Stoicism for the distribution of the logos in the world soul. (Celia Deutsch, *Hidden Wisdom and the Easy Yoke* [Sheffield: JSOT Press, 1987], 59; Burton Mack, *Logos und Sophia* [Göttingen: Vandenhoeck & Ruprecht, 1973], 96ff.) Just as in Stoicism the ordering principle of the universe is the logos, so in Wisdom of Solomon that ordering task is assigned to Wisdom.

12. See the fuller discussion of the role of the spirit in wisdom traditions below. Other associations of wisdom with *logos* and *pneuma* occur at 1:7; 7:22, 24; 9:1-2, 17; 12:1; 16:23, 26; 18:7, 15.

13. Cf. 1 Cor 2:6.

(2:12-24), in whose blindness he appears to be punished and destroyed (3:2-4).[14]

New themes such as the resurrection of the just (5:15), God's arming of creation against the unrighteous enemy (*echthros*) (5:16; cf. 1 Cor 15:25-26), and a preponderance of images of battle and cosmic catastrophe stand parallel to the call of Wisdom (6:9), who "hastens to make herself known to those who desire her" (6:12-13).

Of special interest for the development of wisdom theology is the nearly apocalyptic passage in 18:15-16, where of Yahweh's victory over the Egyptians we read:

> Your all-powerful word leaped from heaven, From the royal throne, into the midst of the land that was doomed, a stern warrior carrying the sharp sword of thy authentic command, and stood and filled all things with death, and touched heaven while standing on earth.

While the author clearly intends a reference to God's historic judgment upon Egypt and Israel's subsequent "salvation" from the Egyptians, the actor is the same cosmic "word" (*logos*) that is implicitly identified with wisdom at 7:23; 9:10; and 18:15. The association of word (*logos*) and wisdom is not new in Wisdom of Solomon, but the setting of these terms amid images such as these (e.g., the warrior wielding the word between heaven and earth) does sound a new tone which will become more and more familiar as we move toward apocalyptic texts. Similarly, the association of terms like *sōma* ("body"), *psyche* ("soul"), and *nous* ("mind"), with the liberating function of *pneuma* ("spirit"), presses the wisdom tradition beyond its accustomed borders.[15] In these respects at least, Wisdom of Solomon stands at the outer limits of the wisdom tradition poised to move forward into the apocalyptic landscape, although much here still reflects ways of knowing associated with the older wisdom tradition.

---

14. One is struck by the Pauline parallel of the suffering fool in 1 Corinthians 1–4 who as "servant of Christ and steward of the mysteries of God" is paradoxically weak, in ill repute, hungry, thirsty, ill-clad and buffeted, homeless, reviled, persecuted—"the refuse of the world" (1 Cor 4:8-12).

15. The resemblance of this "word" to the world-dividing *logos tou staurou* in 1 Cor 1:18 is striking. In both texts, the "word" divides and judges, in both it separates the perishing from the saved. The strongly apocalyptic character of the Wisdom-Logos in Wisdom of Solomon and the parallel clusters of the terms "word," "wisdom," "spirit," "mind," and "salvation" suggest the possibility that Paul and Wisdom of Solomon share a common wisdom context. This possibility is strengthened by other details of Wisdom of Solomon and will be discussed more fully later in chapter 3.

It appears, then, that in Wisdom of Solomon we have come upon a hybrid text, accessible, perhaps, to both wisdom and apocalyptic ways of knowing. It is possible that both Paul and the Corinthians used this text, or other such hybrid texts, to support their rather different epistemological positions. As in the beginning, when wisdom was poured out on the whole earth, essential knowledge is universal. Yet not all are its righteous recipients. There is, in Wisdom of Solomon, an enemy to wisdom against whom God wages war (5:16), and an apocalyptic judgment executed by the warrior with a sharp sword (18:15-16). For the righteous who persevere on God's side of battle, there is life everlasting and a glorious crown (5:15-16). Salvation belongs to wisdom (9:18) and destruction of evil is the work of the "all powerful word."

Finally, in Wisdom of Solomon, wisdom has a new and mystical content (*What*); it is the "pure emanation of God's glory." Now Wisdom is like the *logos* of the Stoics; she permeates the universe, radiates in the souls of human beings and liberates them from the body. Only the sage reaches perfection (*teleios*) in wisdom (*How* and *Who*); this one she frees from the constraints of the present material world (*Why*). Having shed her conventional garb, Wisdom now anticipates both apocalyptic ways of knowing and that epistemology which will later emerge as Gnosticism.

Wisdom of Solomon and Philo of Alexandria

Scholars have long noted the strong affinities of Philo of Alexandria with Wisdom of Solomon. Because Philo was a contemporary of Paul and his Corinthian congregation, I will mention here some suggestive connections. In both writers, we see the development of a new language of the spirit and a new interest in the mystical dimensions of spiritual attainment. As in Wisdom of Solomon the sage alone reaches liberation from the constraints of body (*soma*), soul (*psyche*), and mind (*nous*) to attain perfection (*teleios*) as a "spiritual one" (*pneumatos*), also in Philo we find the *sophos teleios* (perfect or mature sage), who alone is "nobly born" and filled with the divine spirit (*pneuma*).[16] Philo too shows considerable interest in levels and

---

16. See, for example, *Leg.all.* 3.159, *Agr.* 165, and *De Virtutibus*, 187–227, all cited by Richard Horsley in "*Pneumatikos* vs *Psychikos:* Distinctions of Spiritual Status among the Corinthians," *HTR* 69 (1976): 281–283.

demonstrations of spiritial status gained through intimate knowledge of wisdom. The one who is perfect in wisdom, for example, demonstrates perfection in eloquent speech (*eulogia*).[17]

Observations on Ways of Knowing in the Wisdom Tradition

We have come a long way from the immanence of wisdom in the cosmic order (Job and Ecclesiastes), to its identification with Torah (Sirach), to the mystical wisdom whose goal is the liberation of the adept from the constraints of the natural world (Wisdom of Solomon). The shift in ways of knowing is more obvious, however, than its causes. Hellenization is a sure factor. As Hellenism advanced with its intentional dissolution of local identity, its systematic replacement of the non-Greek with the Greek in government, religion, and education, Jews found new ways to exist in and communicate with the new world. The scriptures were translated into Greek, the sages learned Greco-Roman modes of argumentation, philosophical and religious correspondences were recognized in both directions, Jew to Greek and Greek to Jew.

There were less salutary changes, too. The autonomy that Israel had achieved under Persian rule was newly challenged by the Hellenistic powers. Already in Sirach and Wisdom of Solomon we see the separation of wisdom from kingship which had been a mainstay of the wisdom tradition even through the Persian period. Now, as we turn to the apocalyptic literature, we will see the estrangement of wisdom from the political and material world turn to apocalyptic confrontation between the powers of heaven and hell.

The world changed radically but, until the destruction of Jerusalem and the Temple in 70 C.E., not suddenly. Over time, certain convictions about the order of the world gave way. As Wisdom withdrew from her familiar resting places, new ways of finding and knowing her, despite her apparent absence, began to emerge. Now the stage was set for the entrance of the apocalyptic visionary.

---

17. See *Mig.* 70–85 and Richard Horsley, "Wisdom of Word and Words of Wisdom," *CBQ* 39 (1977): 227.

THE APOCALYPTIC TRADITION AND THE
SEARCH FOR KNOWLEDGE

Because of the social and political contexts in which they are written, apocalyptic writings express a greater degree of alienation from the world, including more hostility toward world rulers, than do even the latest wisdom writings. The four texts we survey here all stem, again, from the Hellenistic period; two of them, 1 Enoch and the Dead Sea Scrolls, reflect the unstable time before the destruction of the Temple (ca. 65-70 C.E.). The other two, 4 Ezra and 2 Baruch, are written in direct response to that tragedy in Israel's life.

1 Enoch

1 Enoch, a book entirely extant only in Ethiopic (with Syriac and Greek fragments), is a composite work consisting of five major parts: Book I, the Book of the Watchers (1–36); Book II, the Similitudes (or Parables) (37–71); Book III, the Astronomical Book (72–82); Book IV, the Dream Visions (83–90); and Book V, the Epistle of Enoch (91–105). Because of its composite nature, 1 Enoch is very difficult to date. There is consensus among scholars, however, that the earliest sections of the book (Books I and III) reach back to the third century B.C.E., with the latest extending perhaps into the first century C.E.[18]

The author purports to be a witness of the end time and the final judgment (1:1-9). He assumes the pseudonym "Enoch"—a faithful figure from predeluvian times who, in Genesis 5 and 6, is said to have

---

18. J. T. Milik, *The Books of Enoch* (Oxford: Clarendon Press, 1976) dates the Similitudes/Parables (Book II) to the late first century C.E. This late date is disputed. See Michael Knibb, "The Dating of the Parables of Enoch: A Critical Review," *NTS* 25 (1979):345–69. For "consensus" report, see James H. Charlesworth, *The Old Testament Pseudepigrapha and the New Testament: Prolegomena for the Study of Christian Origins* (SNTS Monograph Series 54; Cambridge: Cambridge University Press, 1985), 106–110. See also Michael E. Stone, "Enoch and Apocalyptic Origins," in *Visionaries and Their Apocalypses*, ed. Paul Hanson (Philadelphia: Fortress Press, 1980), 96. Alan F. Segal, *Paul the Convert: The Apostolate and Apostasy of Saul the Pharisee* (New Haven: Yale University Press, 1990), 47–48 and 318–19 n. 50, has recently joined Milik in assuming a late date for the Similitude (1 Enoch 37–71) as a "control" on his thesis that "the transformation motif originates before the first century within Judaism." If 1 Enoch 37–71 is pre-Christian, as the majority of scholars now hold, the case that Segal wishes to build is strengthened.

walked with and been taken up by God—and proclaims the blessings due the "elect" (1:8-9).

Although wisdom terminology permeates 1 Enoch, wisdom is markedly at the service of a new frame of reference—apocalypticism. Gone is Sirach's keen interest in the vocation of the sage. Gone, too, is the theme of Wisdom's finding her home in Zion (via Torah); instead, we find the myth of *vanished* Wisdom in 1 Enoch 42.[19] In Wisdom's absence, the present, earthly rewards of wise living are no longer emphasized, and there is more attention to the retributive justice of God, whose way will prevail despite present conditions.

As in some wisdom literature, fundamental questions about God and the world's course lead the author(s) to see world events on two levels, that of "appearance" and that of "reality." Book I (1–36) offers a mythological explanation of this dual structure in recounting the exploits of the wicked angels, the Watchers. The "apparent" world of this writer is a rebellious world in which even the elements are turned in folly against God (18:15-16).[20] But the present world simply reflects the "real" rebellion of the angels. They are the cause of all the chaos. They have revealed secrets that should have remained hidden (16:3-4) and have thereby obscured true knowledge (i.e., the true mysteries of God).

The elevating of the trouble to the heavenly realm and the distancing of humanity from direct apprehension of the truth mark a feature new to apocalypticism. In the wisdom texts, although wisdom is a heavenly reality, the answers to the mysteries of the world are to be found in nature, human relationships, the sages, and especially Torah. In 1 Enoch, the pattern changes. Now, what is not understood on earth has its explanation in the heavens and is very selectively revealed. The secrets of Torah are now the special property, not of the sages, but of one who has ascended "high up into heaven" (14:8). For Enoch, what is "real" both originates and remains in the far-off realm of the angels and yet has its effect on the world of mortals.

The wisdom that the visionary Enoch receives in Book I is the story of the fallen angels, their desecration of the earth and the

---

19. Hans Conzelmann, "Paulus und die Weisheit," *NTS* 12 (1965–66): 231–44.
20. But cf. Wisdom's ordering function in 2:1-3.

prophetic vision of God's judgment upon them at the Deluge (10:2), the great cleansing of the earth (10:22). In Books II and III, wisdom is the vision of the end time (37:1), now made available through Enoch's proclamation to "those who dwell on earth, first and last." To this surprisingly inclusive group, Enoch will teach wisdom and recite it "in accordance with the Lord of the spirits" (37:4). Yet, Enoch's universalism is short-lived, for in chapter 48, wisdom is revealed only to the righteous and holy ones who will be saved because they have hated this world of oppression (48:7-8).

At the center of Enoch's saving vision is the Son of Man who was "named before the creation of the world" and "became the Chosen One" (48:2-3, 6). This one, who is revealed by the "Lord of Spirits," bears within himself the "spirit which gives insight and understanding" (49:3). In 63:2,11, he is identified with the "Lord of Glory," a title that elsewhere in 1 Enoch belongs only to God, but he is also named the "Chosen One," "Elect One," and "Messiah." He is both "staff of the righteous" and "light to the Gentiles"; he reveals secrets to those who are worthy (49:3), but confounds and humbles the rulers of the world (46:4-6; 48:8-10).

The relation of the Son of Man to the visionary is somewhat ambiguous. One scholar argues, with good reason, that the Son of Man is Enoch himself, mystically transfigured.[21] We need not make a judgment about this but may simply observe the ambiguity. The visionary in this literature, by ascending into the heavens and witnessing divine secrets, takes on the transcendence of the heavens he visits.

The striking alignment of wisdom, spirit, and insightful understanding in the Son of Man recalls royal messianic traditions similar to those in Isa 11:2: "And the spirit of the Lord shall rest upon him (the messianic king), the spirit of wisdom and understanding."[22] In Isaiah, as in 1 Enoch, the spirit descends not only upon one but also

---

21. Segal, *Paul the Convert*, 46, citing 1 Enoch 71:1, argues that the son of man figure is Enoch mystically transformed. Enoch is likewise identified with the titles "Chosen One," "Elect One," and "Messiah," according to Segal, "since virtually identical functions are attributed to these three figures" and since "Enoch performs various messianic functions." Among these functions Segal lists Enoch's righteousness, knowledge of divine secrets (46:3), sitting on the throne (51:3; 55:4; 61:8; 62:2-6; 70:27), and his ascension at the end of his life to enthroned status.

22. Knibb, "The Dating of the Parables of Enoch," 351–52. Cf. 1 Corinthians 2 where a similar alignment is in view.

upon many "descendants" (Isa 44:3) whose blessing contrasts with the shame of those who "know not, nor do they discern; for he has shut their eyes, so that they cannot see, and their minds, so that they cannot understand" (Isa 44:18) (*How* and *Who*).

But despite the promise of intermediation and inspiration by the spirit through this special messianic agent, in both Isaiah and 1 Enoch, the present remains clouded in mystery. God's plan is essentially hidden to human perception, revealed only to the prophet or the seer who ascends to the heavenly council to receive the mysteries (Isaiah 6 and 1 Enoch 1–36).[23] The ascent to the throne by the visionary now becomes a critical step in the process of revelation. True revelation now relies on visionary experience, removed from the familiar ground of Torah study and observance of the natural order.[24]

While the narration of visionary experience is uniquely characteristic of apocalyptic texts, the theme of divine mystery in 1 Enoch is developed much as it is in the older wisdom and prophetic texts (e.g., Job and Second Isaiah), that is, in rhetorical questions asserting the sovereignty of God. As Isaiah asks, "Who has directed the Spirit of the Lord, or as his counselor has instructed him? . . . [Who] has taught him knowledge?" (40:13-14), so also 1 Enoch questions, "Who is there that is able to ponder his [the Holy One's] deep thoughts? What kind of person can understand the activities of

---

23. Raymond E. Brown, *The Semitic Background of the Term "Mystery" in the New Testament* (1958–59; reprint, Philadelphia: Fortress Press, 1968).

24. For an example of the use of language of transformation in heavenly ascent accounts, see 1 Enoch 14; 39:14; 70–71. See also Segal's treatment of heavenly ascents in *Paul the Convert*. Segal attempts to "fill in the Jewish cultural context informing [Paul's conversion] experience." The context most pertinent to Paul's experience, according to Segal, is what he calls "Jewish apocalypticism and mysticism." Arguing largely (but not solely) from Paul's account of ascension in 2 Corinthians 12, Segal holds that Paul was a "Jewish mystic" whose "ecstatic or paranormal experience" of ascension is like what other apocalyptic Jews were reporting. A critical feature of heavenly ascents, the transformation of the "adept" or "heavenly voyager" into a divine figure, is clearly evident in 1 Enoch 71. Of this text and its relevance to Paul, Segal writes, "1 Enoch 71 gives us the experience of an adept undergoing the astral transformation prophesied in Dan 12:2, albeit in the name of a pseudepigraphical hero. If this is true, then Paul gives us the actual, confessional experience of the same spiritual event, with Christ substituting for the son of man." Even if 1 Enoch 71 is post-Christian, Paul would have been influenced by the pre-first century 1 Enoch 90:37-39 where, in Enoch's vision, "believers are mystically transformed into white cows which appear to symbolize the messiah" (p.42) (Segal, *Paul the Convert*, 39–47).

heaven so that he can see a soul or perhaps even a spirit?" (1 Enoch 93:11-12).[25] The innovation of apocalyptic here is to introduce figures such as the prophet, the visionary, and the Son of Man himself[26] who bear the mysteries of God by way of the spirit.[27]

In summary, while 1 Enoch's epistemology is at several points parallel to the wisdom tradition, it ultimately moves well beyond wisdom's ways of knowing. There are the familiar antitheses of truth/wisdom and falsehood/folly, and with them, the development of the doctrine of the Two Ways (91:1-19). Like wisdom writers, 1 Enoch sees in Torah the essence of truth and wisdom (compare 1 Enoch 5:4; 104:12-13; 100:6; 98:1, 9 to Sir 1:26; 15:1; 19:20; 24:23; 39:1). In 1 Enoch as in Wisdom of Solomon, the spirit makes possible the discernment required of the righteous (*How*).

What is distinctive about 1 Enoch is that it places the *what* of knowledge outside the human, earthly realm, where it is accessible only by special revelation; even Torah interpretation must now be validated by visionary experience. 1 Enoch thereby exhibits an unprecedented hopelessness about human capacity to learn truth or to find meaning in this world. Instead, it posits, more radically than does the wisdom tradition, a "real" world transcending the present. In this "real" world, mysteries are revealed; this is where true and saving knowledge resides. The chasm fixed between these two worlds may be crossed by the visionary, chosen by God, who makes an ascent to the heavens. Through this messenger, true knowledge, although hidden from the world, can be communicated to those who are willing to see and hear (*Who*).[28]

---

25. Notably our Pauline text includes a nearly verbatim citation of Isaiah's question (Isa 40:13), "For who has known the mind of the Lord so as to instruct him?" (1 Cor 2:16).

26. In Segal's view, the visionary becomes the messianic figure and as such bears the mysteries of God (Segal, *Paul the Convert*, 46).

27. Paul's use of the cluster of ideas including spirit, wisdom, discernment (mind), and mystery is close to, if not derived from, this apocalyptic development of the older wisdom theme. See R. G. Hamerton-Kelly, *Pre-existence, Wisdom, and the Son of Man* (Cambridge: Cambridge University Press, 1973), 114.

28. Segal suggests that in 1 Enoch 90, "the believers symbolically share the being of the messiah" (i.e, in Segal's view, the transformed Enoch). "The messiah not only saves but serves as the model for transformation of believers" (Segal, *Paul the Convert*, 46).

4 Ezra and 2 Baruch

These two apocalypses are contemporaneous, both of them reflecting the period after the fall of the Second Temple about 70 C.E. While their perspectives are not identical, they respond in similar ways to the same immediate crisis of knowledge, namely, the destruction of the Temple, the center of Jewish piety and national identity.

It is fitting that both pseudonyms, Ezra and Baruch, recall figures in Israel's past who helped to reestablish cultic and covenantal life after exile. Because these writers too seek the restoration of Israel in a time of catastrophe, concerns of Torah and covenant are central. Neither Baruch nor Ezra was known for heavenly ascent (as opposed to Enoch), nor do these latter-day bearers of their names provide glimpses into heaven. The supernatural knowledge that each gains comes rather through symbolic vision or audition, often interpreted by angels, but without "actual correspondence between what the visionary sees and heaven."[29]

As one would expect, given the circumstances that produced these documents, both make Torah observance the sustaining power of the community through the loss of all other supports in the time of disaster. Torah alone will assure the salvation of the righteous in the end time (2 Bar 44:14 and 4 Ezra 13:53-55). In 4 Ezra, the Torah is supplemented by the seventy secret books, but these books will be accessible in the end only to those who have been faithful to the twenty-four books, including Torah itself (4 Ezra 14:45-47).

Wisdom motifs pervade both apocalypses; 4 Ezra demonstrates so strong a wisdom orientation that it appears to be designed for school instruction in wisdom.[30] In 2 Baruch, similarly, one who studies Torah is accompanied by wisdom "which is in us [and] will support us" (2 Bar 48:23-24). Salvation and immortality are functions of wisdom; those who "plant the root" of wisdom through law observance will be "glorified by transformations, and the shape of their face will

---

29. Christopher Rowland, *The Open Heaven: A Study of Apocalyptic in Judaism and Early Christianity* (New York: Crossroad, 1982), 53.
30. Michael Knibb, "Apocalyptic and Wisdom in 4 Ezra," *JSJ* 13 (1981): 62–64.

be changed . . . so that they may . . . receive the undying world which is promised to them" (2 Bar 51:3) (*Why*).[31]

Yet, despite the emphasis in these texts on conventional means of knowing God's ways and attaining salvation, there emerges a conviction that ordinary human wisdom, prone to corruption by the evil impulse (4 Ezra 3:20), is no longer sufficient to make sense of the world. These are not merely wisdom books; they also bear witness to the necessity of apocalyptic revelation.

Pseudo-Ezra's questions and complaints place the problem in bold relief. Lamenting his own limited powers of perception, he states his lack of interest in heavenly things and his urgent search instead for the meaning of "what we experience daily."

> Why Israel has been given over to the Gentiles . . . the law of our fathers has been made of no effect. . . . And why we pass from the world like locusts, and our life is like a mist, and we are not worthy to obtain mercy. (4 Ezra 4:22-24)

To this query, the angel offers an evasive response. Instead of addressing the present conditions that concern Ezra, the angel points to the approaching end of the age: "For the evil about which you ask me has been sown, but the harvest of it has not yet come" (4 Ezra 4:28). And so Ezra's attention is diverted to the secrets of what is to come, secrets whose revelation, in some implicit way, promises to supply meaning to life in the present (*What*).

Repeatedly, Ezra's anxiety about the pervasiveness of evil in the world ("not just a few, but nearly all who have been created" are corrupt, 7:48) is answered in eschatalogical scenarios. Certain apocalyptic features define the scenes. There will be a period of signs followed by the revelation of the "hidden city" and the messiah, the messiah's reign (four hundred years), his death, seven days of silence, his resurrection, a period of severe judgment, seven days of transition, "as it was at the beginning," and finally the new age

---

31. See Segal, who notes that in 2 Bar 51:3ff. "the theme of angelic transformation sounds loud and strong." The transformation pictured here is not, however, that of the visionary upon ascension but of all believers in a gradual process. Segal, *Paul the Convert*, 50.

(6:25). But through the first part of the book, Ezra remains relatively unmoved by the eschatological information, resisting the message of the wholesale destruction of the unrighteous.

Baruch is more readily convinced by his visions. He too is troubled by the corruption of the world and the apparent meaninglessness of life. "For if only this life exists . . . , nothing could be more bitter than this. . . . Every thing is in a state of dying" (2 Bar 21:12, 22). But for Baruch the vision of things to come beyond this world is more immediately satisfying than for Ezra. Baruch readily admits his inability fully to know the way of God but eagerly seeks insight into the mysteries of the end time. He does not question God's justice—"justly do they perish who do not love your law"—and recognizes without question that the true Israel consists of the law-observant. He warns the people to persevere in the law so that they may see "the consolation of Zion" (2 Bar 44:7) (*How* and *Why*). For this writer, there is comfort in the certainty of reward and punishment in the end time, and the glimpses he is allowed into the future bring comfort and hope in a time of questioning and despair.

Ezra too is finally stilled in his skepticism and caused to see the justice of the plan of God who vindicates Zion. Only in the acceptance of God's verdict, harsh though it may be, lies hope that the "whole earth may be relieved" and may "experience the compassion of its creator" (4 Ezra 11:46). In a vision modeled after Daniel 7, Ezra sees the one "like a man" rising up out of the sea with fiery breath and then coming down a mountain calling the multitudes to him (4 Ezra 13:1-58). When he understands that this messianic vision foresees the judgment of the enemy, and the final restoration of Zion (*What*), he exclaims, "It is better to come into these things, though incurring peril, than to pass from the world like a cloud, and not to see what shall happen in the last days" (4 Ezra 13:20). After the vision, in his response of praise, Ezra seems to come to terms with the limited hope of salvation even among the Jews (4 Ezra 13:48).

To summarize: The perspective on knowledge offered by these two documents bears significant resemblances to both the classical wisdom texts and the apocalyptic perspective of 1 Enoch. On the wisdom side, these apocalypses mirror the identification of wisdom with Torah we noted in Sirach. *What* can be known about God and about the world "as it really is" is a function of one's knowledge of and adherence to Torah. It is Torah observance that assures salvation at the end time. Yet Torah knowledge is only partial knowledge. Even the wisest and most pious, like Pseudo-Ezra and Pseudo-Baruch, are not satisfied with the knowledge available to the obedient, faithful life. Because they have witnessed the destruction of Israel's most sacred institution and the devastation of the land and its people, all of which seems to contradict the covenant itself, they seek a context of knowledge larger than Torah.[32] This context is provided by the distinctively apocalyptic feature of the literature—the revelation of divine mysteries in visions of the future. The world to come gives meaning to the present precisely by extending the scope of meaningful knowledge beyond the present.[33]

In both documents, the extension of knowledge reveals an essential insight about judgment and salvation; observance of the law that will serve as the eternal standard of judgment. While the *scope* within which the Torah is operative as true and saving knowledge has expanded in the revelation of mysteries, the *function* of the Torah has not changed. Rather, the visionary now sees that Torah is, in a sense, more true than history. Although in the present crisis the law may seem obsolete, it is yet, in the mysterious wisdom of God, the solid rock of salvation (*Why*). What one knows when one knows the mysteries is that Torah endures. With this knowledge comes advice to those who seek to know God in an age of despair: "I gave you knowledge while I still live. . . . Learn the commandments of the Mighty One" (2 Bar 84:1-2) (*How* and *Who*).

Yet, more than Torah is revealed in the visions. For the visionary, what is revealed causes *a shift in perception;* having once looked into the open heaven, the seer sees the present world with new perspective. The complaint of 4 Ezra turns to praise; 2 Baruch's lament turns to ethical exhortation; he calls his hearers to live so as to receive what

---

32. In the words of 4 Ezra, "So if the world was created for us, why do we not possess our world as an inheritance?" (6:56), and of 2 Baruch, "Where is all that which you said to Moses about us?" (3:9). Indeed the knowledge of the righteous has profited nothing (2 Bar 14:5).

33. Whereas in the wisdom literature the "mysteries" are more apt to involve cosmology than eschatology, now the two interests are combined, with emphasis on the "mysteries of the times" (e.g., 2 Bar 81:4; 85:8; 4 Ezra 6:32-33; 10:38; 14:5).

"has been preserved for you" (2 Bar 84:7). His change of mind is most pronounced, however, in the speech of consolation (2 Bar 83:4ff.),[34] when he reflects on the inevitable fulfillment of the promise to the righteous and looks toward a time of great reversal, "when every power which exists now changes into weakness . . . every clamor of pride changes into silent dust" (2 Bar 83:15). For these writers, as for apocalyptic writers generally, it is the glimpse into the future and the assurance of God's timely vindication of the righteous that gives meaning and hope to the present.

The Dead Sea Scrolls

The Qumran literature includes a diverse group of documents among which are found both writings of the desert sectarians and copies of documents they used but did not compose. All compositions of the community can be approximately dated to the first century B.C.E.[35] While no document written by the community is in the form of an apocalypse, the presence of other apocalyptic writings (notably, 1 Enoch) in their library, coupled with the demonstration of patently apocalyptic concerns in their own compositions (i.e., interest in an imminent end combined with stark ethical and spatial dualism, and corresponding interest in the divine mysteries,[36] and their special revelation to the sectarians), justifies designation of the Qumran dwellers as an apocalyptic community.[37]

Like other apocalyptic literature of the period, selected Dead Sea Scrolls are in some aspects strongly reminiscent of the late wisdom tradition.[38] In particular, the intersection in these texts of an esoteric

---

34. Cf. John 14:1 to 2 Bar 83:4.

35. William F. Albright, "Recent Discoveries in Bible Lands," Supplement to *Young's Analytical Concordance of the Bible*, 22d ed. (New York: Funk & Wagnalls, 1955), 50; and Frank M. Cross, Jr., *The Ancient Library of Qumran*, rev. ed. (Minneapolis: Fortress Press, 1995), 89–91. Translations provided are from A. Dupont Sommer, *The Essene Writings from Qumran* (Gloucester, Mass: Peter Smith, 1973, orig. 1961).

36. An interest in knowledge, particularly the knowledge of formerly hidden secrets, is prominent throughout the Qumran literature (e.g., 1QS 3:15, "God of knowledge," and CD 9:16-21).

37. Not all literature found at Qumran is apocalyptic, of course. My survey concerns apocalyptic (and wisdom) themes in the compositions of the community.

38. There is surprisingly little *ḥākām, ḥōkmāh* (i.e., "wisdom") terminology, but much other perception terminology present at Qumran.

interest in divine mysteries, on the one hand, and in ethics and piety, on the other (1QS 5:21; 6:14), shows this community's conviction that God's creation is fundamentally good despite its corruption by the unrighteous. Thus, in the *Hodayot* (hymns), as in the wisdom literature, the created order is a cause for praise, especially in its secrets that are hidden from the author's understanding (1QH 1:11-12).

The synthesis of wisdom and apocalyptic perspectives at Qumran contains important clues to the community's prevailing epistemology. On the one hand, there is a conviction that true knowledge is hidden to most of the world but revealed to the elect. At the same time, however, the *foundations* of knowledge are in the original cosmic order (1QH 1:21; 1QH 11:11, 13). A new cosmos is expected, and yet this new creation will realize the conditions intended from the beginning; the new cosmos is Paradise restored. God's will is not to destroy the world but to purge it of evil (1QS 4:19-26). Moreover, the mystery of "what went wrong" in the present cosmos was in the preordained plan of God, who created the two spirits, the spirit of Truth and the spirit of Perversity. In essence, the mystery now revealed is that God, who created and ordained duality, will overcome it in the final days.[39]

The content of knowledge at Qumran is at least tripartite. There is first the knowledge that belongs to God, including God's creation of the universe (1QH 1:21; 11:11, 13), predetermination of the course of the end time,[40] and other "wondrous works" which generally involve God's sustaining Israel in time of trouble. Second, there is the knowledge (generally about the future) that is revealed in Torah ("Torah mysteries") to the Qumran sectaries. This knowledge itself has two dimensions, one temporal (interpreting the signs of the times) and the other ethical (how to live and walk in the true way).

---

39. 1QS 4:18. Just as God predetermined the existence of the opposing powers, so God has set a time for the salvation of the righteous and "annihilation for the lot of Belial" (1QM 1:5). For further discussion of the two spirits doctrine at Qumran, see my treatment of *pneuma* below.

40. In the Community Rule (1QS), e.g., God's "mysteries" and "wisdom" are defined in this way: "God . . . has set an end for the existence of perversity; and at the time of the visitation He will destroy it forever. Then truth shall arise in the world forever" (1QS 4:18-19; trans. A. Dupont-Sommer).

Finally, although references here are scant, there are, as in 1 Enoch, "evil mysteries," which are associated with the community's enemies by whom they have been persecuted.[41] All three types of knowledge are eschatological insofar as the perfection of knowledge now taking place among the sectaries is reserved for the last times.[42] The means by which this eschatological knowledge comes to the community are evident in its structure (*How*).

At the head of the community is the enigmatic Teacher of Righteousness whose role, which we derive primarily from the *Habakkuk Commentary* 7:3-4, is to interpret the "mysteries." He is a historical figure—the *Damascus Document* looks to him as the founder of the community—who is opposed by another historical figure, the "Wicked Priest" (presumably the head of the temple at Jerusalem). Generally, his function is to act as the official mediator of revelation for the community. If he is the same person as the author of the *Hodayot*, he claims to have received revelation directly from God (1QH 1:21).

Judging from the example of the *Habakkuk Commentary*, this revelation took place primarily through the inspired interpretation of scripture, specifically the prophetic scriptures.[43] There is no record of apocalyptic visions among the sect's own writings; insight comes directly from God to one chosen in the last days to receive it, apparently without need of visions or the interpreting angels which characterize other apocalyptic texts.[44]

---

41. Brown, *Mystery*, 28–30.

42. It is the community's self-definition as the sole recipient of God's mysteries (= knowledge) that fuels its sectarian fervor (1QS 9:17-18; 1QH 1:21). Every member is to a degree an initiate into the mysteries, i.e., the knowledge which defines the way of Truth (1QS 9:18-19) (WHO). It is not surprising, then, that the scrolls are filled with references to knowledge, secrets (usually *rāz* or *sôd*), and various means of revelation and modes of perception. Brown points out that "*rāz* is the most frequent term for mystery but *sôd* occurs often in parallelism with *rāz* or interchanged for it. *Nishtarot* also appears" (Brown, *Mystery*, 22 n. 75).

43. At this point the Qumran concept of revelation again reflects a combination of apocalyptic and wisdom traditions. The primary source of revelation is Torah, as in Sirach, and yet the Torah requires a higher revelation than is accessible to any sage we meet in the wisdom corpus.

44. See Segal, who alludes to an unpublished work of Morton Smith and A. J. Pantuck, "Paul and the Dead Sea Scrolls: Ascent and Angelification in First Century Judaism," to the effect that ascension-style transformation experiences are in evidence in the Dead Sea Scrolls. In Segal, *Paul the Convert*, 319 n. 50.

The Teacher's special function is instructive for understanding the community's collective self-perception. Although it is seldom stated explicitly, the community is, collectively, both the recipient of revelation and its propagator (1QS 9:17).[45] In the *Damascus Document* we read:

> But because of those who clung to the commandments
>   of God and survived them as a remnant,
> God established his covenant with Israel forever,
> Revealing to them the hidden things
>   in which all Israel had strayed. (CD 3:13-14)

Presumably, the inspired task of Torah interpretation was passed down to others after the original Teacher's death, but the continuing role of the community is clear. They are to learn the maxims of the law (in their true interpretation), to keep these from the "men of perversity, and to propagate them among those who have chosen the Way" (1QS 19:17-18). Similarly, while it is the role of the Teacher of Righteousness to cause the community to know (*yada*), it is the function of the congregation to propagate knowledge within the community (11QPsa 18:3; 19:2; 1QH 4:27-28).

In addition to the Teacher of Righteousness, there are other special teachers who are uniquely gifted recipients of revelation. These are the *maskil*, the *mebaqqer*, and the priests of Zadok, all of whom are essential links in the transmission of the mysteries.[46] Their task is to keep the community in the path of right action and piety (1QS 1:1-6). Thus, the maskil instructed not only about the mysteries of the eschatological events but particularly about the commandments of Torah.

Toward what end is knowledge at Qumran directed? Repeatedly, the corpus offers the singular answer, perfection (*teliōtes*) of the adherent and of his way (*Why*). This perfection has mainly to do with

---

45. The suggestion by Segal that what believers shared with the transformed visionary in 1 Enoch was, in effect, "symbolically the being of the messiah" has provocative implications for the role of the Teacher at Qumran (Segal, *Paul the Convert*, 46).

46. If the hymn writer is not the Teacher of Righteousness as conjectured by some, then he should be included in this list. See 1QH 2:18, where the Psalmist is a "fountain of knowledge to all men of insight"; and elsewhere on the Psalmist's role 1QH 1:21; 1QH 5:15-16; 1QH 2:18.

the practical and spiritual implications of total Torah observance. The member is exhorted to "walk" in the "way of perfection" (1QS 8:18, 21,25; 9:5-9); indeed, the Supreme Council is composed only of those who are *already* perfect (1QS 8:1-2). But, the attainment of perfection is not the result of human effort alone; the revelation of the perfect way is still God's gracious gift to one who is "but a creature of clay and a thing kneaded with water" (1QH 1:21). The gift quality of perfection is nowhere better expressed than by the Qumran psalmist:

> And I know that righteousness is not of man nor is
> perfection of way of the son of man,
> to the Most High God belong all the works of righteousness,
> whereas the way of man is not firm
> unless it be by the spirit which
> God has created for him
> to make perfect a way for
> the sons of men. (1QH 4:29-32)

To summarize: The Qumran writings demonstrate an intense preoccupation with ways of knowing God. Their doctrines show parallels with both the wisdom tradition and the apocalyptic tradition; indeed, they seem to present a synthesis of the two traditions, developed by a community whose needs were not met by either tradition singly. The two most dominant aspects of the Qumran epistemology—esoteric revelations and a keen interest in Torah observance—reflect these two prior traditions.

Observations on Ways of Knowing in Apocalyptic Texts

Our survey of ways of knowing in apocalyptic literature has revealed this tradition to be both like and unlike the wisdom tradition. Like wisdom writers, apocalyptic writers retain an ethical dualism which, in both traditions, takes the form of "two ways" theology; right knowledge leads to right behavior. For both wisdom and apocalyptic authors, moreover, this right behavior is prescribed by Torah. Whether knowledge of God is immanent in the cosmos or hidden in the transcendent realm, it is revealed at least in part in Torah. But as "knowledge" becomes less accessible to those who seek it in the cosmos and in the written commandments, Torah takes on a much broader meaning to include the mysteries which must be interpreted by uniquely inspired persons in the community. In both wisdom and apocalyptic, then, there are two levels of knowledge—what can be known by ordinary people and what must be revealed by extraordinary means through extraordinary people.[47]

Apocalyptic *differs* from wisdom in its convictions about the availability of saving knowledge in the present world. In apocalyptic, chaos and meaninglessness apparently rule the world. Believers find no confirmation on earth for their belief. At this crisis point, God reveals saving knowledge through extraordinary means; seers have visions whereby they receive knowledge that the present world is coming to an end in the advent of the reign of God. The turmoil of the present and its apparent subjection to the evil spirits is nearing an end. Meanwhile, perseverance in hope is called for; the righteous who persist in their faith and right behavior through the present eschatological battle will be glorified.

The receipt and dissemination of this otherworldly knowledge has two basic effects. First, the vision of the future glory of God and God's new creation gives meaning to the present strife, and complaints turn to praise. Second, the present is reconceived as the eschatological moment for perfection of righteousness among those who know God's plan. One's participation in the ongoing eschatological mystery is guaranteed by strict adherence to God's way in the time of trial.

THE SPIRIT AS AGENT OF KNOWING IN WISDOM AND APOCALYPTIC TRADITIONS

In the survey of wisdom and apocalyptic texts, we have observed an increasing incidence of spirit vocabulary and a corresponding inter-

---

47. Sages and visionaries are always the purest of the people. See Segal: "In apocalypticism and Jewish mysticism ascensions to God were the prerogative only of the more pure, made after the adept went through several ritual preparations, including fasting and cleansings but preeminently through ritual immersion (tevilah)." Segal makes direct reference to Qumran rituals and goes on to associate the tevilah with Christian baptism, citing what he calls 2 Corinthians' "echoes of baptismal liturgy" (2 Cor 4:4-6). Segal, *Paul the Convert*, 61.

est in the Spirit's role in the enlightenment and salvation of human beings. Because the S/spirit plays a central role in 1 Corinthians, it will be helpful to bring into sharper focus the place of spirit (*pneuma*) in the background sources.

In the Hellenistic period, the Hebrew notion of God's Spirit (*rūaḥ*) as both transcendent and immanent (cf. Genesis 1) is revitalized in the idea of the divine Spirit which pervades all things. Just as in the Hebrew Bible the Spirit enlivens every being and yet comes anew in surprising ways upon individuals and nations, so in later wisdom texts, S/spirit is both a property of the human being and "a power that possesses or seizes him."[48]

In Sirach, the two levels of S/spirit work in tandem for the perfection of the sage. Thus, in Sir 39:6, the *pneuma synesis* ("Spirit of understanding") comes from beyond the human being, and yet the one to whom it comes is one prepared by study of the law and the search for wisdom for receiving God's gracious gift. What begins in the human quest for God through law and wisdom ends in God's gracious fulfillment through the Spirit of the righteous search (Sir 51:20).

Similarly in Wisdom of Solomon, the spirit which is the principle of life in the human being and in the cosmos (cf. 1:5 and 1:7) is distinguished from the Spirit identified with *sophia* (wisdom). The latter comes only to those who are morally pure and who open themselves through prayer to God's gift of *sophia* (7:7); these people are called *pneumata* ("spiritual ones"; 7:23). The distinction between the visible and invisible worlds affects the pneumatology here. Real life (and thus, too, salvation) is no longer primarily earthly life. A dualism of flesh and spirit, which is alien to the Hebrew Bible, becomes established in this Hellenistic context; now the soul labors under bondage to the earthly tent of flesh (9:15). Although God created human beings for incorruption (*aphtharsia*), "through the devil's envy, death entered the world" (2:24). Consequently, some fall into sin and perish, while the righteous rest secure in the hand of God (3:1). The gift of God's Spirit comes to one whose own soul (*psychē*), spirit (*pneuma*),

---

48. Eduard Schweizer, *The Holy Spirit* (Philadelphia: Fortress Press, 1980), 13.

and mind (*nous*) are consciously oriented toward the good and who manifests this orientation in purity and virtue.

In several respects, wisdom and apocalyptic traditions of the Second Temple period share common views on the spirit, especially insofar as both are heir to the philosophical and religious innovations of Hellenistic culture. In both, spirit has both anthropological and theological manifestations.[49] What is new in apocalyptic is the conviction, born of oppression under foreign rulers, that history has already entered into its decisive eschatological crisis. With this view of history comes a new level of spiritual dualism. Not only is the human spirit distinguished from the divine Spirit but the human realm is possessed of and by two opposing spirits.[50]

Perhaps the most familiar apocalyptic motif of opposing spirits is the Qumran teaching about the Spirit of Truth and the Spirit of Falsehood (1QS 3:13—4:26). At Qumran these two spirits are developed to moral purpose so that human destiny is determined by the decision to follow one or the other. The Qumran writers (and other apocalyptic writers of the time) adapt the "two ways" doctrine of the wisdom tradition, now with specific reference to the spirit (*pneuma*).

At the same time, however, the dualism is brought into an eschatological schema that limits the significance of human choice. At Qumran, the two spirits are engaged in a battle whose final outcome—the victory of the Spirit of Lights—is already assured. The present crisis, mirrored in the heavenly battle of the spirits, moves inexorably toward conclusion. The end, the focus of the seer's and prophet's visions, will demonstrate God's saving will and finally the overcoming of cosmic dualism in the defeat of the spirit of evil. One who has this

---

49. Cf. 4 Ezra 3:3 to 4 Ezra 6:39-41.

50. In 1 Enoch the evil spirits arise from the "bodies of the giants" born of the union of fallen angels with mortal women (15:8). Their "first origin" is the "spirit foundation" (15:9), but their dwelling is not in heaven but on earth (15:10); they will corrupt the earth until the day of the great conclusion (15:10). In contrast is the Lord of Spirits who sits on the throne of glory to judge the evil spirits at the end. This one is sometimes identified as the Son of Man (62:3), sometimes as the one prior to "his Messiah" (48:10). Before the Lord of Spirits stands the Elect One synonymous with the Son of Man (48:2) who mediates the spirit of wisdom to the elect among the people: "His glory is forever and ever and his power is unto all generations. In him dwells the spirit of wisdom, the spirit which gives thoughtfulness, the spirit of knowledge and strength" (49:3).

saving knowledge is already transposed into the sphere of the Spirit of Truth,[51] even if there he is "still assailed by the 'parts of darkness' in him," and still awaits the final purification possible only after the annihilation of evil.[52]

In both traditions, the Spirit facilitates a new and true perception of all things. In wisdom, it reveals by agency of the sage; in apocalyptic, it guides the adept in the interpretation of scripture and through experiences such as heavenly ascents. In both traditions, the transcendent nature of the revealing power is emphasized. In both, too, the aid and/or interference of a mundane human spirit is operative.

A significant point of distinction between the two traditions, however, is apocalyptic's sharp disjuncture between the two ages. Here the Spirit of God does not, as in the wisdom tradition, meet the human spirit on a continuum that reaches from creation to the present. Rather, God's Spirit is revealed to the seer as the heavenly foe of the Spirit of Falsehood. The battle now raging in heaven will issue (the visionary comes to see) in the new creation. This distinction makes sense only in a framework of two ages where there is posited *a future reign of God* over against the present apparent reign of evil. In apocalyptic thought, then, the Spirit does more than disclose wisdom; it both announces a new creation and claims human beings for eschatological existence in that creation. On the basis of these observations, we are able to suggest the following general sketches of the role of *pneuma* in wisdom and apocalyptic literature.

Spirit in Wisdom Literature

1. The wisdom tradition comes closer than apocalyptic to identifying human and divine spirit. Wisdom/*pneuma* is a creative principle that includes the human being and pervades the cosmos.

---

51. The Spirit of Truth will aid in the process of enlightenment (1QS 4:28). We note too that this enlightenment spirit is characterized as a spirit of humility (1QS 2:24; 4:26). Those who are "proud in spirit" do not receive the Spirit of Truth (1QS 4:9-11; 11:1).

52. 1QS 3:18-19, 22-25; 4:2-8, 20.

2. At the same time, the wisdom tradition demonstrates a strong interest in wisdom/spirit as a gift from God, who is utterly separate from human beings.
3. The net effect of these two trends in wisdom is to posit a meeting of divine and human spirits on the human plane such that the well-prepared human spirit (i.e., the sage) receives the transcendent Spirit as a consequence of moral and intellectual striving for the good. In wisdom literature, the one who seeks and attains the higher Spirit is especially righteous.

Spirit in Apocalyptic Literature

1. By virtue of its heightened cosmic dualism, the apocalyptic tradition resists identifying divine and human spirits. The visionary, possessed by the divine Spirit, is engaged by a transcendent power whose primary effect is to move him beyond the limits of his own worldly consciousness (his own spirit). The divine Spirit is not something he has always had; rather, it newly enters the scene from a foreign realm. It brings the seer into a strange new creation.
2. Despite occasional universalizing overtones, apocalyptic literature attests generally that the Spirit comes, as in wisdom literature, to the specially righteous and not to the ordinary human being.
3. The Spirit in apocalyptic thought serves as mediator of truth and knowledge in the present. It leads the faithful in the path of right action and piety and thus into salvation at the end time.
4. The gift of the Spirit in apocalyptic is attached to certain future eschatological motifs, particularly to ideas of the final judgment of the wicked and glory of the righteous (1 Enoch 62:2-16).

CONCLUSION

At the beginning of this chapter, I noted that several scholars in this century have posited Gnosticism in the church at Corinth on the basis of vocabulary in the letter which coincides with later articulations of developed gnostic systems. Along with many other critics of this thesis, I regard it as unconvincing given the late dating of materials that are certainly gnostic. As critics suggest, Paul is more likely a source for the first articulations of Christian gnosticism than a borrower from such traditions.

Our review of wisdom and apocalyptic literature has revealed another, perhaps more plausible way to reconstruct the Corinthian position. In these traditions, concentrated as they are in the concepts and vocabulary of knowledge and perception, we have found ample resources for the building of "gnostic-like" systems of belief. Paul's hearers are likely to have had some degree of exposure to both traditions if only, in the case of apocalyptic, through Paul's own preaching. Perhaps we need look no further than these two venerable traditions, their conventions and anti-conventions to find adequate background for the debate at Corinth. To return to the expressionist metaphor with which we began, perhaps these traditions are the "stockpile from which the spirit draws what it needs at any given time, just as the cook does from the larder."[53]

---

53. Wassily Kandinsky, "Uber die Formfrage," in *Almanach der blaue Reiter* (Munich, 1912), 75; quoted in Hans K. Roethel, *The Blue Rider* (New York: Praeger Publishers, 1971), 63.

4

Act 1: Word of the Cross, Power, and Perception

This chapter and the next will seek to show how Paul works to create new and effective perceptual structures for the spiritual realities he experienced, so that he might bring others to the "knowledge" or vision he now has through the Spirit. As we look carefully at the language Paul uses to address what he takes to be the Corinthians' malformed perception, we will be attentive first to the "materials" from which his new structures are to be built.

Paul's view of the cross and its effects, we have seen, is characterized by apocalyptic motifs, although some features of Paul's modified apocalyptic schema would render his thought unrecognizable *as apocalyptic* to many of his time.[1] The Corinthian perspective, on the other hand, appears to set forth a type of wisdom piety that is at odds with Paul's apocalyptic perspective. One task of the text analysis is to illuminate the apocalyptic schema that Paul employs and to show how it determines his presentation of the cross in a setting dominated by a particular wisdom perspective.

The reading of 1 Corinthians 1–2 that follows is more thematic than strictly exegetical. In it, I will pay particular attention to three kinds of language in the text that illuminate its potential to act as performative utterance:

1. Language that reflects *what* Paul preaches, especially the phrase *logos tou staurou* (Word of the Cross).
2. Language that reflects the diverse *symbolic systems* or *"worlds"* that provide contexts for hearing the Word of the Cross.

---

1. Paul's apocalyptic, e.g., is remarkably free of pictorial depictions of end time. See the discussion of Pauline innovations in apocalyptic thought in chapter 1 above.

3. Language that reflects the range of *perceptual predispositions and transpositions* attendant to the preaching of the *logos tou staurou.*

THE OPENING AND THANKSGIVING: 1 CORINTHIANS 1:1-9

(1) Paul, called by the will of God to be an apostle of Christ Jesus, and our brother Sosthenes, (2) To the church of God which is at Corinth, to those sanctified in Christ Jesus, called to be saints together with all those who in every place call on the name of our Lord Jesus Christ, both their Lord and ours: (3) Grace to you and peace from God our Father and the Lord Jesus Christ. (1 Cor 1:1-3)

The Corinthian Calling and the Sovereignty of God

A central feature of the opening verses is the emphasis Paul places on God as the source of (1) his apostolic calling (*klēsis*), (2) the calling of the church (local and universal), and (3) the abundance of gifts known within the community.[2] The word *theos*, which appears three times in vv 1-3 alone, occurs six times in the first nine verses. Even where the word itself does not appear, reference to *theos* is implicit, as, for example, in the second two words of the opening, where the verbal adjectives *klētos apostolos* ("called [to be] apostle") describe Paul as the recipient of God's action. Paul is both "the person who is called" and the "person who is sent *from* (*apo-stellō*)." While this compound self-designation is typical of Paul's letter openings, it is significant that here, as elsewhere where he is under attack, he stresses the source of his apostolic calling in the "will of God" (*thelēmatos tou theou;* cf. Gal 1:4; 2 Cor 1:1). Moreover, he emphasizes God's calling of the *church;* the Corinthians are "called to be saints," sanctified by God (inferred from the "divine" passive) and endowed with grace and peace from God. As Paul is called by God, so is the church both "called" (*klētois*) and "sanctified" (*hēgiasmenois*).[3] Calling

---

2. See the discussion of this theme in the Introduction.

3. Some commentators observe that the notion of being called as a holy or sanctified community is characteristic of Jewish eschatology, and in fact, this tradition is much in evidence in Paul's thought here. But for Paul the notion of calling or vocation has taken on new significance in light of the Christ-event. The bracketing of the greeting and thanksgiving (1:1 and 1:9) of the letter by references to God's call signals that, for Paul, this notion is critical to all that follows. The word group *kaleō/klēsis* is heavily represented in 1 Corinthians. If we omit uses of *ekklēsia*, in the first chapter alone there are five uses of words from this group (*kaleō*, 1:9; *klēsis*, 1:26; *klētos*, 1:1, 2, 24). Elsewhere, *kaleō/klēsis* terminology is found in chapter 7 (ten uses), in 10:27 (once), and in 15:9 (once). No other Pauline letter displays this frequency of *kaleō/klēsis* use.

and sanctification, moreover, are not the unique possessions of the church at Corinth but extend to the church universal. The Corinthians are called "with all the churches in every place" (1:2b). They are not unified by their own will but by the will of God who calls.

The call to sanctification as Paul presents it in 1:2 involves both a vertical bond with the One who calls and a horizontal bond between human beings who (by consequence of having been called) call upon God. This is demonstrated particularly at 1:9 where the same calling that brought sanctification in 1:2 brings believers together in fellowship (*koinōnia*). Indeed, the use of the term "all" (*panta*) in 1:2 initiates a series of references in 1:1-9 that highlights the inclusiveness of God's call (perhaps in opposition to the Corinthians' exclusivistic claims).

against Corinth's heirarchy

An Embarrassment of Riches and Paul's End-Time Irony

(4) I give thanks to God always for you because of the grace of God (*chariti tou Theou*) which was given you in Christ Jesus, (5) that in every way (*en panti*) you were enriched in him with all speech and all knowledge—(6) even as the testimony to Christ was confirmed among you—(7) so that you are not lacking in any spiritual gift (*charismati*), as you wait for the revealing (*apokalypsis*) of our Lord Jesus Christ; (8) who will sustain you to the end, guiltless in the day of our Lord Jesus Christ. (9) God is faithful, by whom you were called into the fellowship (*koinōnia*) of his Son, Jesus Christ our Lord. (1 Cor 1:4-9)

Verses 4-9 contain a typical Pauline thanksgiving.[4] Here, in one long sentence with a number of dependent clauses, Paul's thanksgiving is characterized by hyperbole. In the first half of the sentence, for example, *panta* is used four times: Paul gives thanks *always* (*pantote*), that in *every* way (*en panti*) they were enriched, in *all* (*en panti*) word (*logos*) and in *all* (*en panti*) knowledge (*gnōsis*). Considering the controversies that follow the thanksgiving, one suspects that the hyperbole is an expression of polemic against the ones who are boasting at Corinth.[5]

---

4. For a definitive treatment of the thanksgiving form, see Paul Schubert, *Form and Function of the Pauline Thanksgiving* (Berlin: Töpelmann, 1939).

5. On this matter, there are at least three options: (1) Paul is wholly sincere in his hyperbole; (2) Paul is indulging wholly in sarcasm to mimic the boasting of the Corinthians; (3) Paul is sincere to the extent that he recognizes the gifts exhibited at Corinth but wishes to give credit where it is due, namely to God as source (Hans Conzelmann, *1 Corinthians* [Hermeneia; Philadelphia: Fortress Press, 1975], 26). The third option appears most reasonable. The fact that the two gifts Paul mentions (speech and knowledge) are the two most subject to abuse at Corinth, as the letter will later reveal, confirms the polemical tone. But at the same time, the setting of these gifts under the rubric of the "grace of God which was given" indicates a positive evalu-

Paul's mention of enrichment (*plousios*) in 1:5 typifies the ambiguity of the whole section. It may be viewed either as a note of sarcasm or as a positive endorsement of the gifts, either as a designation of social status or as an indication of spiritual wealth. If it reflects Jewish thought about the eschatological blessings of the end time, these blessings may be understood as either social or spiritual in nature.[6] Without making a judgment on the precise meaning of the term here, I simply note its eschatological overtones. Paul writes of riches experienced in the present and yet in a context dominated by future reference: "So that you are not (at present) lacking any gift as you await the (future) apocalypse of our Lord Jesus Christ" (1:7a).

The second half of the thanksgiving, vv 7-9, reveals more definitely apocalyptic concerns. Despite their *plousios* ("wealth") in the gifts of God, Paul now reminds the Corinthians that they are yet the ones awaiting (*apekdekomoi*) "the revelation of the Lord Jesus Christ" (*apokalypsis tou kyriou Iēsou Christou*).[7] The objective *apokalypsis* is further specified by temporal qualifiers. The common judgment that it refers to the parousia is supported by Paul's description of the Corinthians' condition "in waiting" (*apekdechomenous*) and by his assurance of their "confirmation (future tense) until the end (*heōs telous*) in the day of our Lord Jesus Christ" (1:8).[8] The one confirm-

---

ation of the "speech" and "knowledge" per se. (See the bracketing of the gifts between the two passive verb forms, *dotheisē* and *ebaiōthē*.) Furthermore, the linking of the whole thought through the datives "in Christ" and "in him" serves to place the Corinthians' particular gifts positively within the universal context of the sanctified "in Christ Jesus" in v 2.

6. Philo, e.g., writes of the *sophoi* that they enjoy divine wealth (*De post.* 130–39). Elsewhere he writes of the wise as those who look to the divine as their great, glorious, and inalienable wealth (*Quis Her.* 27).

7. The familiar question concerning whether the genitive here (*tou kyriou hēmōn Iēsou Christou*) is used to describe the content of revelation (i.e., objective or epexegetical genitive) or its agent (subjective genitive) is not resolved by the context. Richard Sturm has based his preference for the objective use of the term on the observation that generally "Paul reserves the verb (*apokalyptō*) for use in an active voice with God alone as the subject, never Christ." Sturm concludes that the phrase should be translated "the revelation by God which reveals Jesus Christ" (Richard E. Sturm, "An Exegetical Study of the Apostle Paul's Use of the Words APOKALYPTŌ/APOKALYPSIS: The Gospel as God's Apocalypse" [Ph.D. diss., Union Theological Seminary, 1983], 126).

8. See *apekdechesthai* elsewhere in Paul: Rom 8:19, 23, 25; Gal 5:5; Phil 3:20. The expre ision "Day of the Lord" is analogous to the Hebrew *Yom YHWH* (Amos 5:18 and Joel 2:28-31); here and elsewhere in Paul it is used to denote the final judgment at the coming of Christ (1 Cor 3:13; 5:5; Phil 3:15). There is an especially strong resonance between Paul's thought here and that of the prophet Joel, who prophesied the pouring out of God's spirit and the community's consequent charismatic experience in the days prior to the *Yom YHWH*. Paul similarly associates charismatic gifts with the Day of the Lord only now with the twist that the outpouring of the Spirit preceeds the Day of the Lord.

ing these things (*hos bebaiosei*) could be either Christ or God, but the syntax makes God the more likely antecedent, since otherwise the following reference to Jesus Christ would be redundant.

The word *apokalypsis* (v 7) is pivotal, standing as it does between Paul's thanksgiving for the Corinthians' gifts in the present and his acknowledgment that they still await a future revelation. The pairing of a future apocalypse with the present reality of *charismata* is thought by many interpreters to begin Paul's polemic against a "realized eschatology."[9] Whether or not Paul means to say the Corinthians have overtly rejected the idea of a future eschatological fulfillment, his rhetoric suggests that they have overestimated their present *plousios* to detrimental effect.[10]

We can deduce from their slogans that the gifted Corinthians have experienced the ecstasies of spiritual transformation and that in their ecstasy, they have attained freedom from the weightiness of the world.[11] Bolstered by spiritual experiences, they are pulled dramatically toward the future with its promise of glory, perhaps so much so that they provoke Paul's ironic charge: "Already you are filled! Already you have become rich! Without us you are kings" (4:8). Yet Paul suggests that their obsession with spiritual success has blinded them to the deeper realities of God's presence in this world.

the "hijacked" community

The Corinthians do not see, as Paul does, that God's call to *koinōnia* is a call to redemptive engagement with the world. By calling their attention to the *provisional* nature of God's present revelation, Paul sets the scene for the toppling of what they think they can know in the present. His use of traditional end-time language at this point ("you await the day of the Lord") makes the point and begins to prepare the Corinthians for a change in perspective.[12]

---

9. Conzelmann, *1 Corinthians*, 28. This interpretation receives support elsewhere in the letter, and especially in 1 Cor 4:7-8: "What have you that you did not receive? If then you received it, why do you boast as if it were not a gift? Already you are filled!" The Corinthians' "over-realization" of their gifts has been at the expense of belief in God's future apocalypse. Paul reminds them that despite their manifold gifts, they are yet not complete; they still await a further revelation.

10. The thesis that the Corinthians have a "realized eschatology" has much in its favor. The apparently polemical nature of the thanksgiving in combination with eschatological terminology and emphasis on the sovereignty of God, which pervade vv 1-9, lead logically to this conclusion. Another possibility, however, is that Paul's use of eschatological language here and elsewhere in the letters, especially in 1 Corinthians 15, indicates that he shares the expectation of future revelation with his hearers. This second option must not be ruled out too hastily, since Paul never tells us explicitly that the future eschaton is in question at Corinth.

11. Especially 1 Cor 4:8: "Already you are filled! Already you have become rich!" and 8:1: "All of us possess knowledge."

12. One way of reading Paul's argument here is to posit an *a minore ad maius* argument subtly inverted by the logic of apocalyptic thought. "If you know nothing about

In v 9, Paul brings the thanksgiving to a close with a statement that both recapitulates the opening theme of the letter, that is, the origin of the church in the call of God, and declares *koinōnia* ("fellowship") to be God's intention for the church. By placing both the call and the *koinōnia* (now painfully lacking at Corinth) under the rubric of God's trustworthiness (*pisteōs tou Theou*), Paul at once confirms the Corinthians' identity as the church God calls and challenges them to the unity of fellowship that goes hand in hand with that call.[13]

praise & responsibility

CONFLICTING ALLEGIANCES AT CORINTH: 1 CORINTHIANS 1:10-17

(10) I appeal to you, brethren, by the name of our Lord Jesus Christ, that all of you agree (*to auto legēte*) and that there be no dissensions (*schismata*) among you, but that you be united in the same mind (*en tō autō noi*) and the same knowledge (*en tē autē gnōmē*). (11) For it has been reported to me by Chloe's people that there is quarreling among you, my brethren. (12) What I mean is that each one of you says, "I belong to Paul," or "I belong to Apollos," or "I belong to Cephas," or "I belong to Christ." (13) Is Christ divided? Was Paul crucified for you? Or were you baptized in the name of Paul? (14) I am thankful that I baptized none of you except Crispus and Gaius; (15) lest any one should say that you were baptized in my name. (16) (I did baptize also the household of Stephanas. Beyond that, I do not know whether I baptized any one else.) (17) For Christ did not send me (*apesteilen*) to baptize but to preach the gospel, and not in wisdom of word (*en sophia logou*), lest the cross of Christ be emptied (*kenōthē*). (1 Cor 1:10-17)

The Factions

This section contains the first straightforward reference to a problem in the community, namely, to divisive controversies among self-designated factions in the church. Paul uses two terms to describe the problem. First, in v 10, the term *schismata* ("schisms"), which is evidently his own designation; then, in v 11, the term *erides* ("quarrels") cited in indirect discourse as the substance of what Chloe's people reported.[14] As formulated here, the terms are not equiva-

---

the future, how much less you do know the present." Such an argument, indeed, is not far from the statement of 8:2: "If any one imagines that he knows something, he does not yet know as he ought to know."

13. The phrase *pisteōs tou Theou* ("faithfulness of God") is not frequently used by Paul. Other occurrences are 1 Cor 10:13 and 1 Thess 5:24.

14. But C. K. Barrett shows *erides* to be a Pauline word. See C. K. Barrett, *The First Epistle to the Corinthians* (New York: Harper & Row, 1968), 42.

lents; *erides* points to a current reality, while the *schismata* may yet be avoided. That these factions have not yet split the church in a physical sense is also indicated by the fact that Paul addresses four groups at once (v 12) and by his opening appeal that the community not be divided.[15]

Paul now urges his hearers to agree in speech (*to auto legete pantes*, "that you all say the same thing"), mind (*en tō autō noi*, "in the same mind"), and conviction (*en tē autē gnōmē*, "in the same conviction"). In this subtle variation on the themes of the thanksgiving for the Corinthians' possession of "all speech" and "all knowledge," Paul is at his rhetorical best. The Corinthians' greatest liabilities and greatest strengths lie in their gifts. This paradox and the problems it produces for community life will be a unifying theme of the entire letter.

[handwritten marginal note: The water of baptism can also drown]

The nature of the schism whose competing slogans Paul recites in v 11—"I am of Paul," "I am of Apollos," "I am of Cephas," "I am of Christ"—has long puzzled interpreters of 1 Corinthians. It was the judgment of Karl Barth that, whatever the precise origins of the slogans, the Corinthian conflict results from the exchange of belief in God for belief in particular human leaders and heroes.[16] This much, and little more, is safe to say. What is at *stake* in the "party spirit" is at least the confusion of human with divine authority. More important than the precise nature of the "parties" themselves for Paul's discourse is the fact that such human allegiances have arisen at all.

---

15. The exact nature of the *erides* as reflected in the four slogans "I am of Paul," "I am of Apollos," "I am of Cephas," and "I am of Christ" is uncertain. There is much speculation on this matter in the literature on 1 Corinthians but no consensus. The last slogan poses the greatest difficulty. Conzelmann summarizes three possible meanings of the "I belong to Christ" slogan: (1) the slogan represents a distinct group; (2) Paul adds the slogan to theirs in order to reduce theirs *ad absurdum*; (3) "I am of Christ" is a declaration of Paul's own. Conzelmann finally explains the group phenomenon as arising from a particular interpretation of the creed. In the Corinthians' interpretation, contrary to Paul's, "the cross [of Jesus] is annulled by the [his] exaltation." This doctrinal position allows for the "spiritual elevation of the individual to meet the Lord," which in turn facilitates the formation of groups to which these "pneumatic" individuals freely choose to belong. See Conzelmann, *1 Corinthians*, 33–34. The consequence is fragmentation in the church and perversion of the creed itself. But see Elisabeth Schüssler Fiorenza, who argues that these divisions are considered party strife only by Paul, not by the Corinthians (Elisabeth Schüssler Fiorenza, "Rhetorical Situation and Historical Reconstruction in 1 Corinthians," *NTS* 33 [1987]: 396). See also Dieter Georgi's approach to the slogans. He demonstrates their kinship with the slogans of Hellenistic itinerant prophets. Citing Celsus's lists of the prophets' pneumatic expressions, he argues that such formulae as "I am God" or "I am God's child" were common in Hellenistic religion and in magic. In Dieter Georgi, *The Opponents of Paul in 2 Corinthians* (Philadelphia: Fortress Press, 1986), 104.

16. Karl Barth, *The Resurrection of the Dead* (New York: Fleming H. Revell Co., 1933), 15.

Was Paul Crucified for You?

In v 13, Paul's tone turns abruptly ironic. Now his direct criticism of the Corinthian schism begins. Three rhetorical questions serve with remarkable economy to state his case:

1:13a   Is Christ divided?
1:13b   Was Paul crucified for you?
1:13c   Or were you baptised in the name of Paul?

The first question leaves no doubt about what Paul thinks is at stake at Corinth. It is the unity of Christ's body, the church.[17] The next two questions supply essential links in the chain that reaches from the existing Corinthian divisions to the ideally unified Christ-church. Notably, in v 13b, crucifixion is introduced as the middle term between division *(memeristai,* v 13a) and baptism (v 13c).

One way of reading the three questions is to emphasize the middle term so that it "grounds" the other two, that is, so that both unity and baptism are predicated on the crucifixion of Jesus. In a parallel text, Rom 6:3-6, Paul writes of baptism into Christ's death as the only authentic baptism. Whether one acknowledges it or not (Rom 6:3a), baptism in Christ is baptism into death—and that baptism is said to unite the baptized with Christ (*symphytoi*) in a *death like his*, that is to say, in a death *kata stauron*.[18]

Whether or not one views the crucifixion as the hermeneutical center of the three-pronged question, it is significant that Paul stops short of what might have been a companion question to v 13b: "Was Paul resurrected for you?" For Paul, the story of the *church* is the story of the cross (with its impact in past and present) and not yet the story of the resurrection.[19] Whatever the Corinthians' error (in Paul's view) with regard to exaltation theologies and the like, Paul does not think the way to reconciliation lies in discussion of the resurrection. Reconciliation enters the world by Jesus' death on the

---

17. Ulrich Wilckens, *Weisheit und Torheit: Eine exegetische-religionsgeschichtliche Untersuchung zu 1 Kor 1 und 2* (Beiträge zur historischen Theologie 26; Tübingen: J. C. B. Mohr, 1959), 15.

18. Wilckens (*Weisheit*) remarks on the Romans text in connection with 1 Cor 1:13 that Paul's teaching about baptism stands or falls on the preaching of the cross of Christ. Likewise, the unity of the church depends on this preaching. Restating Paul's message here, one may say that for Paul neither true baptism nor true unity in Christ occurs at all except through entering into a death like Jesus' own.

19. The resurrection hope is, however, sure. In Rom 6:5b, note the future tense: "we shall be resurrected (*anastaseōs esometha*)."

cross. This Word alone works to reconcile human beings to each other and to God.

In v 14, Paul returns to a thanksgiving (*eucharistō*) statement, now stated in the negative. Paul is thankful that he did *not* baptize any except Chrispus, Gaius, and the household of Stephanus. In contrast to his earlier thanksgiving for *God's initiative* in the provision of gifts to the Corinthians, Paul now magnifies his own *lack of initiative* with regard to their baptism. His disclaimer is more sharply stated in the antithetical formulation at 1:17: "For Christ did not send me to baptize (*ou baptizein*) but to preach the gospel (*alla euangelizesthai*), and not with eloquent wisdom, lest the cross of Christ be emptied."

Lest the Cross Be Emptied

The transition in v 17, from preaching the gospel *ouk en sophia logou* to the cross of Christ, anticipates the argument that follows in 1:18—2:5 (and on into chap. 3).[20] Paul's syntax here is difficult. He begins with a straightforward pair of opposites, "not to baptize . . . but to preach," then moves to the first element of what promises to be a similar opposition, "not in wisdom of word (*sophia logou*)," but finally ends with a circuitous subjunctive clause, "lest the cross of Christ be emptied."[21]

The verb in the subjunctive clause, *kenoō*, is used five times in the Pauline corpus, three times in the Corinthian correspondence (1:17; 9:15; 2 Cor 9:3), once in Romans (4:14), and once in Philippians. Only in the Philippians text (2:7) is the term associated (indirectly) with the cross. In the Christ hymn (Phil 2:6-11), Jesus "empties himself" to become a slave (*doulos*) and to suffer death on the cross. In the other two Corinthian references, *kenoō* appears in the context of Paul's grounds for boasting with the meaning "to render ineffective,"[22] and in Rom 4:14 in the argument that faith is empty unless heirs of Abraham are so by promise and not by law. In every case, the meaning "to render powerless or ineffective" fits the context.

---

20. See Richard Horsley on the role of eloquent speech as part of the soul's individual achievement without concern for the vitality of the community. Richard Horsley, "Wisdom of Word and Words of Wisdom in Corinth," *CBQ* 39 (1977): 228–31.

21. See Deut 32:47 where Moses insists that the people not think of God's word as empty (*rik*) and thus implies that man's word is empty by comparison. Also Isa 55:11: "[God's] word will not return empty."

22. See Gal 6:14, e.g., where Paul boasts only in the cross of Christ.

In 1 Cor 1:17 the emptiness of the cross anticipates its opposite, the association of cross with power in 1:18.[23] The term *kenoō* in 1:17 participates in a central Pauline irony. On the one hand, the power of the crucifixion lies in the self-emptying action of Christ, just as in Phil 2:5-11 "emptiness" is understood as a power-rendering condition. Only those who boast of *this* emptiness boast legitimately. At the same time, those who boast in the Christ-event from other than the experience of emptiness (i.e., the Corinthians) are in effect *emptying* the cross. In this second sense, the "emptiness of the cross" is the nullification of its meaning and power. At Corinth, "wise talk," party strife, and exalted ego (1:12-13) empty the cross precisely because people have not experienced the paradigmatic emptiness that the cross, properly perceived, produces.[24]

In summary, it appears that the disunity at Corinth (as reflected in the "party slogans") resulted from a way of thinking and acting which, in Paul's view, undervalued the cross. One manifestation of this way of thinking was the attachment of exalted status to certain leaders and consequently to their adherents. It is difficult to read Paul's indirect claim in v 13 that membership in the unity of Christ is by way of Christ's crucifixion as other than a response to the Corinthians' exalted claims. Finally, the correspondence between the thanksgiving sections in vv 4-9 and vv 14-17 on the opposition of divine agency to human agency seems to counter a view in which human agency in the divine plan is overvalued.

In these first seventeen verses, Paul has touched upon virtually every major theme of the letter. Moreover, he has developed the rhetorical framework for his exposition by introducing a number of paired opposites, all of which contrast God's way of knowing to human wisdom. Now, in 1:18—2:16, primarily through subtle interweavings of wisdom and apocalyptic frames of reference, he will attempt to bring the implications of this contrast home to the divided Corinthians.

---

23. Wilckens, *Weisheit*, 120 n. 1. It also anticipates the function of the word in 1:18, especially if there Paul has in mind the "Word of Yahweh" in the prophetic tradition that "goes out to accomplish Yahweh's purpose and will not return empty" (Isa 55:10-11).

24. Philo, too, criticizes the individualistic spiritual orientation of some who lose touch with the social dimension of philosophy. Against the Sophists he argues that their speeches benefit neither their hearers nor their own souls (Det 72–74).

THE WORD MEETS THE CONVENTIONS OF
WISDOM AND FOLLY: 1 CORINTHIANS 1:18

The principal motifs of Paul's performative strategy are illustrated in the topic sentence of the discourse at 1:18:

> For the word of the cross (*logos tou staurou*) is folly to those who are perishing, but to us who are being saved it is the power of God (*dynamis tou Theou*). (1 Cor 1:18)

On the surface this is a nicely balanced sentence; it has two parallel clauses, each consisting of subject, copulative verb, indirect object, and predicate nominative. The two pairs of opposites together assert something about the single subject, the Word of the Cross (*ho logos tou staurou*). On closer inspection, however, the paired opposites are strangely unbalanced; by standard expectations, they represent an aporia. The first pair, *saved* versus *perishing*, presents no particular perceptual problem; that is an opposite we expect. But the second, *folly* versus *power*, presents an unexpected and destabilizing opposition. Even in the twentieth century, and perhaps all the more in the philosophical and religious context of the first century, the expected partner to "folly" is not "power" but "wisdom."[25]

Paul's choice of opposites is startling, especially in light of his subject, the cross; it is not simply the pairing of folly with power that surprises but the attribution of power to what is otherwise the symbol of weakness, the cross. In making the substitution "power" for "wisdom," Paul has said something new and epistemologically offensive about salvation. It is now not the wisdom of the wise that "saves," despite the high value of wisdom in the traditions of both Jews and Greeks; in fact, this wisdom is equated with "emptiness." Rather, what saves is the "power of the cross," a formulation that is nonsensical in the perspective of worldly wisdom. Moreover, Paul has located the power of the cross not simply in the past event itself but in the present Word about the event that continually re-presents it to the reader. Through the *logos*, the cross continues to break powerfully into the old world's "dominant system of convictions" wherever it is proclaimed.[26]

---

25. The Book of Sirach, a product of the Hellenistic period, rehearses the familiar opposition: e.g., Sir 21:16, "Like a house that has vanished, so is wisdom to a fool."

26. Gerd Theissen uses this phrase to describe the opposition encountered by the Word of the Cross within the human psyche. See Gerd Theissen, *Psychological Aspects of Pauline Theology* (Philadelphia: Fortress Press, 1987), 79.

Already in the structure of the sentence at 1:18, we begin to see how the Word works in a particular linguistic context to dislodge readers from their accustomed perceptual worlds. This is one aspect of its dynamic apocalyptic nature; by this power to dislocate, the Word begins to create the conditions under which readers may be transformed and transferred into a new world. In his transpositions of linguistic signs, and particularly signs associated with ways of knowing—that is, *wisdom* and *folly*—Paul presses previously held cognitions about God, self, and world to the point of collapse. This is the first step of the transformative action of the Word—act 1, scene 1 of the performative drama.

Following the lead of its topic sentence, the entire discourse is patterned on a series of antitheses that oppose the wisdom (or in 1:18, "power") of God to worldly wisdom (or in 1:18, "folly") and repeat the challenge presented by 1:18 again and again:

Antithetical Patterns in 1 Corinthians 1:18—2:5

1:18	folly	vs.	power of God
	perishing	vs.	the ones being saved
1:19-20	wisdom of world	vs.	wisdom of God
1:21	wisdom of world	vs.	folly of kerygma
1:22-24	Jews who seek signs and	vs.	the called for whom
	Greeks who seek wisdom	vs.	Christ = Wisdom of God
1:25	foolishness of God	vs.	wisdom of human beings
	weakness of God	vs.	strength of human beings
1:26	wise (by world's standard)	vs.	foolish chosen by God
	powerful/strong	vs.	weak chosen by God
	nobly born	vs.	lowly and despised
	things that are	vs.	things that are not
2:1	proclamation in lofty words of wisdom	vs.	knowing only Christ crucified
2:3-4	plausible words of wisdom	vs.	Paul's speech and preaching
	plausible words of wisdom	vs.	demonstration of *pneuma* and *dynamis*
2:5	human wisdom	vs.	power of God

Two principal dynamics of the discourse are evident in this unit: (1) the division between ways of knowing, one characterized by standard pairs of opposites and one by the overturning of those opposites, and (2) the power (*dynamis*, 1:18) of the "Word of the Cross" to effect a transition from one way of knowing to the other. Both themes, I will argue, arise from and function within an apocalyptic frame of reference.

The Word as Salvation or Destruction

The datives in 1:18 translated "the ones being saved" (*sōzomenois*) and "the ones perishing" (*apollymenois*) may be read either subjectively or objectively. If they are subjective, the meaning is that the Word is judged by some to be folly (to the effect that they perish) and by others to be power (to the effect that they are saved). If objective, the meaning is that the Word itself brings about the judgment—the Word determines who is being saved and who is perishing. Ulrich Wilckens solves the problem by merging the two meanings; the divine judgment takes place in the hearer's act of perceiving and evaluating the Word.

> The measure of their [the hearers] distinction is therefore, on the one hand, their judgement about the *logos tou staurou*, but on the other hand, the eschatological judgement of God, through which God will separate them as saved and lost.[27]

The joining of divine judgment and human perception presents a challenging theological question. If God acts to save or to damn by calling some to perceive the Word correctly and others to misperceive it, what becomes of human freedom to decide? One approach to this question is to consider once again Paul's surprising substitution of "power of God" for "wisdom" at the end of the verse.[28] At least one effect of this substitution is to take the wind from the sails of human decision. It is the power of God, not the power of human beings, that determines salvation.[29]

---

27. Wilckens, *Weisheit*, 22.

28. Wilckens notes that the *moria* of the perishing is without a genitive, whereas on the "side of the saved," *dynamis* is characterized by the genitive, *tou Theou* (Wilckens, *Weisheit*, 24).

29. Had the standard opposite to folly, "wisdom," appeared here, human decision would receive greater emphasis as in the tradition of the "two ways." J. Louis Martyn argues against the presence of a call to decision in this text: "By means of the surprising imbalance between *moria* and *dynamis tou Theou*, Paul says forcefully that the preached word is not served up as a first step so that as a second step the Corinthians may apply it to their superior powers of discernment" (J. Louis Martyn, "Epistemology at the Turn of the Ages: 2 Corinthians 5:16," in *Christian History and Interpretation: Studies Presented to John Knox*, ed. W. R. Farmer, C. F. D. Moule, and R. R. Niebuhr [Cambridge: Cambridge University Press, 1967], 287). See also the related views of Gordon Fee, who writes, "The Gospel is not a new sophia, not even a divine sophia. For sophia al-

Attribution of such power to God's Word is not new to religious thought. The motif of the dividing power of the Word is found in both Hebrew prophecy and Jewish apocalyptic. In both contexts, the word of Yahweh is power-filled and double-edged; it goes out to accomplish Yahweh's purpose, and it will not return empty (Isa 55: 10-11). The word is "like a fire," a hammer that breaks rocks into pieces (Jer 5:14; 23:29). The word brings life and joy (Deut 32:47 and Jer 15:16) and is "a sharp sword that fills all things with death" (Wis Sol 18:14-16).

In apocalyptic texts, the word both recalls the past and sets the future in motion. In 4 Ezra, the word that went forth and accomplished the work of creation in the beginning now prophesies the end (6:15, 43). In Daniel, the word of the holy ones is revealed in a dream "to the end that the living may know that the Most High rules the kingdom of men" (Dan 4:17). The word is, above all, an active, "performative" word. Its power belongs to God, not to human beings,[30] and its effect is to compel human beings to discern their own relationship to it.[31]

In both prophetic and apocalyptic thought the word acts by revealing something about God and God's plan for the future. Almost always, what it reveals concerns the end of the old order and either the beginning of a new relationship between God and humanity or a new creation altogether (e.g., Jer 31:31-34; Isa 43:19; 65:17-25; Ezek 37:4; Rev 1:2; 4 Ezra 15:1; 16:36). When Paul writes of the power of

---

lows for human judgments or evaluations of God's activity. But the Gospel stands as the divine antithesis to such judgments." On 1 Cor 1:18, Fee develops the point further: "In Pauline theology the new division is not so much predicated on their response to the message of the cross as it is on the event of the cross and resurrection itself. That is, the crucifixion and resurrection of Jesus for Paul marked the 'turning of the ages,' whereby God decisively judged and condemned the present age and is in the process of bringing it to an end" (Gordon D. Fee, *The First Epistle to the Corinthians* [Grand Rapids: Wm. B. Eerdmans, 1987], 69).

30. Gerhard von Rad cites Isa 40:6-8 and notes the opposition of "all flesh" to the "word of our God that stands forever": "The phrase is extremely terse, but it is perfectly clear that by "the word of our God the prophet means to point to that other power which confronts the first one, the power of man. He is not, therefore, thinking of the word which will endure because it calls forth an echo in the inner realm of the heart, but of the word which Yahweh speaks into history and which works creatively on that plane" (Gerhard von Rad, *Theology of the Old Testament* [New York: Harper & Row, 1965], 2:92-95; emphasis mine).

31. Timothy Polk, in an article on the *māšāl* as speech act in Ezekiel, captures the hearer-involving capacity of performative language of Ezekiel 17 as *māšāl*. He writes, "As a paradigm of divine activity, modeling the structure of reality and the ways of God with human beings in such a way as to invite or compel the readers to define their own place within that picture" (Timothy Polk, "Paradigms, Parables and *mĕšālîm*: On Reading the *māšāl* in Scripture," *CBQ* 45, no. 4 [1983]: 578-79).

God revealed in the Word of the Cross, the powerful word of Yahweh known to the prophets and the visionaries is not far from view. It is my judgment, given Paul's bracketing of this whole section between prophetic citations, that this association is direct if not deliberate—in other words, that Paul's understanding of the word was directly influenced by the prophets and visionaries.[32] The Word of the Cross, like the word of Yahweh in prophecy, reveals something about God, that is, God's son suffered crucifixion for the sake of humanity, and about God's plan for the future, that is, who will be saved and who will perish.

Paul demonstrates further contact with apocalyptic thought in his understanding of the double effect of the Word to lead some to true perception and some to blindness. The conviction that God, as Sovereign, allows or even ordains opposition to God's word is evident at Qumran:

> The Angel of Darkness leads all the children of righteousness astray, and until his end all their sin, iniquities, wickedness, and all their unlawful deeds are caused by his dominion *in accordance with the mysteries of God*." (1QS 3:22-23; emphasis mine)[33]

For Paul, as for the Qumran writer, the present is the time of division. We may compare his use of the present participles *sōzomenois* and *apollymenois* and his persistent reference to the future end time to the Qumran writer's conviction that the Angel of Darkness leads some astray *until his end*. Yet, when Paul merges the present and future aspects of judgment, as he does in our text, he works from a distinctive understanding of the sequence of eschatological events. The end is provisionally present, not merely awaited (as at Qumran) in the event and the Word of the Cross.[34] True or false perception of

---

32. There is always the question, of course, whether or not the Corinthian hearers would have "heard" the prophetic overtones here. Perhaps Paul's message about the life-and-death-dealing activity of the word would have made more sense to Jews than to Greeks. The absence of this logos interpretation among the Greeks may be one reason for the apparent (relative) failure of this letter to stabilize the Corinthian church.

33. See the similar thoughts at 1QH 5:36 and the helpful discussion of the double effect of the revelatory word in Joel Marcus, *The Mystery of the Kingdom of God* (SBLDS 90; Atlanta: Scholars Press, 1986), 49–51.

34. Conzelmann (citing W. Foerster, *TDNT*, 7:992) prefers not to interpret the present tense here in such a way as to "read mysterious hints into them to the effect that the present tense 'expresses the unfinished character of the road to *sotēria* and apoleia respectively'" (Conzelmann, *1 Corinthians*, 41). Barrett observes, on the other hand, that Paul's eschatological perspective, already explicit at 1:8, requires that "neither process can be thought of as complete. . . . Destruction and salvation . . . are consummated at the last day" (Barrett, *The First Epistle to the Corinthians*, 51). Wilckens too emphasizes the future reference of the terms given the "strong eschatological context" of this usage. See Wilckens, *Weisheit*, 22.

this event brings one actually into salvation or destruction, not merely into the predisposition toward one or the other.

I have suggested that the *logos tou staurou* in 1:18 functions in ways that recall the function of the "word of Yahweh" in Semitic thought. About that earlier word, Gerhard von Rad has written,

> It is an event, a unique happening in history, which a man is looking for, or which takes him by surprise, and which therefore in either case sets the person concerned in a new historical situation.[35]

In Paul's view, the "new historical situation" effected by the Word of the Cross is none other than the end of the old world. One who perceives what the cross reveals is dislocated from that world and relocated in God's new creation. While he still awaits the parousia and the final subjection of all things to God (1 Cor 15:27-28), he now waits in the life-giving apocalyptic perception of God's present and future redemption. To wait here is to wait in a newly defined territory, from which one's view of the world (and thus one's way of living in the world) is totally transformed.

PROPHECY REVISITED: 1 CORINTHIANS 1:19-31

(19) For it is written, "I will destroy the wisdom of the wise, and the cleverness of the clever I will thwart." (20) Where is the wise man? Where is the scribe? Where is the debater of this age? Has not God made foolish (*emōranen*) the wisdom of the world?

(21) For since, in the wisdom of God, the world did not know God through wisdom, it pleased God through the folly of what we preach to save those who believe. (22) For Jews demand signs and Greeks seek wisdom, (23) but we preach Christ crucified, a stumbling block to Jews and folly to Gentiles, (24) but to those who are called, both Jews and Greeks, Christ the power of God and the wisdom of God. (25) For the foolishness of God is wiser than [human beings], and the weakness of God is stronger than [human beings].

(26) For consider your call, brethren; not many of you were wise according to worldly standards, not many were powerful, not many were of noble birth; but God chose what is foolish in the world to shame the wise, God chose what is weak in the world to shame the strong, (28) God chose what is low and despised in the world, even things that are not, to bring to nothing things that are, (29) so that no human being might boast in the presence of God. (30) He is the source of your life

---

35. von Rad, *Theology of the Old Testament*, 87.

in Christ Jesus, whom God made our wisdom, our righteousness and sanctification and redemption; (31) therefore, as it is written, "Let him who boasts, boast of the Lord." (1 Cor 1:19-31)

The unit 1:19-31 is composed of three subunits, in which prophetic citations in 1:19-20 (A) and 1:26-31 (C) "frame" the kerygmatic statement in 1:21-25 (B). Verse 19 consists entirely of a quotation from Isa 29:14, which Paul has modified slightly from the LXX, replacing, in v 19b, *krypso* ("I will hide") with *atheteso* ("I will set aside/bring to nothing"). The standard comment on this verse is that here Paul offers a proof text for his own thesis by showing that already in scripture, God has rejected the world's wisdom.[36] Few commentators go on, however, to explore Paul's deeper indebtedness to Isaiah—and later in this section, Jeremiah traditions—for the formulation of his discourse on the cross. Because these traditions appear to inform Paul's revised apocalyptic, I will consider them in some depth.

In the discussion of 1:18, we noticed a parallel between the Word of the Cross and prophetic traditions about the active, judgment-rendering word of God. The Isaiah citation at 1:19 makes those traditions even more evident. Isaiah 29:14 reads, "I will destroy the wisdom of the wise and the understanding of the discerning ones I will hide." Paul cites the verse essentially as it appears in the LXX but intensifies the divine negation of human wisdom by changing its final verb from *krypso* ("I will hide") to *atheteso* ("I will set aside/bring to nothing"). His use of the verse, moreover, seems to echo its larger context in Isaiah, for Isaiah goes on to outline the false, self-exalting perceptions of Israel:

> You turn things upside down!
>   Shall the potter be regarded as the clay;
> that the thing made should say of its maker,
>   "He did not make me";
> or the thing formed say of him who formed it,
>   "He has no understanding"? (Isa 29:16)

But at 29:18, Isaiah describes the new day:

> In that day the deaf shall hear
>   the words of a book,

---

36. See F. Lang, *Die Briefe an die Korinther* (Das Neue Testament Deutsch; Göttingen: Vandenhoeck & Ruprecht, 1986), 29; Conzelmann, *1 Corinthians*, 52–53; and Barrett, *The First Epistle to the Corinthians*, 52–53.

and out of their gloom and darkness
   the eyes of the blind shall see.
. . . .
And those who err in spirit will come to understanding,
   and those who murmer will accept instruction. (Isa 29:18, 24)

The prophet's word (= the word of Yahweh), like Paul's Word of the Cross, is two-edged. It destroys the illusions of self-determination by declaring human wisdom and understanding to be blindness and incomprehension, but it also declares the will of Yahweh to open eyes and unstop ears.[37] Similarly, in 1:18 the word reveals who is blind and who perceives. But unlike Isaiah's word, the Word of the Cross does not meet utter failure, followed by God's reversal. Rather, the Word of the Cross creates comprehension and obduracy *simultaneously*.

In v 20, Paul draws much more freely from Isaiah, alluding to texts like Isa 19:12 and Isa 33:18 ("Where then are your wise men?"; "Where then is he who weighed the tribute?"), now fashioning the rhetorical questions for his own audience. The three questions demand the same negative answer (e.g., "There is none wise") and, in each case, amplify the opposition of worldly wisdom to divine wisdom. The three "occupations" mentioned—sage, scribe, debater—may be meant to cover the bases of both Jewish and Greek intellectual pride. That Paul has both Jews and Greeks in mind becomes obvious in vv 22-23.[38]

The blind and the deaf in Isaiah are above all the religious leaders, the prophets and seers, precisely those whom one would expect to be exegetically astute. The apocalyptic qualifier that Paul places on the third occupation, "debater *of this age*," probably applies to all three stations. Opposed to this age is another, in which all the structures of the present age, including those that define who is sage,

---

37. Cf. Isa 6:9-11, where God decrees the sentence of blindness, deafness, and incomprehension, which is, at 29:18-21, at least in part, repealed.
38. Nils Dahl finds in v 20a indication that the Corinthians "exercised their wisdom as interpreters of scripture." See "Paul and the Church at Corinth According to 1 Cor 1:10—4:21," *Studies in Paul* (Minneapolis: Augsburg Publishing House, 1977), 54 n. 32. J. A. Davis has cited Dahl to support his idea that Paul addresses a Torah-centric wisdom at Corinth. See J. A. Davis, *Wisdom and Spirit: An Investigation of 1 Cor 1:18—3:20 against the Background of Jewish Sapiential Tradition in the Greco-Roman Period* (Washington, D.C.: University Press of America, 1984), 73 n. 29. While I do not accept Davis's conjecture of a Corinthian Torah-centrism, the suggestion that the Corinthian side of the debate may have been bolstered by scriptural exegesis (perhaps according to principles Paul himself had taught them) is plausible.

scribe, or philosopher, will pass away.[39] The last question in v 20, "Has not God made foolish the wisdom of the world?" echoes Isa 44:25:

> I am the Lord . . . who turns [the] wise . . . back, and makes their knowledge foolish.

For Paul, as for Isaiah before him,[40] God's power to create anew *dislocates* and supersedes the traditions of the wise.[41] Unlike Isaiah, Paul uses the past tense to indicate that this power has been exercised definitively in the past (i.e., in the cross event).

God's Resolve to Save Through the Folly of Preaching

(21) For since, in the wisdom of God, the world did not know God through wisdom, it pleased God through the folly of what we preach to save those who believe. (22) For Jews demand signs and Greeks seek wisdom, (23) but we preach Christ crucified, a stumbling block to Jews and folly to Gentiles, (24) but to those who are called, both Jews and Greeks, Christ the power of God and the wisdom of God. (25) For the foolishness of God is wiser than [human beings], and the weakness of God is stronger than [human beings]. (1 Cor 1:21-25)

Verse 21a begins with the causal "for since" (*epeidē*), which links it both to v 20b, as if to explain God's action to "make foolish the *sophia tou kosmou*," and to v 21b, to supply the condition under which God resolved to save through the folly of the cross kerygma.

> 1:20b Has not God made foolish (*emōranen*) the wisdom of the world?
> 1:21a For since (*epeidē*) in the wisdom of God (*en sophia tou Theou*) the world did not know (*egnō*) God through wisdom,
> 1:21b God resolved (*eudokēsen*) through the folly of what we preach (*dia tēs mōrias tou kērygmatos*) to save (*sōsai*) the ones having faith (*pisteuontes*).

---

39. Conzelmann observes that the expression *tou aiōnos toutou* comes from Jewish apocalyptic and "has its counterpart in the expectation of the coming aeon," but then he denies (on the basis that the expression "the coming aeon" is lacking in Paul) that Paul's eschatology is "constructed on an apocalyptic outlook" (Conzelmann, *1 Corinthians*, 43). The thrust of my argument, of course, is toward the firm establishment of the expression in apocalyptic thought.

40. Cf. Isa 43:19, "Remember not the former things, nor consider the things of old. Behold, I am doing a new thing; . . . Do you not perceive it?"

41. Conzelmann notes the emphasis on the act of God here; "God *makes* the wisdom of the world foolish" (this as opposed to showing worldly wisdom to be already foolish). In fact, it is a consistent theme in Isaiah that God's act supersedes even tradition. See Conzelmann, *1 Corinthians*, 46.

The aorist verbs *emōranen, egnō, eudokēsen* (made foolish, knew, was pleased) reveal two activities of God that bracket one human activity. In v 20b, God *made foolish* (*emōranen*) the world's wisdom, in v 21b God *resolved to save* (*eudokēsen . . . sōsai*) through the foolishness of preaching. Between these two divine actions stands the world's failure: it *did not know* (*ouk egnō*) God through wisdom, with the result that God resolved to save through the folly of preaching. The aorist indicates that the crucial turning point in God's affairs with the world came *in the past*. The *present* tenses of v 22—the Jews *demand . . .* the Greeks *seek*—indicate that the world persists in ignorance even beyond God's past resolve (in the cross event) "to save."

Considerable controversy surrounds the interpretation of 1:21a and particularly the two uses of the term *sophia* in that verse. Are two kinds of wisdom in view here, the wisdom of the world and the wisdom of God? Or is only *one* wisdom in view, the wisdom of God, which is unrecognized as such by the world?[42]

The context supports a distinction between two kinds of wisdom in v 21a. The first, God's wisdom, is in sharp *contrast* to the wisdom through which the world fails to know God. In context, the latter wisdom is equivalent both to the "wisdom of the wise," which God will destroy in v 19, and the "wisdom of the world God made foolish" in v 20b. Such a distinction brings the logic of v 21 into conformity with the surrounding verses, each of which is structured by the contrast of worldly to divine wisdom as illustrated here:

---

42. The controversy centers on the meaning of the dative in 1:21a: *en tē sophia tou Theou*. Is the preposition *en* to be taken with spatial meaning, "in the midst of wisdom," or with temporal meaning, "during the epoch of wisdom"? Or is the *en* best understood in relation to *ginōskein*, so that the verse renders the meaning "the world did not recognize God in the light of his wisdom (as it has shown itself in creation)"? (Conzelmann, *1 Corinthians*, 45). The temporal solution is the least plausible, since, as Conzelmann notes, Paul nowhere discusses a temporal epoch when God's wisdom was directly manifested. The spatial solution is a stronger one, supported by both Wilckens and Conzelmann, who connect *en* and *dia* in v 21 to the effect that *en* reflects a sphere of existence (in the midst of wisdom), and *dia* the means of knowledge (through wisdom). In this reading, the wisdom of God is both the "sphere" in which one lives and the means by which one comes to the knowledge of God (Conzelmann, *1 Corinthians*, 45, and Wilckens, *Weisheit*, 34). In this interpretation, however, there is no sharp distinction between the sophia through which the world failed to know God (*dia tēs sophias*) and the "folly of what we preach" in v 21. The antithesis between worldly sophia and divine sophia is erased. Instead, the sentence reads: "Since in the midst of God's wisdom, the world did not know God through God's wisdom (God's act in Christ), God resolved to save through the preaching of God's wisdom (act in Christ)." This is a difficult and obscure reading.

1:19b I will destroy the wisdom of the wise
1:20a God made foolish the wisdom of the world

1:21a God's wisdom (in the wisdom of God)
1:21b World's wisdom (world does not know *dia* wisdom)

1:21b God's wisdom (folly of what we preach)
1:22b Greeks seek wisdom

1:23a We preach Christ crucified (= folly of what we preach = wisdom)
1:24b Christ = wisdom of God

1:25a Christ = foolishness of God
1:25b Wiser than wisdom of human beings

A related dichotomy emerges in v 21 in the juxtaposition of human and divine activities represented by the terms "to know" and "to save"—since the world did not know, God decided to save through the proclamation. Whatever the *content* of the world's ineffective wisdom, what it failed to deliver was true knowledge of God. The statement reminds us of Rom 1:18-22 and the fall from knowledge brought on by willful refusal to recognize God. But our verse lacks the Romans emphasis on human willing. Instead, we find the surprising implication that *God* willed the world's inability to know *so that* (*epeidē*) God could save (i.e., give the true and saving knowledge of God) through the cross. God's saving act makes futile any attempt to know God through "perceptual criteria developed apart from the gospel."[43]

Again, as in 1:18, the hearer is perceptually dislocated by God's power to save. The dislocating and relocating power of the Word is illustrated formally in vv 21-25. These verses may be schematized on the pattern A → B → C → B′ → A′ → D:

A – A′ = God's initiative to save
B – B′ = Human expectations about salvation/knowledge
C   = kerygma, Christ crucified
D   = Transformed human perception about salvation

Our verses conform to this pattern as follows:

---

43. The expression is J. Louis Martyn's in reference to Gal 1:16-17. Martyn continues: "[Paul] implies that the patriarchal traditions did not provide him with criteria of perception that enabled him to recognize the gospel when it came along." What brought Paul to the gospel was not his decision about God, based on criteria learned *en tē Ioudaismō*, but rather what one might call God's apocalyptic decision about him: "But when [God] was pleased to apocalypse his Son to me . . . " (J. Louis Martyn, "Paul and His Jewish-Christian Interpreters," *USQR* 42 [1988]: 13–14).

1:21	God was pleased to save believers	A
1:22	Jews ask for signs	B
	Greeks seek wisdom	
1:23	We preach Christ crucified	C
	to the Jews, scandal	B′
	to the Greeks, folly	
1:24	But to the called	A′
	Christ,	D
	the Power of God	
	the Wisdom of God	

At the center of the diagram (C) is the heart of the kerygma, Christ crucified (C). On the near side of center is divided human expectation [Jews demand . . . Greeks seek . . .] (B); on the far side is the unperceiving human response to the kerygma (B′). Beyond the unperceiving response is true perception (D). The schema demonstrates three perceptual events effected by the cross:

1. The movement from sign to scandal. The Jews who seek signs and the Greeks who seek wisdom perceive the cross as scandal or folly (B–B′).
2. The creation of a new entity, "the called," which includes Jews and Greeks (A′).
3. The movement from human expectations (B) to the "apocalyptic perception" that the crucified Christ is the Power and Wisdom of God (D).

The opening *hoti* ("For") in v 25 brings resolution to the train of thought in vv 21-25:

(25) For the foolishness of God is wiser than [human beings], and the weakness of God is stronger than [human beings].

The dual designation, Jew and Greek, is now dissolved into the single expression, human being (*anthrōpos*). The "folly of God" (*mōron tou Theou*) now takes its meaning from what precedes; it is the kerygma of Christ crucified. Together with v 24, this verse forms a summary chiasm in which the wisdom of God (*sophia tou Theou*) is equal to the folly of God (*mōron tou Theou*) and the power of God (*dynamis tou Theou*) is equal to the weakness of God (*asthenes tou Theou*):

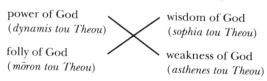

power of God   wisdom of God
(*dynamis tou Theou*)   (*sophia tou Theou*)

folly of God   weakness of God
(*mōron tou Theou*)   (*asthenes tou Theou*)

Having now stated the paradox of the cross in vv 21-25, Paul will turn again to the prophetic tradition, this time to Jeremiah, to work out its applications for community life.

Jeremiah and the Tradition of Counter-Wisdom: Jeremiah 9:22-23

(26) For consider your call, brethren; not many of you were wise according to worldly standards, not many were powerful, not many were of noble birth; (27) but God chose what is foolish in the world to shame the wise, God chose what is weak in the world to shame the strong, (28) God chose what is low and despised in the world, even things that are not, to bring to nothing things that are, (29) so that no human being might boast in the presence of God. (30) He is the source of your life in Christ Jesus, whom God made our wisdom, our righteousness and sanctification and redemption; (31) therefore, as it is written, "Let him who boasts, boast of the Lord." (1 Cor 1:26-31)

Paul now moves from the more formal exposition of the Word of the Cross (vv 21-25) to its application in the social order of the church at Corinth. This section of his argument returns to the concrete problem at Corinth (vv 10-17), now applying the Word of the Cross explicitly to it. It is perhaps the social/political nature of the problem that puts Paul in mind of the prophet Jeremiah, whom he cites at 1:31: "Let him who boasts, boast of the Lord" (Jer 9:23).

Both the citation formula, "as it is written," and the verbal proximity to the Jeremiah text suggest an intentional citation of the Septuagint text of Jer 9:23.[44] Since the citation serves as Paul's summation of 1 Cor 1:26-31, we are led to inquire about the extent and effect of Jeremiah's influence on the section as a whole (1:26-31).[45]

In an article devoted to the study of "intertextuality"[46] in biblical exegesis, Gail O'Day argues that Paul's exposition of the cross is heavily influenced by "the rhetoric and logic of Jer 9:22-23." O'Day points out that while scholars often note the Jeremiah citation, they neglect Paul's larger debt to Jeremiah. The entire section 1:26-31,

---

44. Barrett, *The First Epistle to the Corinthians*, 61: "The quotation is not exact, but the Semitic use of the conditional participle as subject . . . is due to the LXX."

45. In what follows I will assume that whether or not Paul knew what Jeremiah was up to in his critique of Israel, Paul effectively applies Jeremiah's words to his own epistemological purposes.

46. Drawing on the work of a number of literary critics, Gail O'Day defines intertexuality as "the interaction between a received text and a fresh social context [which] brings a new textual and symbolic world into being" (Gail O'Day, "Jeremiah 9:22 and 1 Corinthians 1:26-31: A Study in Intertextuality," *JBL* 109, no. 2 [1990]: 259).

she argues, is an example of "inner-biblical exegesis," in which "Paul both makes explicit reference to the received text (Jer 9:22-23), and interweaves it thoroughly into the fabric of his new text." O'Day concludes that "Jeremiah's critique of wisdom, power, and wealth as false sources of identity that violate the covenant are re-imaged by Paul as a critique of wisdom, power and wealth that impede God's saving acts in Jesus Christ."[47]

A principal source for O'Day's study is Walter Brueggemann's article on Jer 9:22-23, "The Epistemological Crisis of Israel's Two Histories (Jer 9:22-23)."[48] In his analysis, Brueggemann shows Jeremiah to be engaged in a critique of what he calls the "illusionary epistemological consensus" of the "royal definers of reality," that is, the traditioners of wisdom. The two "histories" whose conflict produces crisis, according to Brueggemann, are the Mosaic-covenantal history that is "radically concerned for justice" (represented in Jeremiah's critique) and the "Davidic royal" history that is more concerned for order. Each history is "powered by a different memory," each provides a "different lens through which life may be experienced."[49] The wisdom tradition, he argues, is more apt to assume the epistemological position of the royal history since that history strives for stability and continuity, even if at the price of human freedom and justice. Brueggemann writes of the wisdom tradition that characterized the royal epistemology:

> The royal (sapiential) tradition, inevitably conservative, fashions a life-world which is essentially settled. What is valued, i.e., true and life-giving, consists in the resources managed by the king and his retinue. Alternatively, the Mosaic-covenantal tradition is characteristically in tension, as it finds the core of a legitimate epistemology in the Exodus-sojourn-Sinai memories, stories of intervention by Yahweh on behalf of the politically disenfranchised against the Egyptian royal reality. The royal consciousness developed a consensus which screened out such an unbearable concern. It was unbearable because, on the one hand, it kept raising to consciousness those very elements in society which had been declared non-existent. On the other hand, it was un-

---

47. O'Day, "Intertextuality," 260, 267.
48. Walter Brueggemann, "The Epistemological Crisis of Israel's Two Histories (Jer 9:22-23)," in *Israelite Wisdom: Theological and Literary Essays in Honor of Samuel Terrien*, ed. J. G. Gammie, W. A. Brueggemann, W. L. Humphreys, and James W. Ward (Missoula, Mont.: Scholars Press, 1978).
49. Brueggemann, "Epistemological Crisis," 86.

bearable because it articulated a freedom and sovereignty for God which would not be domesticated by the royal apparatus.[50]

At times of crisis in Israel's history, Brueggemann suggests, the epistemological consensus achieved by the "royal definers of reality" broke down. At these times there rose up in Israel two other figures, the prophet and the apocalyptic visionary, who saw things very differently. For them, the center claimed by the traditioners of wisdom did not hold. God was free to invade and disrupt the status quo on behalf of the outsider, the dispossessed, those whose inexplicable tragedies found no place in the cosmic order.

Brueggemann articulates something very near the epistemological conflict we see 1 Corinthians. There too the primary source of the crisis is dispute about the nature and sovereignty of God. Seen as a demonstration of conflicting epistemologies, that is, royal wisdom against the prophetic critique, the Jeremiah text appears to be much more than a "proof text" for Paul's insights about boasting. The combined insights of O'Day and Brueggemann, that the Jeremiah text substantively informs Paul's argument in 1 Cor 1:26-31, and that the Jeremiah text itself concerns an epistemological crisis resulting in a critique of wisdom traditions (even while using wisdom forms), support, then, our reading of 1 Corinthians 1–2 as Paul's apocalyptic critique of a wisdom epistemology.

The Epistemological Challenge in 1 Corinthians 1:26–31

Verse 26 begins with an imperative: "Brothers, consider your call (*klēsis*)" which echoes Paul's emphasis in 1:1-9 on the Corinthians as the ones "called by God" and thus utterly dependent on God's sovereignty.[51] To demonstrate the paradox of God's electing will, Paul proceeds, now in parallel with the Jeremiah text (Jer 9:22 [LXX]), to a discussion of the conditions under which they were called.

---

50. Brueggemann, "Epistemological Crisis," 86–87. See also the thesis of Robert Gordis on class origins of wisdom literature. "Wisdom literature, which reached its apogee during the earlier centuries of the Second Temple, roughly between the fifth and the first half of the second centuries BCE was fundamentally the product of the upper classes in society, who lived principally in the capital, Jerusalem" (Robert Gordis, "The Social Background of Wisdom Literature," *HUCA* 18 [1943/44]: 81).

51. The initial *gar* in v 26 is best left untranslated. I agree with Gordon Fee that the *gar* is an inferential or explanatory conjunction "indicating that this paragraph (and the next) will offer specific illustrations further to demonstrate the point of vv 18-25" (Fee, *The First Epistle to the Corinthians*, 79).

Not many of you were wise according to worldly standards
   (*gar*) *ou polloi sophoi kata sarka*[52]
Not many were powerful
   ou polloi dynatoi
Not many were of noble birth
   ou polloi eugeneis

The verse suggests that the congregation is composed largely of the lower classes. But, as Gerd Theissen points out in his treatment of the sociological implications of this text, "If there are not many . . . who were wise, powerful and well-born, then this much is certain: there were some."[53] In Theissen's view, the "some" were the source of the trouble in Corinth. Theissen argues that class distinctions are in view in all three designations, "wise," "powerful," and "noble," and, moreover, that the Corinthian "*gnōsis*" demonstrates a class-based elitism typical of later Gnosticism.[54] The presence of very similar vocabulary in Philo gives reason to think that these distinctions may have been at issue in his Jewish community as well.[55]

If Theissen is correct, the controversy at Corinth arises from socioeconomic distinctions that have developed into religious distinctions. It is not necessary, however, to posit socioeconomic roots for the controversy to see that it involves some sort of elevation of some members of the community over others. Whatever the history of this development, it is now being supported by a religious practice and language that Paul opposes. In the next chapter, we will consider in more detail how people who consider themselves "pneumatics" might have utilized the language of the Hellenistic Jewish wisdom tradition in the service of a spiritual and social elitism.

My concern at this juncture is to show that Paul's threefold negative statement in v 26 is a statement of challenge, not simply a state-

---

52. The initial *gar* is probably an explanatory conjunction to indicate that 1:26 ff. elucidates what has gone before. See Herbert W. Smyth, *Greek Grammar* (Cambridge: Harvard University Press, 1956), 639.

53. See Gerd Theissen, *The Social Setting of Pauline Christianity* (Philadelphia: Fortress Press, 1982).

54. Among the elitist ideas of later Christian Gnostics already in view in Corinth, Theissen lists the stratification of the Christian community that happened when the upper classes separated themselves as Gnostics from the common Christians. Here he cites the example of Valentinians in Rome and argues that "in Corinth there were the beginnings of such differentiation" (Theissen, *Social Setting*, 135).

55. Stephen M. Pogoloff cites Philo, *De somn.* 155–158. In Stephen M. Pogoloff, *Logos and Sophia: The Rhetorical Situation of 1 Corinthians* (Atlanta: Scholars Press, 1992), 207.

ment of fact. It may be paraphrased: "Your election by God did not in the beginning and does not now depend on your status, religiously or socially; neither wisdom, nor power, nor nobility is a prerequisite to salvation."

The Jeremiah text that parallels Paul's first negation triad begins at 9:22 (LXX) with three negative admonitions, all introduced in the Hebrew text (9:23) by the negating particle *'al* and in the LXX by *mē:*

JEREMIAH 9:22 (LXX):

1. (9:22a)—Let not (*'al*) the wise man glory in his wisdom
   (LXX)—*Mē kauchasthō ho sophos en tē sophia autou*
2. (9:22b)—Let not (*'al*) the mighty man glory in his strength
   (LXX)—*Mē kauchasthō ho hischouros ev tē hischui autou*
3. (9:22c)—Let not(*'al*) the rich man glory in his riches
   (LXX)—*Mē kauchasthō ho plousios en tō ploutō autou*

In Jeremiah, the three negative admonitions (whose subjects are roughly parallel to those in Paul's triad) are followed by three positive assertions, all introduced by the disjunctive particle *kî* in 9:23:

JEREMIAH 9:23 (LXX):

1. (9:23a)—But (*kî'im*) let him who glories glory in this,
   (9:23b)—that he understands and knows me
   (LXX)—*all' he en toutō kauchasthō ho kauchōmenos, syniein kai ginōskein*
2. (9:23c)—Surely (*kî*) I am the Lord who does *kindness, justice,* and *righteousness* in the land (9:24b)
   (LXX)—*hoti egō eimi kyrios poiōn eleos kai krima kai dikaiosynēn epi tēs gēs*
3. (9:23d)—Surely (*kî*) in these things I delight, says the Lord.
   (LXX)—*hoti en toutois to thelēma mou, legei kyrios*

In v 27, Paul adds a second triad of his own that has no parallel in Jeremiah. Here he strategically inverts the conditions of the first triad in order to demonstrate the true standards of God's election. The section is set apart (as is Jeremiah's second triad) by the strong disjunctive *alla:*

1. (1:27a) But (*alla*) God chose the foolish things to shame the wise
   alla ta mora tou kosmou exelexato ho Theos hina kataischynē tous sophous
2. God chose the weak of the world to shame the strong
   kai ta asthene tou kosmou exelexato ho Theos hina kataischyne ta hischyra
3. God chose what is low and despised in the world, even the things that have no being, in order to bring to nothing things that are
   kai ta agenē tou kosmou kai ta exouthenēmena exelexato ho Theos ta me onta hina ta onta katargēsē

The Denouement of Paul's Epistemological Challenge at Corinth

What provokes the epistemological crisis of the discourse is that God is said to elect according to criteria that are utterly contrary to what one expects (whether one is a Jew or a Gentile). God chooses the weak, the powerless, the ignoble, the "nothings and nobodies." Moreover, these choices have a double edge; they also bring to shame and extinction the wise, the powerful, the noble and the "people who *are* somebody" in the world's perception.[56]

Paul's vocabulary in vv 27-28 reflects his apocalyptic worldview. Gordon Fee notes that the term *kataischyne* ("to shame") is used in the Septuagint to express "the vindication of God over his enemies, . . . a vindication that is related to God's righteous judgments (e.g., Ps 6:10; 31:17; 35:4, 26-27). . . . In choosing the Corinthians God has already begun the final vindication over his enemies."[57] The term *katargeō* ("to nullify") in v 28 carries even stronger apocalyptic overtones. Paul will use this term seven more times in 1 Corinthians in contexts that have to do with God's bringing to nothing of the present age.[58]

Comparing what Paul omits to what he adds to the Jeremiah text illustrates the dramatic extent of the change in world orders Paul narrates.

> Omission—Jer 9:23b: "(Let him who glories glory in this), that he understands and knows me . . . "
> Addition—1 Cor 1:27-28: "God chose the foolish in order to shame the wise; God chose the weak in order to shame the strong; . . . "

In Jeremiah, the knowledge of God is available to those who do not "refuse to know" (Jer 9:6), that is, to those who "hear the words of the covenant" and do them (Jer 11:6-8). Knowledge in Jeremiah

---

56. Gail O'Day sees these terms reflected later in 1 Corinthians: The wise are in view in 1 Corinthians 1–4; the strong in 1 Corinthians 8–10; and the nobly born in 1 Corinthians 11. See O'Day, "Intertextuality," 263–65.

57. Fee, *The First Epistle to the Corinthians*, 83.

58. 1 Cor 2:6; 6:13; 13:8 (twice); 13:10; 15:24, 26. Fee writes, "This verb occurs throughout 1 Corinthians in decidedly eschatological contexts to express Paul's conviction that in Christ God has already set the future in motion, whereby the present age is 'on its way out', is being done away with by God himself" (Fee, *The First Epistle to the Corinthians*, 83).

has primarily to do with recognition and observance of the sacred tradition that defines true knowledge and wisdom. The definition is not itself foreign to the consciousness of Israel, however far astray the people may have gone. Jeremiah can appeal to sacred memory (Jer 9:7). He calls Israel back to the covenant they once knew and observed, albeit a covenant in need of mending (Jer 9:10).[59]

Paul, on the other hand, makes no appeal to the Deuteronomic past, nor even, as in the wisdom tradition, to the myth of the creation of the world (cf. Jer 9:12). For Paul, God's faithfulness (1:9) stands now on wholly new premises. While it is still Yahweh alone who rules, Yahweh is now "pleased" to save believers through means other than salvation history, or the acquisition of wisdom or reason. As Paul sees it, God "in God's wisdom" has chosen to save through the *apokalypsis* of something entirely apart from history, tradition, and reason. This something new, moreover, is expressed in language that points unmistakably toward the dissolution of the world defined by sacred, social, or intellectual traditions, and toward the creation of a new world.[60]

The language of 1:26-29 evokes creation images that move from anticreation to new creation. God brings to nothing what is, in order to bring into being what is not. For Paul, as for Jeremiah[61] and for at least some Greek philosophers,[62] the word has creative power. But the world created by the Word of the Cross is not merely the physical world, whose majesty reflects God's sovereignty. The world of the cross is characterized by strange reversals; it is a world in which wisdom is folly, the least become the greatest, strength resides in weakness, and fullness of being arises from emptiness. To say that the

---

59. Jeremiah is critical of the Levites who are "still participating in the increasingly corrupt Jerusalemite cult and [who] had violated their Deuteronomic principles. Without directly claiming to be a Mosaic prophet, Jeremiah . . . places his oracle in the tradition of past Mosaic prophets whose words had proven to be true" (Robert Wilson, *Prophecy and Society in Ancient Israel* [Philadelphia: Fortress Press, 1987], 246).

60. For a full discussion of Paul's idea of the death of the old world, see Paul Minear, "The Crucified World: The Enigma of Galatians 6:14," in *Theologia Crucis, Signum Crucis: Festschrift für Erich Dinkler zum 70 Geburtstag,* ed. Carl Andresen and Günter Klein (Tübingen: J. C. B. Mohr, 1979), 395–407.

61. Cf. Jer 10:12: "It is he who made the earth by his power, who established the world by his wisdom, and by his understanding stretched out the heavens."

62. In Stoic thought, e.g., the logos is an active, creative power. See Gerhard Kittel, *TDNT,* 5:84–85 (1967).

Word of the Cross creates a new world is to call an end to the present world. This is creation out of nothing.[63]

Paul brings this world-ending and re-creating Word when he preaches Christ crucified. In 1:27-29 as in 1:18, it does not move the reader onto a higher plane of existence. Rather, it thrusts one deep into the new creation that is first comprehended as anticreation. Verses 27-28 present the same sort of aporia presented by 1:18. They move the reader to the edge of an abyss. When the wisdom of God is crucified, the wisdom of human beings is without foundation, without grounds for boasting, empty (1 Cor 9:15).

Justice, Sanctification, and Redemption

The offense of vv 27-29 to standard conventions is further illuminated by vv 30-31. The elements of the triad in v 30 are traditional, and yet its arrangement is Paul's own and reflects his new world. The parallel with Jer 9:23 (LXX) is only partial; Paul shares Jeremiah's term *dikaiosynē* ("righteousness"), but instead of Jeremiah's "loving acts/mercy" (*ḥesed/eleōs*) and "justice" (*mišpaṭ /krima*), Paul writes "sanctification" (*hagiasmos*) and "redemption" (*apolytrōsis*).

> 1:30: out of whom [God] you are in Christ Jesus who
> *Ex autou de humeis este en Christō Iēsou hos*
> was made wisdom
> *egenēthē sophia*
> for us from (*apo*) God
> *hēmin apo Theou*
> (1)   righteousness
> *dikaiosynē*
> (2)   and sanctification
> *kai hagiasmos*
> (3)   and redemption
> *kai apolytrōsis*

Jeremiah's triad—righteousness, mercy, justice (Jer 9:23)—recalls God's saving acts in covenant history and thereby reconfirms Yahweh's power over royal presuppositions.[64] But Paul has already challenged the notion of saving history in his apocalyptic presentation of

---

63. On Paul's understanding of the cosmos and its end, see Minear, "The Crucified World," 395–407.
64. Brueggemann, "Epistemological Crisis," 99; and O'Day, "Intertextuality," 12.

God as the one who elects "out of nothing" (*ta mē onta*). Moreover, in Paul's formulation, righteousness, sanctification, and redemption are all *present* consequences for the believer of being "in Christ," for it is Christ who *is* righteousness, sanctification, and redemption. In context, the offense is that these attributes are in no way dependent on human action. The God who chooses the foolish, the weak, and the nonbeings does not limit his election to those who are faithful to tradition. Rather, through the "folly of the kerygma," God has *already* justified (2 Cor 5:21), sanctified (1 Cor 1:2), and redeemed (Rom 6:19) humanity.

Paul's amendments to Jeremiah illuminate his apocalyptic epistemology. By adding the catalog of the "called" in vv 27-28 and then omitting Jeremiah's positive reference to boasting in knowledge, he significantly reorients Jeremiah's claims. While both writers understand the word of God as a word of judgment against prevailing epistemologies, for Paul the word is not the familiar word of Yahweh that judges Israel's faithfulness to the *former* covenant but the strange and powerful Word of the Cross (*logos tou staurou*) that depends on nothing that came before. Because it stands against expectations based on covenant allegiance, this Word presents a challenge to both "histories," covenantal and sapiential, by which Brueggemann defines the epistemological crisis in Jeremiah. The cross kerygma does not, like Jeremiah's "word of Yahweh," *reroute* the hearer's train of thought from royal epistemology to covenant epistemology; rather, it *derails* the train altogether. In other words, the cross forces a disjuncture with prior salvation schemas and, ultimately, an end to the accustomed ways of knowing God. Paul's reworking of the Jeremiah text thus reflects a more profound epistemological crisis than that presented by Jeremiah himself. This crisis comes fully to expression where Paul departs most radically from the Jeremiah text, in vv 27-29.

Paul as Apocalyptic Prophet

Jeremiah 8:4—10:25 is characterized, as is 1 Corinthians 1–4, by the recurrent themes of "knowing" and being "wise." While Paul is far removed from the social and political world of Jeremiah, and seemingly from the concerns of the "royal epistemology" against which the prophet spoke, the underlying critique of human securities posed by Jeremiah's understanding of Yahweh's sovereignty and covenant faithfulness is echoed, yet radically revised, in Paul's own theology.

We have seen that while Paul borrows substantially from Jeremiah, he moves beyond Jeremiah's critique when he calls into question the most basic structures of the old world. For Paul, it is not just a competing or corrupt wisdom that is destroyed (i.e., the wisdom of Israel's corrupt sages, as in Isa 29:14); rather, all wisdom previously known to humanity (Jew and Gentile) gives way to God's new revelation in the cross. God does not simply *humble the boastful*, but *elects the nonexistent* by bringing to nothing whatever and whomever claims existence apart from God's new creative act (*ta onta*). Paul's witness to the utter dissolution of one world at the advent of the new moves his theology beyond prophetic and into apocalyptic categories. The epistemological crisis he encounters in the Word of the Cross both puts him in mind of the Jeremiah text and causes him to reshape it according to the demands of the apocalyptically conceived new creation.

good distinction

Summary: The Workings of the Cross in 1 Corinthians 1:18-31

Thus far in Paul's discourse the cross has functioned in three central ways. First, it has dislocated its hearers by calling into question their ways of knowing (1:18). Second, it has revealed God's purpose to save, not through wisdom, but through the "folly" of the cross itself (1:21-25); and third, it has demonstrated God's destruction of the old world (with its valued human assets of strength, wisdom, nobility) and creation of the new world (into which he calls the weak, the ignoble, the nonexistent; 1:26-31).

Each of these functions contributes to the system of thought I have designated "Pauline apocalyptic," and especially to Paul's distinctive conviction that the new age has been inaugurated in the death of Jesus. Because in Paul's view people now live at the juncture between the ages, that is, before the new is fully and unmistakably manifested, *perceptions* of who God is and what God is doing are critically important. At Corinth, Paul sees signs that the God to whom the Corinthians think they belong is not the God revealed in the cross. This is why his challenge is directed toward their ways of knowing God and why its focus is God's act to inaugurate the new creation in Christ crucified.

THE WORD OF THE CROSS AS APOCALYPTIC
MYSTERY: 1 CORINTHIANS 2:1-5

(1) When I came to you, brethren, I did not come proclaiming to you the mystery of God in inflated word or wisdom. (2) For I decided not to know anything among you except Jesus Christ and him crucified. (3) And I was with you in weakness and in great fear and trembling. (4) And my word and my preaching were not in persuasive words of wisdom but in demonstration of the Spirit and of power (5) that your faith might not rest in human wisdom but in the power of God. (1 Cor 2:1-5)

In this section, Paul restates and condenses the antitheses of 1:18-31. Once again, the overarching pair of opposites is human wisdom versus divine power. But the section is more than a recapitulation of what precedes; it also sets the stage for the instructions on mystery and spirit to follow in 2:6-16 and for the apostolic defense in chapters 3 and 4. As one would expect in a pericope that acts in part as a summary of 1:18-31, the vocabulary of wisdom and power is prevalent in 2:1-5. Moreover, in this section, Paul's use of perception-related terminology intensifies. As demonstrated below, each verse contains at least one perception-related term:

1. *hyperochēn logou sophia* exalted word of wisdom (2:1)
2. *mystērion* mystery (2:1)
3. *ekrina* I decided (2:2)
4. *eidenai* to know (2:2)
5. *phobos* fear (2:3)
6. *tromos* trembling (2:3)
7. *peithois sophias logois* persuasive wisdom words (2:4)
8. *apodeixis* demonstration (2:4)
9. *sophia* wisdom (2:5)

Several *apocalyptic* terms are newly introduced here. In 2:1, Paul declares the kerygma he brings to be the *mystērion tou Theou*,[65] in 2:2, he uses the term *krinō*, which elsewhere in his writing occurs in apocalyptic contexts;[66] and in 2:3, when he describes his own state of "fear

---

65. On this text variant, see note 68 below.
66. E.g., Rom 2:3, 16; 1 Cor 4:5, 6.

and trembling," he uses language that belongs to apocalyptic traditions about the last judgment.[67]

The presence of this new terminology in 2:1-5, the increased incidence of perceptual vocabulary, and the consequent sharpening of
the central antithesis—human wisdom/divine power—cause this passage to stand as an apocalyptic bridge for the whole of Paul's argument in chapters 1–2. The unit focuses on the relation of *what* Paul
proclaims to his *mode* of proclamation. In this way it points both back-
ward to the preliminary statement of the kerygma's content, Christ
crucified (1:18, 23), and forward to the unfolding mystery of that
preaching (2:6-16).

The Preaching of the Cross as Mystery

When I came to you, brethren, I did not come proclaiming to you the
mystery (*mystērion*) of God in lofty words or wisdom. (1 Cor 2:1)

Although the explicit equation, gospel = mystery, awaits the
deutero-Pauline epistles, several implicit references to such an
equation in Paul's thought support the reading of *mystērion* rather
than the variant *martyrion* in 2:1.[68] According to 1 Cor 4:1, for example, Paul understands himself to be a "steward of mysteries." In a re-

---

67. See, e.g., 1 Enoch 14:13-14: "Fear covered me and trembling took hold of me.
And as I was shaking and trembling, I fell on my face." Translated by Michael Knibb in
The Apocryphal Old Testament, ed. H. F. D. Sparks (Oxford: Clarendon Press, 1984).
68. The apparent identification of the kerygma as "mystery" at 2:1 is one of the
most debated aspects of the text. Although there is early and strong evidence for the
variant reading *martyrion* ("witness") instead of *mystērion* at 2:1, I follow the twenty-sixth
edition of Aland and a number of authorities on 1 Corinthians, including Bornkamm,
Leitzmann, Lührmann, and Lang in choosing *mystērion*. Bornkamm argues that the
term *mystērion* refers back to *keryssein Christon estauromenon* in 1:23 and that Paul's use
of the term is further explained by 2:6-16. See Bornkamm, "*Mystērion*," *TDNT*, 4:819 n.
141; Conzelmann notes to the contrary that *mystērion* may have intruded itself from
2:7, but he also notes that *martyrion* could be the intruder from 1:6 (Conzelmann,
1 Corinthians, 53). Since there can be no certainty on text-critical grounds and since I
find the interpretation of the larger context to be better served by *mystērion*, I read
mystērion for the reasons Bornkamm suggests. Fee argues against mystery in part because this rendering "would seem to deflect his [Paul's] present concern" (Fee, *The
First Epistle to the Corinthians*, 91). What Paul calls *mystērion* is none other than the
gospel of Jesus Christ crucified. The manuscript evidence is inconclusive. Raymond E.
Brown comments: "The ms. evidence is divided on whether to read mysterion, 'mystery', or martyrion, 'witness,' and no solution seems possible on textual grounds"
(Raymond E. Brown, *The Semitic Background of the Term "Mystery" in the New Testament*
[Philadelphia: Fortress Press, 1968], 48).

lated text, the gospel is said to be veiled (2 Cor 4:3-4; *kekalym-menon*), and in 1 Cor 2:7 and Rom 11:25-35, God's wisdom and mystery are associated closely with the gospel.[69] A brief review of Paul's references to the gospel as mysterious (*mystērion*) or veiled (*kekalymmenon*) may contribute to our understanding of the "mystery" Paul proclaims in 2:1.[70]

A text that is very close to 1 Cor 2:1 conceptually, although it does not contain the term *mystērion*, is 2 Cor 4:3-4:

> And even if our gospel is hidden, it is hidden only to the perishing. In their case, the god of this world has blinded the minds of the unbelievers to keep them from seeing the light of the gospel of the glory of Christ. (2 Cor 4:3-4)

Several features of this text recall the argument in 1 Cor 1:18—2:16. What renders one blind in 2 Corinthians 4—the god of this world (*ho theos tou aiōnos toutou*)—is not unlike the reason or *sophia* of this age (*toutou aiōnos*) that renders one unperceptive in 1 Cor 1:18—2:5. The theme of eschatological judgment also enters here, as it does in 1 Cor 1:18 and 2:7. In these three cases, it is the faulty perception of, respectively, the "perishing" (1:18 and 2 Cor 4:3), the "rulers of this age" (2:7), and the "unbelievers" (2 Cor 4:3) that determines their destruction. Similarly, in Rom 11:25-26, faulty perception itself appears to be a part of the divine mystery, that is, it is integral to God's mysterious plan that some are blinded to the truth of the gospel:

> Lest you be wise in your own conceits, I want you to understand this mystery, brethren: a hardening (*pōrōsis*) has come upon part of Israel, until the full number of the Gentiles come in, and so all Israel will be saved. (Rom 11:25-26)

The mystery of which Paul speaks here is the blindness of that "part of Israel" that is, as yet, unbelieving. More mysterious still (even

---

69. At Rom 16:25—a text probably not authentic to Paul—revelation (*apokalypsis*) and mystery (*mystērion*) are listed as synonyms. In this text, the "mystery which was kept hidden for long ages" (Rom 16:25) is synonymously parallel with the phrases "my gospel" and "the preaching of Jesus Christ." Here, as in 1 Cor 2:7, the mystery is hidden ("before the ages") but not finally hidden. It has been "revealed and made known to all the nations" (Rom 16:26; cf. 1 Cor 2:6).

70. Elsewhere, however, Paul uses the term *mystērion* to mean something other than the gospel itself (see 1 Cor 13:2; 14:2; 15:51).

to Paul), is that *God has ordained* the blindness of Israel (for a time) for the salvation of the Gentiles, even as in 1 Cor 2:8 the misunderstanding (*oudeis egnōken*) of "the rulers of this age" is the cause of the saving death by crucifixion of Jesus.[71] The fact that blindness or incomprehension *constitutes* divine mystery, rather than simply reflecting the willful failure of human beings to accept the mystery, is a feature of apocalyptic thought that leaves little room for the saving *choices* available to the world in the wisdom literature.[72] The absence of imperatival language (i.e., language urging choice)—as obvious here as anywhere in the Pauline corpus—will be noted again in the enigmatic section 2:6-16.[73]

We have seen that Paul's mode of argumentation involves a reappropriation of Corinthian language to the new standard set by the cross kerygma. It is reasonable that he should begin the reappropriation of *mystērion* in 2:1 to set the stage for the strong identification between *kerygma* and *mystērion* that he will need in the next phrase of the argument in 2:6-16.[74] There, it makes a great deal of difference whether we read the "secret and hidden mystery of God" (2:7) as a reference to the cross kerygma in 1:23 or as a reference to some other esoteric teaching of Paul's, apart from the kerygma.[75]

---

71. Cf. the "hardening (*pōrōsis*) of the minds" of the Israelites in 2 Cor 3:14.

72. This is not true of all strands of apocalyptic. For contrast, see the Two Ways language of the Community Rule at Qumran.

73. In reference to 1 Cor 4:16, W. A. Beardslee writes, "Paradoxically, part of what he [Paul] intends by his imperative that they should be imitators of him (4:16; 11:1) is that they move into a style not dominated by the imperative" (W. A. Beardslee, "Response to Gordon Fee" [Paper delivered to the Pauline Theology Group at the Society for Biblical Literature in Anaheim, California, 1989], 6.

74. In this assessment I challenge the judgment of Fee and others that the use of *mystērion* here "would seem to deflect [Paul's] present concern" (Fee, *The First Epistle to the Corinthians,* 91). Scroggs argues that Paul intends a sharp disjuncture between the kerygma and the sophia/mystery he speaks in 2:6-16, and in support of this argument chooses *martyrion* where the connection with kerygma is explicit. See also Scroggs, "Paul: Sophos and Pneumatikos," 37.

75. The paucity of such references may be interpreted in several ways. Perhaps Paul avoided the equation in order to steer his gospel away from the kind of interpretation that it had, in fact, already received at Corinth. If so, however, it is odd that he should use the term more intensely in the Corinthian correspondence than elsewhere, unless his intent there was to correct what he saw as a misuse of the equation gospel = mystery. Another possibility is simply that Paul uses the term less self-consciously than scholars generally assume. His several uses of *mystērion* to mean something other than gospel prevent us from pressing his mystery language consistently into the service of apologetic or polemical discourse about the cross kerygma. Käsemann argues that the kerygma-mystery association is characteristically deutero-Pauline: "Apart from the disputed passage 1 Cor 2:1 . . . Paul himself never specifically as such calls the gospel the mystery, as happens in the deutero-Pauline epistles" (Käsemann, *Commentary on Romans,* 425).

The unit 2:1-5 is defined by three pairs of opposites:

1. lofty words or wisdom   vs.   kerygma of Jesus Christ crucified
2. plausible words of wisdom   vs.   my word and kerygma in weakness, fear, trembling
3. human wisdom   vs.   power of God

As in earlier parts of Paul's discourse, the oppositional patterns of this passage supply the fundamental rubric for interpretation. The summary antithesis in 2:5 amplifies the beginning antithesis of the section at 1:17–18, forming an inclusio with those opening sentences. The "power of God" on which faith rests in 2:5 is none other than the power manifested in the cross of Christ. The human wisdom in which faith must *not* rest is the wisdom that perceives the cross as folly and thus "empties" it.

The movement we observed in 1:18 from the preached word to the perceived word is mirrored in 2:4-5 where we see a transition from Paul's *preaching (logos* and *kerygma)* to the Corinthians' *pistis* ("faith"). Moreover, in 2:1-5, where Paul's self-defense is more obvious, Paul makes it clear that the misperception at Corinth is the fault not of his preaching but of the Corinthians' hearing.

Word as Demonstration

Paul's strategy in 1:18-31, we have suggested, was to strike directly at the perceptual faculties of his hearers in order to "capture" their perceptions.[76] In 2:1, with the entry of the term *katangelein* ("to proclaim") other dimensions of that battle come into view. Paul uses this term almost exclusively in polemical contexts: in 1 Cor 9:14 and Phil 1:17-18 (two of only five uses besides 1 Cor 2:1), it occurs in the context of apostolic defense. In 1 Cor 11:26, it occurs again in a polemical setting,[77] this time in the words of the institution of the Lord's Supper: "As often as you eat this bread and drink this cup, you proclaim the Lord's death until he comes." In only one case, Rom 1:8, does it occur without polemical overtones: "Your faith is proclaimed in all the world."

---

76. Cf. 2 Cor 10:4.
77. Paul is criticizing the Corinthians for their divisive behavior at the Lord's Supper.

The unusual use of the term in 1 Cor 11:26 may help to illuminate its use here. In that text, the proclamation is not verbal, but rather issues forth from the concrete *action* of persons in the setting of the Supper. It is what they *show*, not what they *say*, that *proclaims the Lord's death*. Notice that what is shown is the *death of Jesus*—for Paul, an *apocalyptic* and *paradigmatic* act. As the death of Jesus on the cross is for Paul the revelation of God's struggle with and victory over hostile forces (1 Cor 15:24), so is bearing and demonstrating that death the apocalyptic sign of the victory whose fruit is reconciliation.[78]

It now becomes clear why Paul turns in 2:1-5 to the language of paradigm and demonstration. In 1:18-25 he has stated in a preliminary way the paradox that attends his preaching of the *logos tou staurou*. In 1:26-31 he has begun to *show* the paradox by pointing to the evidence of God's call in the concrete circumstances of the community. Finally, in 2:1-5, he brings the initial statement of paradox (1:18-25) more directly and personally into the language of *showing*. Thus, in 2:2 he has resolved (*ekrina*) to know nothing except Jesus Christ crucified.[79] In 2:3 this "knowing" proves itself, not in words, but in Paul's demonstration of weakness, fear, and trembling. In 2:4, although he returns to *logos* and *kerygma*, these terms themselves become metaphors for something beyond speech; they are parallel to the term in the same verse, *apodeixis* ("demonstration").[80] To know and to proclaim Jesus Christ crucified is to *show* (demonstrate) the power of the cross by one's own weakness, fear, and trembling—conditions, we must note, that typically describe apocalyptic visionaries awed by their visions. In such demonstrations and not in persuasive words is the true *logos* (2:4), the true *kerygma*.[81] It must be said, then,

---

78. Here the theological insight of Gustav Aulen is helpful: "This victory of Christ over the destructive powers appears to faith as an act of reconciliation. As a matter of fact, the triumph of Christ is at once a victorious and reconciling act which involves a transformation of man's estate and a new situation for 'the world,' and implies a reconciliation between God and man" (Gustav Aulen, *The Faith of the Christian Church* [Philadelphia: Fortress Press, 1960], 201).

79. On *krino* in apocalyptic contexts, see Sturm, "Apokalyptō/Apokalypsis," 246–250.

80. David Lull discusses *apodeixis* as a reference to the empirical evidence of the spirit in the ecstatic experience of the Corinthians. Paul compares persuasive argument to empirical evidence. See David Lull, *The Spirit in Galatia* (Chico, Calif.: Scholars Press, 1980), 58–59.

81. This theme is present elsewhere in Paul. See especially 2 Cor 4:7-8 where the afflictions of the apostle reflect divine power: "But we have this treasure in earthen vessels to show that the transcendent power (*hē hyperbolē tēs dynameōs*) belongs to God and not to us. . . . (We are) always carrying in the body the death of Jesus so that the life of Jesus may also be manifested in our bodies."

that for Paul the "fear and trembling" that authenticate his *kerygma* point well beyond ordinary human weakness. Rather, his weakness is the apocalyptic "fear and trembling" that reflect the epiphany of God.[82]

Bridge to Act 2: The Entry of the Spirit

In 2:4, Paul mentions the Spirit as the authenticating medium of the mystery he proclaims in fear and trembling. The mention of Spirit is risky in this context among self-professed "spiritualists," but its introduction at just this point is strategic. At the point of the hearer's greatest uncertainty, gazing upon the "weak and trembling" form of the visionary who preaches God's power of the cross, Paul links the cross with the Spirit. Without this link, surely the Corinthians would be apt to retreat to their accustomed spiritualism—without the cross.[83] But once this link is established in 2:1-5, it causes all that Paul says about the Spirit in 2:6-16 to be read in light of the cross kerygma.

Looking ahead for a moment, we see that the link is reiterated in the next section. In 2:6 we read the apparently contradictory statement, "Yet among the perfect we do impart wisdom." Now the "wisdom" in question is immediately qualified as the apocalyptic wisdom hidden in the cross, that is, the "secret and hidden wisdom of God . . . which the rulers of this age did not understand, for if they had, they would not have crucified the Lord of glory."

The second act of the Word's performance begins with the introduction of the Spirit in 2:4. Having dislodged his audience from their customary world by deconstructing time-honored paired opposites in 1:18-31, Paul now illumines the Spirit's role as guide to a newly constructed universe. Without the link between 2:6-16 and the cross kerygma, however, the "performance" of the Word would be cut short. It is the Spirit refigured in light of the cross—for Paul, the only true Spirit—that brings the work of the Word to completion. In

---

82. See also the passion and resurrection narratives in the Gospels where the Christ-event regularly provokes this reaction.

83. Fee notes what he takes to be the "especially pointed irony" of 2:6-16, that "since the Corinthians are *pneumatikoi* (spirit people), they should have understood the cross as God's wisdom; for the Spirit alone knows the mind of God and thus has revealed what was formerly hidden" (Gordon Fee, "Toward a Theology of 1 Corinthians," in *Pauline Theology, Volume 2*, ed. David M. Hay [Minneapolis: Fortress Press, 1993], 45–46).

his study of the psychological aspects of this text, Gerd Theissen suggests that this level of the discourse moves the hearer to a "higher stage of consciousness." He remarks on the two-stage development that occurs between 1:18 and 2:16:

> In the "initial preaching" (i.e., 1:18—2:5), Christians are seized by the symbol of the cross. But it is only through the "doctrine of perfection" that they grasp what seizes them. Both the immature and the perfect are affected by the same revelation, but only the perfect penetrate what happens to them and in them. In brief, perfect wisdom consists in making conscious a previously unconscious content.[84]

As we turn now to 2:6-16, the relation of the Spirit to the mystery of the kerygma and the perceptual transformation it mediates will come more clearly into focus.[85] The second act of the Word's performance, having begun with the Spirit's entry, will reach its ideal conclusion in the hearer's realization of the cruciform "mind of Christ."

---

84. Theissen, *Psychological Aspects*, 352.
85. "Paul values revelation not as something private or hidden, but, like prophecy, as God's communicating endtime understanding, so as to commission an apostle or to build up the congregation as a new creation" (Sturm, "Apokalyptō/Apokalypsis," 251).

5

Act 2: The Cross, the Spirit, and the Mind of Christ

COMING TO CONSCIOUSNESS IN THE MIND OF CHRIST

It should come as no surprise that in 1 Corinthians 2, where Paul attempts to show *what* is revealed in the crevasse that the Word of the Cross creates, he resorts to heightened apocalyptic—indeed, mystical imagery. For here the performance moves into its second act, beyond the concerns of conventional language, even beyond the image of the cross, and into the shared experience of the Spirit who transcends human cognition to communicate the depths of God. Now Paul seeks to bring the new world to consciousness by invoking the presence of its vital force, the Spirit of God, in the experience of the believer. Here he must move to a heightened mystical discourse, taking with him those who have been prepared for this move through the course of 1:18—2:5.

First Corinthians 2:6-16 is notorious for its exegetical and hermeneutical difficulties. So vast are its problems that at least one interpreter resorts to the tempting solution that it was not written by Paul.[1] In the scholarly literature on 1 Cor 2:6-16 some argue that when Paul comes to this section, he delves suddenly and inexplicably into gnostic or mystical thought.[2] Indeed, a new terminology appears: now Paul uses the distinction "this age/before the age," and paired terms that will be echoed in later gnostic writing on spiritual status, for example, *psychikos* versus *pneumatikos* and *teleios* versus *nēpios*. Now the wisdom of

---

1. M. Widmann, "1 Kor 2:6-16: Ein Einspruch gegen Paulus," *ZNW* 70 (1979): 44–53. See J. Murphy-O'Connor, "Interpolations in 1 Corinthians," *CBQ* 48 (1986): 81–84. Since Widmann argues on some rather spurious grounds, his theory is not considered a plausible option by the majority of scholars.

2. There is a division in secondary literature, we recall, between those who divorce 2:6-16 conceptually from 1:18—2:5 and those who think 2:6-16 "unfolds" the message of 1:18—2:5.

God is said to be "hidden in mystery" and the vocabulary of knowledge (*gnōsis*), mystery (*mystērion*), spirit (*pneuma*), and wisdom (*sophia*) fills the discourse. The absence of an explicit cross motif leads many to conclude that at this point Paul abandons the cross, turning instead, perhaps in desperation against his opponents, to a gnostic-like position approximating theirs or to an esoteric teaching intended only for a few advanced believers.[3]

Despite its new vocabulary and mood, however, this passage builds unmistakably on patterns already established in 1:18—2:5. I have already argued for the conceptual integrity of 1:18—2:16 as a unit devoted to the themes of true and false ways of knowing.[4] Now I will argue that in both structure and theme 2:6-16 presupposes and develops the antitheses of 1:18—2:5. The pairs of opposites that give shape to each section of the argument are illustrated below:

1. 1:18-31 *sophia tou kosmou* vs. *dynamis tou Theou* (wisdom of human beings versus power of God)
2. 2:1-5 *sophia tōn anthropōn* vs. *pneuma/dynamis* (*tou Theou*) (wisdom of human beings versus Spirit/power of God)
3. 2:6-16 *sophia tou aiōnos toutou* vs. *apokalypsis dia tou pneumatos=nous tou Christou* (wisdom of this age versus apocalypse through the Spirit-mind of Christ)

By attending to the apocalyptic strategies that link the two sections, we see that both are focused on the cross (although certainly at two

---

3. It is Rudolf Bultmann's opinion, e.g., that Paul becomes so enmeshed in the worldview of his audience that his theology of the cross here gives way to a theology of *gnōsis* (Rudolf Bultmann, *Theology of the New Testament* [New York: Charles Scribner's Sons, 1951, 1955], 175, 181). Ulrich Wilckens too initially argued this line, although he later retracted his thesis on Gnosticism at Corinth (Ulrich Wilckens, *Weisheit und Torheit: Eine exegetische-religions geschichtliche Untersuchung zu 1 Kor 1 und 2* [Tübingen: J. C. B. Mohr, 1959]). Robin Scroggs takes a different turn that acknowledges the apocalyptic cast of the section (Robin Scroggs, "Paul: Sophos and Pneumatikos," *NTS* 14 [1967]: 33–35). He argues that in 2:6-16, Paul leaves the cross kerygma to engage in an esoteric discourse on apocalyptic mysteries designed for a few advanced believers, the spiritual *teleioi*. Although Scroggs avoids the dubious assignment of Gnosticism to Corinth, he, like Bultmann and Wilckens, posits a sharp disjuncture between the two sections of the argument. This break signals the failure of the cross proclamation to bring the Corinthians into the unity of mind toward which the whole discourse is aimed. While for Bultmann the proclamation of the cross appears to have fallen prey to the Gnostics, for Scroggs it seems merely too elementary a doctrine for the spiritually advanced believer who now turns with Paul to the esoteric, secret doctrines of spiritual "perfection." While I admit that Paul is no stranger to rhetorical failure, there is no other place known to me where his failure is attributable to confusion about which side he is on. For both Bultmann and Scroggs, the discourse that begins with a strong plea for unity of mind in Corinth ends with a gnostic-like confirmation that the transformation of Spirit offered by the gospel is, seemingly by design, more accessible to some than to others.

4. See pp. 96–104 above.

different levels of discourse) as the agent of true perception. Neither section alone is sufficient to complete the shift Paul intends. Act 1 brings the reader into range of transformation and sees its beginnings through the strategies of convention and image we have observed. Act 2 narrates its completion through the transcendent action of the Spirit.[5] Having brought the eagle clearly into view (to recall the speech-act example from Walt Whitman), Paul now incites it to fly.[6] Now the transfiguring of language that Paul began in 1 Corinthians 1 reaches its full effect.

The Apocalyptic and Epistemological Features of 1 Corinthians 2:6-16

The terminology of perception reaches its greatest concentration in 2:6-16. In the eleven verses of this passage, there are thirty-one perception-related terms.[7] This is by far the greatest concentration of such language anywhere in the Pauline corpus. Corresponding to this terminology is a similar concentration of apocalyptic terms that sets the framework for Paul's final evaluation of the two opposing ways of knowing. The two kinds of wisdom are now not merely human and divine but the "human wisdom *of this age*" and the "wisdom of God *hidden before the ages*" (2:6-7). Now the ones who misperceive are "the rulers of this age" who, in apocalyptic fashion, are "doomed to pass away" (2:6).[8] Apocalyptic themes are likewise in view in the idea of the glory already possessed by the Lord of glory and set aside for the righteous in the future.[9] Finally, the most direct apocalyptic reference of the passage consigns knowledge of all these mysteries to the revealing power of God who, through the Spirit,

---

5. It may be helpful to repeat at this point that the two-act structure of the performance I am suggesting should not be interpreted mechanically, as if the reader literally experiences a break in modes of consciousness between the two sections, or as if the performing literally changes from text to Spirit as Act 2 begins. Rather, the unit works as a whole to elicit a response whose constituent parts, however they are ordered or experienced, may be described in sequence. The effect is the same as that presupposed in the hymn, "I once was blind, but now I see." The two stages need not be arrived at by the same processes, but each stage, blindness and sight, must be arrived at for the idea in the song, or the conversion of the singer, to be meaningful.

6. Chapter 2, note 11, above.

7. The perception vocabulary in 2:6-16 includes *sophia, apokekrymmenēn, egnōke* (twice), *apokalypsen, erauna, oida, eidōmen, didaktois anthrōpinēs, didaktois pneumatos, dechetai, anakrinō, sygkrinō, egnō, nous.*

8. Compare similar passages in 1 Enoch where world rulers are brought to nothing by the Son of Man.

9. Dan 12:3; 1 Enoch 38:4; 62:15-16; 2 Bar 51:3; cf. 2 Cor 3:19.

revealed (*apokalyptein*) to us "what no eye has seen, nor ear heard, nor the human heart conceived" (2:9). In this context, Paul's closing words at 2:16, "But we have the mind of Christ," stand as a definitive statement of his apocalyptic epistemology.[10]

The "Opponents" in 1 Corinthians 2:6-16

It is typical of Paul's way of thinking, even where he has bona fide human opponents (e.g., the Galatians), to see his real opposition in cosmic "powers and principalities" which are opposed to God.[11] What appears to be a merely human disagreement is often, for Paul, a reflection of the cosmic battle between God and Satan. The same principle is operative in 1 Cor 2:6-16 where the realm and agency of the enemy appears in Paul's references to "this age" and its wisdom, the "spirit of the world" and the "rulers of this age." The power of this opponent is demonstrated in its hold on the perceptions, allegiances, and actions of actual human beings. While particular campaigns in the war are directed against these manifestations of evil, the real enemies for Paul are always the "powers and principalities" that hold human beings prisoner. The Corinthians are not themselves the enemy, but they are held hostage by enemy forces!

Paul's letters demonstrate that, for him, the enemy forces often hold territory by skillfully subverting the language of the gospel he preaches. It is perhaps for this reason that his writing in 1 Corinthians 1–2 is filled with double entendre, irony, and sometimes biting sarcasm. By such means he seeks to expose the false *logos* of his opponents and thus to win people back to the territory already claimed by God. Since both Paul and his opponents make effective use of linguistic camouflage, it is at points exceedingly difficult for the outside reader of 2:6-16 to determine the true identity of either side.

We may learn, however, from Paul's use of a similar rhetorical strategy in a less polemical context in 1 Thessalonians. In that text, in order to keep his congregants in the fold, Paul adopts the language of the Greco-Roman cults to which the Thessalonians may be

---

10. This observation has also been made by Richard E. Sturm, "An Exegetical Study of the Apostle Paul's Use of the Words APOKALYPTŌ/APOKALYPSIS: The Gospel as God's Apocalypse" (Ph.D. diss., Union Theological Seminary, 1983), 153.

11. See, e.g., 1 Thess 2:18; Gal 4:9.

tempted to return.[12] To people who know the comfort of the nurse figure in mystery cult initiation, Paul becomes "gentle as a nurse" (1 Thess 2:7). For those who know the sensual passion associated with the Dionysus cult, Paul is "affectionately desirous" (2:8).[13]

In these cases and others, the use of the "foreign" motif is skillfully crafted to seal allegiance to Paul's gospel. Similarly in 1 Cor 2:6-16, Paul attempts to seal his kerygma against the rise of (what he takes to be) a perverse spiritualism and elitism in Corinth. That he uses the language of *sophia* and *mystērion* and *gnōsis*, probably key terms in the Corinthian vocabulary, need not be seen as a concession to the problems he combats. It may, rather, be a shrewd way of getting to the core of the problem—the perception of his hearers. It is not the terms per se to which Paul objects but the particular meanings the Corinthians assign to them. Paul brings one set of meanings into conflict with another; the symbolic world defined by God's revelation at the cross challenges a worldview that is centered elsewhere.

In order better to understand the position Paul opposes in 2:6-16, we will examine Paul's allusions to the substance of the argument of his "opponents."[14] In 1:18—2:5, for example, obvious indicators of their position occur in the negative constructions in 1:19b; 1:20; 1:21a; 1:23; 1:26-29; 1:31; 2:1; 2:4; and 2:5. In each of these verses, Paul sets his position over against another position, usually in the form "not . . . but . . . ." In 2:6-16, as in 1:18—2:5, Paul's antithetical formulations contain a not-so-veiled reference to another point of view. In 2:6, Paul's proclamation concerns "not the wisdom of this age" but a hidden and secret wisdom of God; in 2:9, not the knowledge of rulers but the foreknowledge of God; in 2:7-8, not natural human perception but the revelation of God: "no one has seen (but God has revealed)"; in 2:11, not the thoughts of the human being but "thoughts of God"; in 2:12, "not the spirit of this world, but the Spirit of God"; in 2:13, "not human-taught doctrines but Spirit-taught

---

12. Since they now face persecution and death before the parousia. See Karl P. Donfried, "The Cults of Thessalonica and the Thessalonian Correspondence," *NTS* 31 (1985): 336–56.

13. On the relation of Paul's rhetoric to the social and especially religious background of his hearers, see Donfried, "The Cults of Thessalonica," 336-56.

14. On "mirror-reading" as a method for discerning the Corinthian position, Gordon Fee has written, "It seems neither possible nor desirable to analyze the theology of a letter like this without some degree of "mirror-reading" of the historical situation presupposed by the text." In "Toward a Theology of 1 Corinthians," *Pauline Theology, Volume 2*, ed. David M. Hay (Minneapolis: Fortress Press, 1993), 37.

doctrines"; in 2:14, "not *psychikos* but *pneumatikos*"; and finally, in 2:16, "not knowing the mind of God but having the mind of Christ."

The viewpoint that emerges from the negative terms of the formulae is characterized by human claims to wisdom, right doctrine, direction by the *pneuma,* knowledge of God, and a related possession of the divine *nous.* We may add to these features derived in the same way from the antithetical formulations in 1:18—2:5, namely, claims to eloquence, nobility, strength, and abundance of spiritual gifts, including exceptional noetic powers.

In contrast, Paul's own viewpoint requires the obliteration of the social, intellectual, and (in 2:6-16) spiritual distinctions the world deems important. For him, only one distinction remains secure—this world versus God's world as defined by the revelation of the cross and, more explicitly in 2:6-16, by the entry of the Spirit.

In 2:6-16 this distinction is demonstrated in its depths. The mystery revealed by the cross is a mystery that must take hold in the deep realm of Spirit; *only* insofar as it takes hold here and not merely in the realm of speech or behavior will its recipient be liberated from the imprisoning structures of received paradigms. And so Paul concludes his treatment of the power of the kerygma with the penetrating, symbolic language of spirit.

But spirit language in this text is complicated by the clear evidence that, on another level and toward different ends, it functioned at least as powerfully for Paul's enthusiastic "opponents" as it did for Paul. Assuming that Paul knew this, we look for the distinguishing marks of Paul's spirit discourse. What makes this particular use of language therapeutic for the Corinthian hearers? Once again we are called back to the central thread of the entire discourse, the message of the cross, for it is the cross that distinguishes what Paul calls the *pneuma ek tou Theou* from the *pneuma tou kosmou.*

The analysis of 2:6-16 will follow the tripartite structure of the passage by focusing on the major themes of each section.

    I. *Sophia tou Theou* vs. *Sophia tou Aiōnos Toutou* 2:6-8
      (Wisdom of God versus Wisdom of This Age)
        <<Apocalyptic Signal 2:9-10a>>
    II. *Pneuma tou Theou* versus *Pneuma tou Kosmou* 2:10b-14
      (Spirit of God versus Spirit of the World)
   III. *Nous tou Christou* 2:15-16
      (Mind of Christ)

By following the contours of this section, as it builds from the familiar antithesis at the foundation to the unfamiliar term *nous tou Christou*, we discover the structure of the cognitive transformation the text requires of the reader. Within this structure, I will argue, vv 9-10a function to signal the crucial transition without which the whole text remains obscure.

> But, as it is written, "What no eye has seen, nor ear heard, nor the heart of man conceived, what God has prepared for those who love him, God has revealed to us through the Spirit." (2:9-10a)

Here the discerning reader is implicitly enjoined to "see" and "hear" what follows as revealed (apocalyptic) knowledge. The signal warns us that our text and its symbols are liable to misinterpretation (as is often the case in apocalyptic texts). The double language of the spirit and *nous* in 2:9-10a reflects an ambiguity common to apocalyptic thought; only those who truly discern the mystery (the cross kerygma) will correctly perceive the identity and the role of the Spirit. It is these who have the "mind of Christ" (*nous tou Christou*). The designation "mature/perfect" ones (*teleioi*) in 2:6 now can be understood to function not as limitation of the audience to a specific few but rather, true to apocalyptic teaching, as a call to discernment within conflicting worlds. "Let him who has ears to hear, hear."

THE WISDOM OF THIS AGE VERSUS THE WISDOM OF GOD

> (6) Yet among the mature (*teleioi*) we do impart wisdom (*sophia*), although it is not a wisdom of this age (*sophia tou aiōnos tou kosmou*) or of the rulers of this age, who are doomed to pass away (*katargoumenōn*). (7) But we impart a secret and hidden wisdom of God (*sophia tou Theou*), which God decreed before the ages (*pro tōn aiōnōn*) for our glorification (*eis doxan hemōn*). (8) None of the rulers of this age understood this; for if they had, they would not have crucified the Lord of glory. (1 Cor 2:6-8)

Several themes within this statement of the familiar antithesis (wisdom of God versus wisdom of world) signal the new context into which Paul has brought it. First, the wisdom that Paul speaks (the wisdom of God) is directed for the first time to a specific group, the "perfect"(*teleioi*). Moreover, divine wisdom is now characterized as "hidden in mystery before the ages for our glorification." On the other side of the antithesis, the "wisdom of this age" is associated with the "rulers of the world who are doomed to be destroyed." All of wisdom's qualifiers are common to apocalyptic thought, bringing this section of Paul's discourse firmly into that context.

The appearance of the opposites, "wisdom of this age" (*sophia tou aiōnos toutou*) versus "wisdom of God" (*sophia tou Theou*), in 2:6-7 establishes a strong conceptual link to 1:18—2:5. Specifically, it recalls the antithesis inherent in 1:21: "For since, in the wisdom of God, the world did not know God through [its own] wisdom, it pleased God to save believers through the folly of what we preach." But in this text, the qualitative distinction between these two uses of *sophia* is extended into the temporal categories characteristic of apocalyptic. Now the worldly wisdom is said to be "of this age" even as God's wisdom is decreed "before the ages."[15]

The Glory of God Manifested in Mortal Flesh

The stated purpose of God's decree reveals another apocalyptic motif. Paul writes that God decreed this "secret and hidden wisdom for our glorification" (*eis doxan hemōn*). The theme of glory, typical of Jewish eschatology, denotes the radiance of God and the manifestation of God's power, as in Isaiah 6 (LXX), where the glory (*doxan*) of God fills the whole earth.[16] But for Paul, the concept has more than a future reference.[17] In 2 Cor 4:17, for example, the "eternal weight of glory" for which current afflictions are preparing believers is the culmination of the *present* transformation from "one degree of glory (*doxan*) to another" (*metamorphoumetha apo doxēs eis doxēs*) which results when believers "behold the glory of the Lord" in Christ (2 Cor 3:18). Divine glory is already breaking into the world in the Christ-event.[18] Furthermore, it is reflected in the *diakonia* (service) of God

---

15. The temporal designation of God's wisdom is notable in its merging of protology ("before the ages") and eschatology ("for our glorification"). See Sturm, "Apokalyptō/Apokalypsis," 139.

16. See *doxa* as "catchword for apocalyptic"; title used for God in 1 Enoch 63:2, and see Ps 110:3 and Micah 5:11 as Paul's sources.

17. A point made by Rudolf Bultmann, *The Second Letter to the Corinthians* (Minneapolis: Augsburg Publishing House, 1985), 82.

18. Alan Segal reads Paul's reference to "the glory of God in the face of Christ" (2 Cor 4:6) in light of his later description of a heavenly ascent (2 Corinthians 12): "For Paul, as for the earliest Jewish mystics, to be privileged to see the *Kavod* or Glory (*doxa*) of God is a prologue to transformation into his image. . . . One could conclude that Paul's conversion experience involved his identification of Jesus as the image and Glory of God" (Alan F. Segal, *Paul the Convert: The Apostolate and Apostasy of Saul the Pharisee* [New Haven: Yale University Press, 1990], 60-61).

by believers who are "daily given up to death for Jesus' sake, so that the life of Jesus may be manifested in our mortal flesh" (4:11).

An explicit characteristic of the experience of glory in 2 Corinthians 3–4 is that it transforms human beings. Implicitly, the transformation involves a change of perception by which the believer, although outwardly weak and afflicted, becomes the vessel in which the transcendent power of God is manifested (4:7). Likewise, in 1 Cor 2:7, when Paul writes that God decreed the secret wisdom for our glorification, he has in mind both the eschatological glory (with its present and future connotations) and the transformed perception that results when one beholds the glory of God in the face of Christ *crucified*.[19]

Wisdom Hidden in Mystery

It is within this overtly apocalyptic context that Paul locates the wisdom of God (*sophia tou Theou*) "hidden in mystery" (2:7). But the pairing of wisdom with the address of this section to the *teleioi* ("mature" or "perfect ones") causes some interpreters to doubt that Paul speaks the *same* wisdom here that he speaks in 1:18—2:5.[20] Even if Paul does call that earlier wisdom a "mystery" (2:1), some argue, he is clear that he did not proclaim *it* in "lofty words or wisdom." So, the argument goes, at 2:6, when he speaks "wisdom hidden in mystery," he must mean something quite apart from the wisdom of the cross, which he spoke not in mystery but plainly.

This argument may be challenged, however, by noting that the expression about wisdom in 2:1 ("not in lofty words or wisdom") refers to the *mode* of expressing the kerygma (i.e., the way that we speak is "in wisdom"), while the expression about wisdom at 2:7 ("we impart a wisdom hidden in mystery [to the *teleioi*]") refers to the *content* of the kerygma. The "wisdom hidden in mystery" (2:7) is associated *di-*

---

19. See the association in 1 Cor 2:8 of "Lord of glory" with the crucifixion. Richard B. Hays makes reference to a paper by John T. Koenig, "The Knowing of Glory and Its Consequences: 2 Corinthians 3–5," now published in R. T. Fortna and B. R. Gaventa, ds., *The Conversation Continues: Studies in Paul and John in Honor of J. Louis Martyn* [Nashville: Abingdon Press, 1990], 158–69), to support the idea that what is behind Moses' veil in 2 Cor 3:12-16 "is none other than the Glory of God which is made visible in Jesus Christ" (Richard B. Hays, *Echoes of Scripture in the Letters of Paul* [New Haven: Yale University Press, 1989], 146 n. 67).

20. See discussion of Scroggs's thesis above, p 106n.3.

rectly with the "mystery not (communicated) in wisdom" (2:1) and therefore *indirectly* with the Word of the Cross in 1:18-25.

Despite the material association between mystery in 2:1 and wisdom in 2:7, however, we must concede an important distinction between the two expressions in 2:1 and 2:6-7. In 2:1, Paul claims to speak a "mystery," which, in context, can be none other than the "Word of the Cross" (*logos tou staurou*), and to proclaim it plainly without recourse to the conventions of formal rhetoric or "wise speech." In 2:6, however, he claims to speak a "wisdom" whose qualifier, "hidden in mystery," seems to exempt it from expression in plain speech.

Could it be, however, that the wisdom "hidden in mystery" is capable of direct expression and yet does not always result in direct communication to human perception? In other words, may not the divine wisdom of 2:6 retain its quality of hiddenness even as it is plainly proclaimed by the apostle? Indeed, we recognize here a commonplace about preaching. *Expression* (what the preacher *says*) of the gospel through speech or action is a human possibility and calling. But *communication* (what the hearer *hears*) of that gospel to the hearts of hearers remains in the mysterious capacity of God who alone reveals (or conceals) the truth of God's self to (or from) the hearer. We need look no further than the parables of Jesus for parallels to the phenomenon of plain speech communicating divine mysteries which are sometimes grasped, but more often not grasped, by the hearers. In the same way, the Word of the Cross in 1:18 is preached to all, and yet its saving truth is selectively revealed. To some it is folly but to others, power. In 2:1, when Paul vows to say what he says plainly despite its character as "mystery," he makes a statement about the means of expressing the gospel. In 2:7, when he claims that what he says plainly is nevertheless hidden in mystery before the ages, he points to the mystery of communication which is finally controlled, not by the preacher's expression, but by God's power to reveal.

Finally, the ambiguity about the *capacity* of the hearers to hear remains one of this text's great enigmas.[21] It is clear only that Paul both leaves communication to God's sovereign will and calls hearers to readiness for receiving the mystery behind his message.

---

21. On God's willing that some remain ignorant, see Isaiah 44 and 1 Enoch 46. See also Mark 4:11-12.

The Wisdom of This Age

Turning to the other side of Paul's antithetical expression in 2:6-8—
"the wisdom of this age"—we are again guided by qualifiers in the
parallel genitive clause. The primary characteristic of this wisdom is
that it is "of the rulers of this age who are doomed to pass away."

There is debate in the literature on 1 Cor 2:6-8 over the identity of
the rulers (*archontes*). Again, we find ample apocalyptic parallels in
1 Enoch.[22] But are the rulers the human beings who crucified Jesus
or are they cosmic, demonic powers?[23] Some scholars recognize the
possibility that both kinds of rulers are intended.[24] About this possibility Gerd Theissen writes:

> The two interpretations are not sharp alternatives. The historical
> rulers could be heightened symbolically to mythical powers. They are
> doubtless shrouded with a mythical aura in 1 Cor 2:6ff, inasmuch as
> they participate in a dramatic event that encompasses heaven and
> earth.

Theissen concludes that in 1 Cor 2:6-8 the *archontes* are historical
figures who have become transparent to the demonic powers just
as the worldly-wise in 1:26-31 who are being brought to nothing
(*katargein*) are "transparent to being in general, to all 'flesh' that
seeks to boast of itself before God."[25] The historical rulers are in the
foreground, but the opposition to Christ they represent is the opposition of the demonic powers to the Lord of glory. Walter Wink
concludes similarly:

> Both human and demonic powers are meant. Every *archon* involved in
> Jesus' death is intended. This, in fact, is actually what the *Ascension of
> Isaiah* itself says; "the adversary envied Him and roused the children of
> Israel against Him, not knowing who he was, and they delivered Him
> to the king, and crucified Him" (11:19; also 9:13-15).[26]

---

22. See 1 Enoch 63, for example, where the rulers of the world appeal to the Lord
of glory for mercy. For the relation of Paul to 1 Enoch, especially with regard to the
rulers, see Robert G. Hamerton-Kelly, *Pre-existence, Wisdom, and the Son of Man* (Cambridge: Cambridge University Press, 1973), 114.
23. Martin Dibelius concludes that Paul may have meant both heavenly and
earthly rulers. Martin Dibelius, *Der Staat im Neuen Testament*, 1961.
24. See Gerd Theissen, *Psychological Aspects of Pauline Theology* (Philadelphia:
Fortress Press, 1987), 374; and Walter Wink, *Naming the Powers* (Philadelphia: Fortress
Press, 1984), 44.
25. Theissen, *Psychological Aspects*, 376.
26. Wink, *Powers*, 44–45.

That the rulers are not *merely* human powers who oppose God's plan is supported by the intensification of apocalyptic images in this section (2:6-16). In apocalyptic thought, we recall, cosmic rulers struggle for sovereignty over, and are manifested in, human life. At Corinth, they seek sovereignty over the mind; with "wisdom" on their front line of battle, they capture human perception and hold it hostage. In 2:6, Paul announces the doom of the *archontes* much as 1 Enoch had announced the defeat of the rulers by the Son of Man.[27]

In v 8, Paul characterizes the world's wisdom as a wisdom ensconced in ignorance, the same ignorance out of which the "rulers" crucified the "Lord of glory."[28] That of which they are ignorant is clear from the context; it is the "wisdom of God," indicated by the use of the relative pronoun *hēn* in vv 7 and 8:

2:7b   [the wisdom of God]
      which (*hēn*) God foreknew
2:8   which (*hēn*) none of the
      rulers of this age knew (*egnō*),
      for if they had known, they would not
      have crucified the Lord of glory. (2:7-8)

The association of worldly ignorance with the act of crucifixion strengthens the link between the wisdom at 2:6 and the wisdom of the cross kerygma defended in 1:18—2:5. Yet, one aspect of Paul's logic here is problematic. If the "wisdom of God hidden in mystery" is equivalent to the cross kerygma, that is, to the whole narrative of redemption that comes from the cross event, how can it be that the rulers crucified the Lord of glory out of ignorance of the kerygma?

---

27. The term he uses, *katargein*, appears frequently in his letters (Rom 3:3, 31; 4:14; 6:6; 7:2, 6; 1 Cor 1:28; 2:6; 6:13; 13:8, 10, 11; 15:24; 2 Cor 3:7, 11, 13, 14; Gal 3:17; 5:4, 11) and may be translated with passive or active meaning, thus, "to pass away" or "to abolish/to break the power of." Almost certainly in this context Paul thinks of the more active meaning. The rulers are not just passing away, they are being abolished, and their power is destined to be broken. Cf. the use of *katargein* in 2 Cor 3:7, 11, 13, 14 where the "softer" term "passing away" or "deteriorating" seems the better translation. Even here, the term reflects an apocalyptic antinomy. What is deteriorating is the material of the old age: the tables of stone. The gramma passes away as the pneuma enters the scene. In the words of Richard Sturm, "The antinomy between *gramma* and *pneuma* reveals for Paul the battle being fought between two competing epistemologies." Sturm, "Apokalyptō/Apokalypsis," 186. Richard B. Hays notes that in Paul's lexicon *katargein* means "to nullify, to abrogate, to invalidate, or to render ineffectual" (Hays, *Echoes*, 134).

28. Again, relevant apocalyptic background appears in 1 Enoch 63.

The Identity of the Rulers

Exactly what Paul had in mind when he wrote in 2:8, "The rulers of this age did not know this, for if they had, they would not have crucified the Lord of glory," is finally not clear. Several solutions have been offered. One proposed by Bultmann and largely adopted by Wilckens and others[29] posits Paul's dependence, following the Corinthians' own language, on the gnostic myth of the disguised Redeemer who descends through the spheres passing the demonic guardians of the spheres unrecognized. Because he is disguised, the rulers are ignorant of his true identity, and not recognizing him, they crucify him. The Corinthians, and now Paul too, identify the Wisdom of God with the Lord of Glory (unrecognized by the rulers) and with the myth of the descending redeemer. But while the gnostic redeemer myth explains ignorance of the rulers, it does not account for their hostile action, the crucifixion.

A more satisfying solution is proposed by R. G. Hamerton-Kelly who argues that vv 6–9 should be seen, rather, from the viewpoint of apocalyptic:

> One can explain all except one[30] of the vicissitudes of I Cor. 2:6–9 on the basis of passages from Enoch. The secret wisdom is the apocalyptic plan of salvation; the "rulers of this world" are the earthly rulers, . . . quasi-spiritual forces opposing the advent of the new aeon; the contents of the divine plan are the things prepared for the righteous, now pre-existent, then to be revealed; among these things is the Son of Man, the heavenly judge and redeemer, with whom Paul compares the pre-existent Christ, the "Lord of Glory."[31]

Theissen holds that Paul's opposition of the Lord of Glory to the world rulers is, in fact, "more radical than gnostic statements about

---

29. Bultmann, *Theology of the New Testament*, 175; Wilckens, *Weisheit*, 71; and Martin Dibelius, *Die Geisterwelt im Glauben des Paulus* (Göttingen: Vandenhoeck & Ruprecht, 1908), 92. For the Gnostics, according to Wilckens, Christ is equal to the Lord of glory and Wisdom of God. He is the redeemer who came down from heaven, the conqueror before whom all powers of darkness must give way but who cannot himself fall a victim to death." "The wisdom of the powers is brought to naught at the cross, at the place of their supposed victory because they were deceived by the fleshly goals of the heavenly redeemer" (Wilckens, *Weisheit*, 75, 97).

30. The one unexplained element is the term "perfect ones" (*teleioi*). Hamerton-Kelly argues that this term comes from Hellenistic mystery traditions, not apocalyptic. But he finds the clearest parallel in Philo, not in Gnosticism. Hamerton-Kelly, *Pre-existence*, 120–21.

31. Hamerton-Kelly, *Pre-existence*, 117.

the descent of the redeemer." Unlike the gnostic redeemer whose descent requires a compromise (through disguise) with the rulers, the crucifixion of Jesus reflects the dramatic and direct *conflict* between Jesus and the rulers. For Theissen, moreover, this conflict mirrors the social and psychological conflicts of human beings.[32]

In Theissen's psychological interpretation, the wisdom of God is "that aspect of God programmed into creation[33] that always wanted to be recognized (as we see in the wandering, wooing wisdom of the Jewish wisdom tradition) but which achieved its aim only in the paradoxical form of the cross."[34] The ignorance that leads to the crucifixion is ignorance about this God, namely, the God who wills the salvation of the creation. While, for Theissen, the cross kerygma takes its bearings from the literal event of the crucifixion, it presupposes the scandalous, loving and wooing God to whom the rulers are chiefly and fatally opposed. The crucifixion is the inevitable result of the utter antagonism of the world (the present evil age) to God's redeeming love.

Paul expresses the hostility of the world in epistemological language. It is "not knowing" the (God of the) cross that causes the world fatally to oppose Christ. Only knowing God, whose love for humanity comes to a culmination in the cross, can bring people into their right mind (i.e., the *ho autos nous* of 1:10 and the *nous tou Christou* of 2:16).

Paul's remarks on worldly ignorance take on special meaning in light of Corinthian boasting in their enlightened knowledge (1:5; 8:1-7). For them, the Christ-event has indeed brought a shift of perspective—they are now "in the know" (8:1). But in 2:6-16, Paul shows that their change of mind has left them vulnerable to the enemy forces. When he identifies the enemies of Christ as those who in ignorance crucified Jesus, he places knowledge of the cross, its power, and effects at the center of correct perception. Whoever among the Corinthians, therefore, does not "know" the power of the cross in God's battle plan is necessarily allied with the rulers of the world who are doomed to be destroyed.

---

32. Theissen, *Psychological Aspects*, 383.
33. Its temporal dimension is "before the ages" (2:7); its spatial dimension, "the depths of God" (2:10).
34. Here Theissen refers to the failure of the set of convictions that constitute "the received paradigm" of the wisdom tradition. The parenthetical expression is mine.

It is not the concrete act of crucifixion about which the Corinthians are ignorant. They, like the "rulers" who perpetrated it, must certainly have recognized the act (see 15:1-3). It is their ignorance about the *meaning of the act* that constitutes the epistemological error at Corinth. Here, Paul is sharply ironic; the Corinthians' "knowledge" is no better than the rulers' ignorance.

The Apocalyptic Signal in 2:9-10a

But, as it is written, "What no eye has seen, nor ear heard, nor the heart of man conceived, what God has prepared for those who love him," God has revealed (*apokalyptein*) to us through the Spirit.

Paul's treatment of the knowledge/ignorance dichotomy becomes more ironic still with his addition of the allusion in 2:9. Here he begins more formally to correct the faulty epistemology he has exposed in 2:8. Against what may have been the Corinthians' claim to know what "no eye has seen, nor ear heard," Paul argues that the human faculties of sight, hearing, and intellect are unable to grasp the mystery of God's wisdom. At the same time he issues a subtle apocalyptic warning; it is as if he says, "Let the one who has eyes to see, let the one who has ears to hear, hear what is revealed in the kerygma of the cross."

The strong adversative "but" (*alla*) in 2:9a sets vv 9-10a in distinct opposition to what precedes it. Against the ignorance of the world, Paul sets the apocalypse of God. Yet, despite the disjunctive *alla*, there is a structural continuity from v 8 to v 10a based on the relative pronouns *hēn* and *ha*. Just as in vv 7-8, the *hēn*, as object of the rulers' ignorance, corresponds to the *hēn* of God's foreknowledge, namely, the cross kerygma, so in v 9 the *ha* stands for both the object of ignorance (vv 9a and b) and the object of God's preparation (v 9c). Given the similar structure and content of the relative clause in vv 7-9, it appears that what God reveals in v 10a corresponds to that of which the rulers were ignorant (i.e., the *hēn* of vv 7-8 and the *ha* of v 9), namely, the power of the cross in God's plan of salvation.[35]

The citation in v 9 is found nowhere in this form in the Old Testament or extracanonical literature, but reflects a conflation of ideas

---

35. Sturm, "Apokalyptō/Apokalypsis," 35.

from texts like Isa 64:3; Ps 31:20; Sir 1:10; and Wis Sol 9:13. The same ideas are found also in rabbinic sources,[36] at Qumran,[37] and in Hellenistic literature concerning hiddenness and unveiling.[38] Origen, in his *Commentary on Matthew* (27:9), cites the text as an excerpt from the no longer extant apocryphal writing of Elijah the prophet. A very similar saying was transmitted in the early church as a saying of Jesus (Gospel of Thomas 17). Indeed, the wide range of sources for this citation in early Christian literature proves that Paul is one among many Christian writers to have made use of it.[39] It is possible that the Corinthians themselves used the citation to bolster their claims to a special, esoteric knowledge. Whether or not the Corinthians appealed to this text, Paul's task is to distinguish the Corinthian mode of spiritual knowing from his own apocalyptic knowledge revealed *by* the Spirit (2:10).

Knowing God, Loving God

The apocalyptic overtones of the quotation provide a key to its interpretation. Context requires that we read the object (*ha*) of blindness, deafness, and so forth, with reference to (1) the protological and eschatological mysteries of God's wisdom (2:7) and (2) the revealing power (*apokalypsis*) of God (2:10). It is not what human faculties innately perceive that liberates but what God reveals through the Spirit. Moreover, this revelation is prepared not for "*knowers* of God"

---

36. H. L. Strack and Paul Billerbeck, *Kommentar zum Neuen Testament aus Talmud und Midrasch*, 5 vols. (Munich: Beck, 1974), 3:327–29.

37. In his work on the Markan Parable theory, Joel Marcus examines the exhortation, "Let him who has ears to hear . . . ," in Mark 4:9, and points to a reminiscent passage in the Qumran literature "which speaks of the sectaries as those 'whose ear is uncovered' (1QM 10:11)" (Joel Marcus, *The Mystery of the Kingdom of God* [SBLDS; Atlanta: Scholars Press, 1986], 58); cf. Conzelmann, *1 Corinthians* (Hermeneia; Philadelphia: Fortress Press, 1975), 64–65, who also points out that the conflation of texts that Paul uses here reflects ideas at Qumran. He cites 1QH 1:21; 12:12-14; and 1QS 11:13.

38. Conzelmann calls the motif "widespread in religious literature of the period" (Conzelmann, *1 Corinthians*, 63).

39. Cf. 1 Clement 34.8; 2 Clement 11.7; Clement of Alexandria, *Protr.* 10. 94.4; and, in gnostic texts, Hippolytus 5. 23.3; 24.1; 26.16; Acts of Thomas 36; and in apocalyptic, Ascents of Isaiah 11. In Wilckens, *Weisheit*, 75–76. See also M. Philonenko, "Quod oculus non vidit, 1 Cor 2:9," *TZ* 14 (1958): 51-52.

but for "*lovers* of God" (2:9c; cf. 8:3). Against the background of the Corinthians' *gnōsis* theology, the citation presents another aporia. It is not *gnōsis* but love (*agapē*) that qualifies one for God's revelation.[40] With this qualification comes a dislocation for those whose *gnōsis* has overshadowed or replaced love for God. In the parenesis in 1 Cor 8:1-2, he will again pose love as the proper alternative to elitism and boasting in knowledge:

> (1) Now concerning food offered to idols: we know that "all of us possess knowledge" (*gnōsis*). "Knowledge" puffs up, but love builds up. (2) If any one imagines that he knows something, he does not yet know as he ought to know. (3) But if one *loves God, one is known by him.*

Similarly, in 1 Corinthians 13, human knowledge is qualified by *agapē*. Knowledge will pass away, but love never ends (13:8-9).

The replacement of *gnōsis* by *agapē* does not undermine Paul's interest in knowing correctly *kata stauron*. Rather, for Paul, loving God is a *sign* that one has correctly perceived who God is. Again, Paul demonstrates apocalyptic insight; in apocalyptic literature, the knowledge one receives about God generally confirms amidst disconfirming events in history what the seer already knew to be true about God. Paul goes somewhat further in that the revelation he receives redefines *who God is.*[41] In light of the cross, human beings may cease to be oriented to God primarily in intellectual or moral ways. Thus freed of the pretension to know God apart from the cross, they are

---

40. As C. K. Barrett puts it, "Not *gnōsis* but love is the touchstone of Christian maturity and spirituality" (C. K. Barrett, *The First Epistle to the Corinthians* [New York: Harper & Row, 1968], 73). Cf. Sir 1:10, where a similar claim is made about wisdom: "He supplied her [Wisdom] to those who love him (*tois agapōsin autōn*)." See the recent dissertation on this text and its exegetical history by C. Evans, *To See and Not Perceive: Isaiah 6:9-10 in Early Jewish and Christian Interpretation* (Sheffield: JSOT Press, 1989), 82. Most uses of this conflation postdate Paul.

41. Robin Scroggs grounds authentic Christian transformation, which he calls "world-switching" in the new cognition of who God is, namely, the One who justifies the ungodly. He writes, "A new self is created because a new world is being entered, because of a change in the perception of reality. . . . Justification by grace as a creative act frees persons for just such world-switching, and thus the new noetic situation for the believer is an integral part of that new reality. It is to understand God, the world, and the self in a totally new way. Part of that new view of the world is a new view of the neighbor. What Paul has really done, however, is to redefine God" (Robin Scroggs, "New Being: Renewed Mind: New Perception. Paul's View of the Source of Ethical Insight," in *The Text and the Times* [Minneapolis: Fortress Press, 1993], 170).

enabled to "love God with God's own love"[42] and thus to be reconcilers in the world.[43]

If the quotation in v 9 focuses on the impotence of human beings by their own perceptual criteria to receive God's wisdom, v 10a points toward the antidote to that impotence. What God reveals is apprehended not through human capacities but with the help of God's own Spirit.[44] The agency of the Spirit in revealing God is the subject of the next section of the discourse.

THE SPIRIT OF THE WORLD VERSUS THE SPIRIT OF GOD

(9) What God has prepared for those who love him (10) God has revealed to us through the Spirit (*pneuma*). For the Spirit searches everything, even the depths of God. (11) For what person knows the things of the human being except the spirit of the person within him? So also no one comprehends the things of God except the Spirit of God. (12) *Now we have received not the spirit of the world but the Spirit which is from God,* that we might understand the gifts (*ta charisthenta*) bestowed on us by God. (13) And we impart (*laloumen*) this in words not taught by human wisdom but taught by the Spirit, interpreting spiritual truths in spiritual ways. (14) The *psychikos* does not receive the gifts of the Spirit of God, for they are folly to him, and he

---

42. We recall Meister Eckhart's famous saying, "We love God with God's own love." Philo's discussion of the mind (*nous*) possessed by divine love is pertinent in view of the end of our text 2:16 ("but we have the mind of Christ"). Philo writes, "When the mind is possessed by divine love, when it exerts itself to reach the innermost shrine, . . . it forgets everything else, it forgets itself and retains memory and attachment for him alone whose attendant and servant it is. But when inspiration is stilled . . . it races back to human interests that lie in wait for it in the outer court to snatch it away should it venture forth from within" (Philo, *De somn.* 2.232, cited in David Winston, *Philo of Alexandria: The Contemplative Life, the Giants, and Selections* [New York: Paulist Press, 1981], 165–66). This way of viewing the mind, I will argue, is opposed to Paul's own understanding of *nous*.

43. The emphasis I place in this section on the relatively minor mention of *agapē* is justified by Paul's own emphasis on the term elsewhere in 1 Corinthians. I would simply remind us that in chapter 2, Paul is headed toward chapter 13 and that the idea of *agapē* is never far from Paul's mind as he writes this letter (see 4:21; 8:1; 13:1-16; 14:1; 16:14, 24; *agapē*, 1 Cor 2:9; 8:3).

44. That Paul may think of the Spirit as the very source of *agapē* in "those who love God" is suggested by Rom 5:5, where it is the Spirit's role to "pour love into our hearts." In this connection, too, see Joel Marcus's observation that at Qumran (1QS 2:2-3) an exhortation to hear is combined with a recognition that such hearing arises only through an act of God (Marcus, *The Mystery of the Kingdom of God*, 58). In this case, the act of God includes the sending of the Spirit.

is not able to understand them because they are spiritually discerned. (15) The spiritual person (*pneumatikos*) judges all things, but is judged by no one. (1 Cor 2:9-15)

In this long section, Paul moves into the heart of his revelation discourse. He has already, in 1:18—2:5, stated the kerygma and demonstrated its effects in the concrete images of social and political life. In 2:6-8, he has demonstrated the utter opposition of the world's rulers to the Lord of glory, the result of this antagonism in the crucifixion, and the continuing antipathy of the cosmos to the wisdom of God. In 2:9-10a he has alerted the reader/hearer that the truth about God is veiled to human perception until God reveals it.

Now, in 2:10b-15, Paul brings to language, albeit heavily symbolic and ambiguous language, the deep mysteries of the Spirit's operation in the transformative event of apocalypsis. That the cross kerygma functions to transform perception is the subject of 1:18—2:5. *How* it functions is the subject of 2:10b-15. Now Paul takes up the mysteries, the understanding of which, like the understanding of the mysteries at Qumran, requires the lifting of the veil, God's apocalypse.

"To Those Who Love God": What the Spirit Reveals

Already in 2:4, Paul has placed the Spirit in antithesis to the world's wisdom, particularly as that wisdom is manifested in persuasive speech. In 2:10a, the Spirit is again, as in 2:4, associated with the *communication* of what is revealed (in 2:4, what is preached). Here, as in 2:4, the content of revelation is the gospel, the wisdom of God, but now this gospel is said to be communicated "to us" (*hēmin*) through the Spirit. This reference to Spirit as *agent of revelation*[45] moves Paul's argument beyond the contrast between God's wisdom and the world's wisdom that dominated 1:18—2:5.

Paul now considers the *instrumental power* that makes God's wisdom effective in the lives of human beings, the Spirit (*pneuma*). This power is firmly linked to a specific content; it always communicates the saving knowledge of the cross (i.e., that which [*hēn*] God pre-

---

45. The preposition *dia* with the genitive often denotes agency or instrumentality. Nigel Turner, *A Grammar of New Testament Greek*, vol. 3: Syntax, ed. J. H. Moulton (Edinburgh: T & T Clark, 1963), 267.

pared before the ages). Moreover, for Paul, the Spirit not only makes accessible true knowledge of God according to the cross but pulls the knower toward a new realm of existence, namely, the lordship of Christ. The Spirit both discloses this realm as God's new creation (it is in this sense apocalyptic) and empowers the knower to live in obedience to its Sovereign. The one who knows by the Spirit is empowered to exchange the false reality of allegiance to worldly powers for the reality of the living and loving God.[46] To be thus reoriented is to enter the new creation.[47]

Again Paul is apocalyptically innovative. He presupposes the two ages/aeons of apocalyptic thought but alters the traditional concept. Now he places the dividing line between the ages in the *past* event of the cross (i.e., that which "God has prepared for those who love him"). This situates human life in the present at the very *juncture* of the ages rather than before the juncture where God's glorious reign is merely anticipated or after the juncture where God's glory is fully realized (1 Cor 10:11). At this juncture, the Spirit has a mediating function that it does not have in apocalyptic texts before Paul. Whereas in the Dead Sea Scrolls the Spirit of Light opposes the Spirit of Darkness in a heavenly battle which mirrors the *future* battle to be played out on earth, in Paul the Spirit of God has *already* initiated the battle on earth (God has revealed . . . through the Spirit).[48]

The identification of the Spirit as agent of apocalypse (i.e., the revelatory communicator of the gospel) raises important questions about the relation of human spirit to divine Spirit, both designated here by the word *pneuma*. The Spirit's enabling of correct perception

---

46. Scroggs uses the language of true and false reality in his exposition of Rom 1:18-32: "What humankind has denied is that basic reality of God and God's world, which has been revealed not so much in the physical order itself as in the powerful acts of God in the world. . . . . The rebellion against the true God has created a false world, within which false gods play their role as securing and validating the very falsity itself" (Scroggs, "New Being," 177).

47. As Paul Meyer notes, the Christian has not yet been fully transferred to the new creation; in 1:18 the perceivers of God's *dynamis* are "the ones being saved," not the ones already saved. See Paul Meyer, "The Holy Spirit in the Pauline Letters," *Interpretation* 33 (1979): 3–15.

48. In battle language it may be said that through the crucifixion of Jesus, the Spirit has invaded territory previously held by demonic powers; human beings are now being brought into the Spirit's field of force and thus provisionally into the new creation. What is anticipated as a future reality in apocalyptic thought is in Paul's formulation already inaugurated by the Spirit's invasive entry into the world.

may be viewed either as an external force breaking into human consciousness or as the awakening of a spirit already in the human being. There is considerable debate about Paul's intent here.[49] It is my view that in vv 10b-12 Paul develops his view of *pneuma* polemically in such a way as to distinguish clearly between the human spirit and God's Spirit:

> For what person knows (*oiden*) a person's thoughts except the spirit of the person (*pneuma tou anthrōpou*) that is within him? Likewise, no one knows (*egnōken*) the things of God (*ta tou Theou*) except the Spirit of God (*pneuma tou Theou*). (1 Cor 2:11)

In this formulation it seems self-evident that God's Spirit is not the natural endowment of the human being.[50] The Spirit of God, on the one hand, searches everything, even the depths of God (*ta bathē tou*

---

49. The Jewish and Hellenistic background sources on *pneuma* are ambiguous enough to keep the *pneuma* debate alive indefinitely. In particular, various notions about the merging of transcendent and human spirits which arise in philosophical and religious writings of the Hellenistic period present a tangled web of cross-references and mixed influences. While many scholars are willing to leave Paul in a sort of pneumatic limbo between the Stoics and the Gnostics, the text before us offers what seems to be a coherent pneumatology in Paul, if not yet a pneumatology without ambiguities. The debates that have arisen from the question of the relative measures of divine and human activity in revelatory experience have dominated the discussion of this text. Conzelmann (*1 Corinthians*) thinks Paul moves in the direction of Hellenistic mysteries in identifying the power to reveal with the power to receive revelation. The spirit within man in a sense meets the Spirit of God in the moment of revelation. Other scholars note the proximity of Paul's thought on spirit to that of the Stoics, but if Stoic thought is in view, it is "filtered" through something like the mysteries, for no longer does the meeting of human and divine *pneumata* concern primarily the rational discernment of the cosmic order and the place of human beings in it. Now the Spirit is associated with supernatural and nonrational revelation. We see this idea taken to its extreme when in Philo spiritual experience is said to entail the displacement of the principal rational faculty, the *nous* ("mind"). That Paul has not taken this route, however, is clear in 1 Corinthians 14, where he encourages the simultaneous exercise of the *nous* and the spiritual gifts.

50. The Corinthian view, by contrast, may have been that they had always had the divine Spirit but that in Christ that Spirit was awakened, the true self brought to consciousness. Hamerton-Kelly sees this as an aspect of the Hellenistic wisdom expressed by Philo: "Shining through his writings one can see a conception of salvation, based on a consubstantiality between the divine being and the human soul, and taking the form of an ascent of the divine in man to its source in God. The divine in man is a 'natural' endowment, given at creation; indeed, the real 'man' is the divine spirit, or Logos, or Wisdom, in man." Hamerton-Kelly cites several texts in Philo, including *De op.* 134–136; *Leg. All.* 3.161; *Quis Her.* 55–57; *Quod Det.* 80–90. See Hamerton-Kelly, *Preexistence*, 121. On the Philonic parallels, Hamerton-Kelly cites the extensive study on this terminology in 1 Corinthians by Birger A. Pearson, *The Pneumatikos-Psychikos Terminology in 1 Corinthians* (Missoula, Mont.: Scholars Press, 1973).

Theou), and knows the things (*ta*) of God. The human spirit, on the other hand, knows only human things. Admittedly in v 12 the lines of disjuncture are somewhat blurred. Paul writes:

> But we (*humeis*) have received (*elabomen*) not the spirit of the world, but the Spirit which is from God (*pneuma to ek tou Theou*), that we might understand (*eidōmen*) the gifts bestowed on us by God. (1 Cor 2:12)

The "we" (*humeis*) in v 11a identifies the recipients of the "Spirit which is from God" with the recipients (*hemin*, "to us") of the *apokalypsis* in v 10a. This identification leaves open two interpretive options: (1) Paul singles out a specific group, the "we" of v 11a, as the ones naturally endowed with God's Spirit, and thereby capable of being enlivened toward understanding God's subsequent gifts (including the preaching of the kerygma); or (2) in light of the previous association of *pneuma* with both *apocalypse* and *dynamis*, Paul attests to the Spirit's invasion by way of the kerygma into a realm (the human spirit) previously empty of that (divine) Spirit.

The second option is easier to correlate with Paul's argument elsewhere in the letter and helps to establish the continuity between the two major sections, 1:18—2:5 and 2:6-16. In this reading, the spirit of the human being is radically distinct from the Spirit of God; nevertheless, the endowment of the human being with the Spirit of God takes place in such a way as to newly create a kinship with God's Spirit. As the spirit of the human being was breathed into a physical shell at the first creation, now the Spirit from God comes to inspire humanity toward the new creation, making the person, too, a new creature.[51]

The Spirit Searches the Depths of God

The discourse on spirit continues enigmatically in 2:10b and c: "For the Spirit searches everything, even the depths of God (*ta bathē tou Theou*)." Paul's use of the term *bathē tou Theou* in 2:10c has been

---

51. Cf. Jeremiah and the language of the endowment of the new covenant now written "on their hearts." Likewise Paul in 2 Cor 3:6 speaks of a new covenant, not in a written code but in Spirit: "For the written code kills, but the Spirit gives life." The new creation in 2 Cor 5:17 is the work of the Spirit who comes to replace the human point of view. This idea is not far from the formulation of our text. God's Spirit does not supplement the human spirit but replaces it.

taken to indicate variously his "gnostic" leanings, his Jewish wisdom background, and his apocalyptic background.[52] But whatever possible meanings *ta bathē Theou* might carry in the abstract, there is little doubt that the term here extends the context of the *ha* in 2:9 (the object of God's revealing in 2:10a):

2:9   What (*ha*) God has prepared

2:10a ...,God has revealed to us through the Spirit,

2:10b *for* (*gar*) the Spirit searches everything (*ta panta*)(2:10c), even the depths of God.

The opening "for" (*gar*) in 2:10b shows that the following phrase means to explicate 2:10a. The "what" (2:9, *ha*) that is revealed by God "to us" through the Spirit in 2:10a is thus parallel to both the "all things" (*panta*) and the "depths of God" (*bathē tou Theou*) in 2:10b and c. The *panta* and *bathē* must then refer to the wisdom of the cross which is hidden to the world's reason in 1:21 but revealed by God in 2:10a. If my judgment is correct, even if the Corinthians had a gnostic framework by which they interpreted the *bathē tou Theou*, they nonetheless would have been challenged by Paul's train of thought from 1:18—2:10 to read "depths of God" as a designation for the *content* of the *kerygma tou staurou*.

---

52. See Hans Schlier, "*Bathos*," *TDNT*, 1:517 (1964), who agrees with Wilckens, below. Dibelius says the expression "the deep things of God" is a technical term for something "profoundly mysterious," a wisdom reserved for the few who are "perfect," as in Greek mysticism and mystery religions" (Dibelius, *Die Geisterwelt*, 89–98). Scroggs ("Paul: Sophos and Pneumatikos," 51) shows that the expression is at home in wisdom and apocalyptic literature (Eccl 7:24; Job 11:8; 2 Bar 54:12; 1 Enoch 63:2). Wilckens (*Weisheit*, 216–17) takes the term to be "typically gnostic" and yet finds ample background for the term in Jewish apocalyptic (1 Enoch 63:2; 1QS 11:18ff.; 4 Ezra 4:10, 21; 10:35; 2 Bar 14:8). According to Wilckens, the *bathys* in 2:10 brings out the "gnostic" views of the Corinthians and charts Paul's first steps into the adoption of Corinthians' perspective. Wilckens holds that in contrast to Paul's use of apocalyptic tradition, which conceives hidden mysteries as future eschatological events (cf. 2:7, 9), here he posits a present pneumatic revealing of salvation which is already taking place for "us" (*hēmin*) and thus for pneumatics. In the gnostic thought that Wilckens saw behind this text, the revealer himself is Spirit, so that the receipt of the Spirit (at baptism?) changes the receiver into a pneumatic, a being of Spirit. For Wilckens, both *nous* and *sophia* are designations in Corinthian terminology for the divine revealer of gnostic myth. Paul's own theological conviction moves along different lines, according to Wilckens, but he has fallen into the Corinthians' system by his decision to use their vocabulary of *sophia* and *pneuma*. To understand "depths of God," we need not press into gnostic traditions alone. Suggestive parallels in apocalyptic thought are found in Dan 2:22 and 2 Bar 14:8f.

Verses 11 and 12 also reflect this train of thought. Just as in 1:18—2:5 the wisdom of God is hidden to the world, so here the Spirit of God is by nature hidden to the human being. There seems no doubt in v 11 that Paul sees a sharp disjuncture between the human capacity to know the *human* spirit and the human capacity to know *God's* Spirit. There is no implied ontological identification, no continuum between the two.[53] The deep division that Paul develops between human and divine spirits is further supported by the ancient argument "like by like," which is often cited in connection with this passage.[54] If the first half of the argument (1:18—2:5) has to do with the *content* of God's wisdom and the second primarily with its *communication,* then Paul establishes clearly at the outset of the argument concerning communication (2:6-16) that the *human* spirit is not the agent of the communication of the *divine* Spirit. The difference between the "know" verbs of the two "like by like" clauses (*oiden* in 2:11a, *egnōken* in 2:11c) may further press the distinction.[55] The *knowing* of human by human stands in contrast to the *comprehension* of God by God.

How, then, given the strength of the "like by like" clause, can Paul go on immediately to say, "But we have received not the spirit of the

---

53. See Käsemann, who writes of 1 Cor 2:11, "The first clause reminds the reader of the Stoic and popular philosophical view according to which man arrives at true self-understanding by means of the spirit which participates in the divine pneuma. Under the influence of its own tradition, the idealist interpretation misunderstood the trend of the verse and put the stress on the analogy. The spirit was thus fundamentally defined—in God and man alike—as self-understanding, and this determined the interpretation of Pauline anthropology as a whole: as a spiritual being man is called to knowledge of himself. . . . Moreover, it is highly doubtful, not only in the light of our own experience but also in the context of Pauline anthropology, whether the spirit of man possesses an adequate self-understanding apart from the revelation in Christ. Generally speaking, we know ourselves least of all" (Ernst Käsemann, "On Paul's Anthropology," in *Perspectives on Paul* [Philadelphia: Fortress Press, 1971], 14–15).

54. Conzelmann cites ancient uses of the principle by Democritus (*Fragmente* 2:176) and Plato (*Prot.* 377c–338a; *Resp.* 508a–511e; *Tim.* 45a). See Conzelmann, *1 Corinthians,* 66.

55. Both verbs are perfect active forms with present meaning. Koenig draws attention to the distinction when he comments about the word *eidōmen* in 2:12 that "the word the RSV translates as 'understanding' in v 12 (*eidōmen*) implies a change of consciousness which takes place in believers" (John Koenig, "From Mystery to Ministry: Paul as Interpreter of Charismatic Gifts," *USQR* 33 [1979]: 169). In both 2:11a (*oiden*) and 2:12 (*eidōmen*), the same root for human knowing is used opposite (*ginōskō*) for the human inability to know the nature of God (in 2:11) or, in 2:14, for the nature of the divine Spirit.

world but the Spirit which is from God"? Does he not violate his own principle? There is no strong adversative in 2:12 (no *alla*, only *de*) to indicate that Paul intends to make a radical change in direction. The receipt of the Spirit which is "from God" is not treated as a contradiction of what precedes.

We can better understand Paul's distinction between the human and divine spirits by attending to his syntax. Paul proceeds carefully here; the Spirit we receive is not simply "God's Spirit" (*pneuma tou Theou* or *pneuma Theion*) but the Spirit which is *received from* God (*to pneuma to ek tou Theou*).[56] Perhaps he does not say simply "We received God's Spirit," because this would allow an easier identification of human spirit and divine Spirit. Rather, by inserting the preposition *ek*, Paul derives the Spirit that human beings *receive* from God, yet without allowing the natural personal divinity often attached to spirit-bearing in Hellenistic and Jewish circles.[57] The force of the distinction is, "We *receive* the Spirit, we do not already *possess* it."

That We Might Know What Is Bestowed

The *effect* of receiving this Spirit is the subject of the next phrase of v 12: "in order that we might understand the things that are given to us (*ta charisthenta*) by God." A principal problem of this phrase, according to Barrett, is "that Paul makes no attempt to define what these things (i.e. the *charisthenta*) are."[58] C. K. Barrett settles on the cryptic definition of the *charisthenta* as "the undefinable and undescribable things of v 9, things proper (in ordinary Jewish eschatological thought) to the life of heaven, but freely given to Christians." Hans Conzelmann, with no greater confidence, says the *charisthenta* are either pneumatic powers bestowed on individuals or the con-

---

56. Elsewhere Paul uses more the common *pneuma tou Theou*. See 3:16; 6:11.

57. Some scholars see the reference to "the things given by God" in 2:12c as Paul's response to a gnosticizing tendency toward self-identification with God's *pneuma*. In mystery religions, *charis* ("gift") can point to the mystery and denote the power within the pneumatic to become synonymous with *pneuma*. See Conzelmann, *1 Corinthians*, 66. Wilckens, however, thinks Paul uses gift language polemically to avoid the gnostic self-identification as pneumatics with Christ; i.e., it is not because they are ontologically pneumatic, Paul means to say, but because they have received the gifts of God that they now possess the Spirit. See Wilckens, *Weisheit*, 85.

58. Barrett, *The First Epistle to the Corinthians*, 75.

tents of the event of salvation. Of the latter option he argues that "the deliberate allusion to *charis* points in this direction."[59] The most compelling route toward identifying the *charisthenta* follows Conzelmann's (undeveloped) second option.

The term *ta charisthenta* means literally "the things bestowed graciously on us by God." The RSV adds the word "gifts," calling to mind the more prevalent *charis* word in Paul, charisma. John Koenig makes the connection to *charismata* ("spiritual gifts") explicit by arguing that the "things" Paul speaks of understanding here are the *pneumatika* of v 13 and *pneumatika* is, as Koenig observes, "precisely the term Paul uses for the charismatic gifts enumerated in 1 Corinthians 12–14." On these grounds Koenig renders the enigmatic phrase *pneumatikois pneumatika sygkrinontes* in v 13 as "we interpret spiritual gifts to spiritual people." Koenig concludes:

> Here Paul is outlining his ministry to the Corinthians. He claims that the Spirit's teaching work is being accomplished through their spiritual gifts. This interpretation, for its part, consists of two kinds of gifts: future eschatological ones, which wait for believers on the far side of the parousia and must therefore be proclaimed "in a mystery" (2:7); and present ones, *charismata* which believers are currently experiencing.[60]

One compelling option is to combine Koenig's association of "spiritual gifts" to *charisthenta* with Conzelmann's observation of the *charis* allusion. In this case, the verse principally concerns the Spirit's role in communicating the kerygma of the cross, which is the substance of both the mystery that Paul proclaims in vv 6-10 and the spiritual "things" (or, with Koenig, "gifts") that Paul interprets in v 13.

Following Conzelmann, this reading regards the *charis* association as a deliberate allusion to the "salvation event," that is, both the concrete act of Christ's death on the cross and the effects of that death realized in the church (Rom 3:23; 5:10; Gal 2:17-21; Rom 11:32; 2 Cor 5:1). According to Conzelmann, the related word *charisma* in Paul is "linked with *charis* on the one side and *pneuma* on the other,"

59. Conzelmann, *1 Corinthians*, 67.
60. Koenig, "Ministry," 169.

and occurs regularly in soteriological contexts (e.g., Rom 11:29).[61] Similarly, in our text, the term *charisthenta* is linked on one side with *pneuma*, the agent of understanding, and on the other with the kerygma, the soteriological content of the understanding given and received. What one comes to understand by agency of the Spirit is the gifts of salvation through the cross, here stated in the plural to pick up the neuter plurals of v 9.

As Koenig demonstrates, vv 12 and 13 give us reason to associate the *charisthenta* language with the proper evaluation and practice of the *charismata* ("spiritual gifts"). Koenig notes that whereas elsewhere in 1 Corinthians, Paul reflects upon abuses of charismatic gifts (e.g., 4:8; 12:20; 13:1-12; 14:26), here his stress on *understanding* (*eidomen*) the *charisthenta* seems intended to lead toward more authentic behavior in the Spirit. When *charismata* are seen in their right relation to God's *charis*, they too reflect the gospel of unmerited giftedness whose source is God and whose emblem is the cross. In our verse, then, Paul identifies the Spirit as the interpreter of the gifts of salvation, both the kerygma itself and the charismatic service of believers in the world.

The understanding to which Paul refers in v 12b is not, then, a merely intellectual matter (i.e., the *gnōsis* of the *pneuma tou kosmou*)[62] but a spiritual *charisma*, the receipt of which causes the receiver to comprehend authentically and *palpably* the nature of God's grace. It thereby enables the receiver to embody the cross and its salvific power in ministry to the world.[63]

---

61. Conzelmann, "*Charis,*" *TDNT*, 8:403 (1974). Gordon Fee too moves in this direction when he notes that the verb behind the neuter plural *charisthenta*, namely, *charizomai*, "seems to be a deliberate allusion to the 'grace' (*charis*), or the "gift" (*charisma*) of salvation (as in Rom 6:23); it appears here in the neuter plural . . . because it is reflecting the neuter plurals of v 9" (Fee, *The First Epistle to the Corinthians* [Grand Rapids: Wm. B. Eerdmans, 1987], 113). In 1 Corinthians, Paul uses *charis* frequently (9 times: 1:3, 4; 3:10; 10:30; 15:10 [twice]; 15:57; 16:3; 16:23). In 3:10 and 15:10 the term is directly associated with Paul's preaching of the Gospel.

62. The polemical context is clear from 2:12a and b; only the Spirit of God, not the spirit of the world, supplies true knowledge of the gifts. The spirit of the world, already charged with ignorance about the cross, is, by virtue of that ignorance, ignorant also about the gifts from God. The two charges reflect a common theme. The world is blind to *ta charisthenta* (and thus to the meaning of *charismata*, i.e., *logos, gnōsis*), because it has not received the kerygma of God's *charis*, the "word of the cross."

63. "The Spirit is—scandalously—identified precisely with the outward and palpable, the particular human community of the new covenant, putatively transformed by

Human Teaching versus Spiritual Teaching

In v 13, Paul continues his discussion of *pneuma* with the statement,

> (that) . . . which (*ha*) we speak (is) not in words taught by human wisdom but taught by the Spirit, [that is], we interpret (*sygkrinō*) spiritual things by spiritual means (or, to the spiritual ones) (*pneumatikois pneumatika sygkrinontes*).

The statement is confounding in part because of the multiple options for translating *sygkrino* and in part because of the ambiguous dative plural *pneumatikois*. On the first matter, the Bauer, Ardnt, and Gingrich lexicon lists three definitions for the term and shows how each may be used in the translation of this verse.[64] Thus,

1. "To bring together" or "to combine" yields the translation "giving spiritual truth a spiritual form."
2. "To compare" yields "comparing the spiritual gifts and revelations (which we already possess) with the spiritual gifts and revelations (which we are to receive, and judging them thereby)."
3. "To explain" or "to interpret" yields "interpreting spiritual truths to those who possess the Spirit," the meaning chosen by the translators of the Revised Standard version of the Bible.[65]

Options 2 and 3 are most appropriate in the context. If we translate *sygkrinein* as "to compare," the phrase highlights the polemical context of the verse and emphasizes that the authentic criteria for comparisons are determined by the Spirit of God, not by the spirit of the world. Paul uses the term in a similarly polemical setting in 2 Cor 10:12 to eschew the practice of comparing himself to others.

God's power so as to make Christ's message visible to all" (Hays, *Echoes*, 131). Of the Corinthians' failure properly to understand the spiritual gifts, Koenig writes, "Understanding would lead them to mutual service in the community—in other words to hard work" (Koenig, "Ministry", 167–68). What Paul thinks he is doing in his language about the *charisthenta* is encouraging the Corinthians to the ministry of building up the church.

64. William F. Arndt and F. Wilbur Gingrich, *A Greek-English Lexicon of the New Testament and Other Early Christian Literature* (Chicago: University of Chicago Press, 1957), 782.

65. John Koenig proposes "interpreting spiritual gifts to spiritual people" (Koenig, "Ministry," 169). F. Blass and J. Weiss propose emendation of the text: See James H. Moulton and George Milligan, *Vocabulary of the Greek New Testament* (Grand Rapids: Wm. B. Eerdmans, 1949). Another option is to allow all three meanings at once. This is the choice of Robert Funk, who says that the term "covers the range of speaking the word of the cross, interpreting, comparing, combining" (Robert Funk, *Language, Hermeneutics and the Word of God* [San Francisco: Harper & Row, 1966], 205); Wilckens chooses only the meanings "compare" and "connect" (or combine). See Wilckens, *Weisheit*, 84.

For we do not venture to class or compare ourselves (*sygkrinai heautous*) with some of those who commend themselves. But when they measure themselves by one another, and compare themselves (*sygkrinontes heautous*) with one another, they are without understanding (*syniasin*).[66]

If, however, we translate *sygkrinein* as "to interpret," the verse denotes criteria for communication of spiritual matters. This more dynamic reading of the phrase implies a ministry of interpretation within the community. If the *pneumatika* denote spiritual gifts, there is an obvious and urgent need for this ministry in Corinth's present situation.

In either translation of the phrase, Paul's message is more practical than esoteric. Whether he calls for an end to boastful comparisons or a beginning to the edifying interpretation of spiritual gifts, the spiritual healing of the community is in view.

But what of the *pneumatikois*? Shall we translate "spiritual *people*" in anticipation of the *pneumatikoi* in v 14 or "by spiritual *means*" in reference to the "words not taught by human wisdom" of v 13a? Either option is possible grammatically, but the second renders a unity of meaning in the whole clause by allowing v 13b to directly explicate v 13a; the spiritual things are taught not in words of human wisdom but by spiritual means, that is, words taught by the Spirit.[67]

THE PSYCHIC VERSUS THE PNEUMATIC

(14) The psychic (unspiritual) person does not receive the things of the Spirit of God, for they are folly to him, and he is not able to understand them because they are spiritually discerned. (15) The spiritual person judges all things, but is himself judged by no one. (1 Cor 2:14-15)

---

66. It is not without significance for our study that 2 Cor 10:12-18 is prefaced by one of the most profoundly apocalyptic passages in Paul, in which the battle lines between worldly perception and divine perception are clearly drawn: "For though we live in the world we are not carrying on a worldly war, for the weapons of our warfare are not worldly but have divine power to destroy strongholds. We destroy arguments and every proud obstacle to the knowledge of God, and take every thought captive to obey Christ, being ready to punish every disobedience, when your obedience is complete" (2 Cor 10:3-6).

67. In support of this reading, Fee notes, "The participial construction, modifying *laloumen*, argues for the closest possible ties to what has already been said, not a loose additional anticipating what follows" (Fee, *The First Epistle to the Corinthians*, 115).

The discussion of *psychikos* and *pneumatikos* in vv 14 and 15 functions in part to restate the central antithesis of the unit, the spirit of the world versus the Spirit of God (*pneuma tou kosmou* versus *pneuma tou Theou*).[68] But now Paul takes up a new and somwhat puzzling vocabulary. Some interpreters suggest that at this point he falls victim to the Corinthians' language in a way that fatally confuses his own theological position.

But it is also possible that at 2:14 Paul is ironically and *polemically* quoting a Corinthian slogan that contrasted *psychikoi* and *pneumatikoi*. We are once again on the perilous path of speculation on the Corinthian position. Those who see Gnosticism in the text argue that this sentence reflects the gnostic anthropological divisions of humanity into *hylics, psychics* and *pneumatics*.[69] A more conservative approach seeks the distinction's origin in Hellenistic Jewish tradition. The wisdom tradition, in particular, attests to the division of human beings into two groups, the sages and all others. Philo is perhaps the master of the period in assigning people to various stages of and capacities for spiritual enlightenment.[70]

Whatever the origin of the idea, those who use it suppose they are the *pneumatikoi*, who are especially endowed to receive the spirit. The *psychikoi*, on the other hand, do not receive the things (gifts?) of the Spirit and, moreover, are *unable* to know (*ou dynatai gnōnai*) them because they lack what they need to discern its gifts. For a Valentinian Gnostic, the psychic's state is a congenital condition for which there is no cure. Some are capable of receiving the Spirit, others are not.[71]

---

68. Sturm writes of this passage, "Unlike others in Corinth, then, Paul sees the *psychikos/pneumatikos* dichotomy less as a differentiation between kinds of human beings than as a differentiation between all humanity (*hoi psychikoi*) and what is from God (*to pneuma*)" (Sturm, "Apokalyptō/Apokalypsis," 152).

69. Wilckens states the position strongly in his early work, citing *psychikos* as "ein gnostischer Terminus technicus" (*Weisheit*, 89).

70. E.g., Philo discusses the *teleios* as one on the border line between divine and human existence (*De somn.* 2.234) and the *prokopton* as one making progress (*Fuga*, 38.213).

71. For the gnostic anthropological divisions, see Nag Hammadi Corpus II, 5, 117, James M. Robinson, ed., *The Nag Hammadi Library in English* (San Francisco: Harper & Row, 1978), 173. Kurt Rudolph writes, "Only the pneumatics are gnostics and capable of redemption" (Kurt Rudolph, *Gnosis* [San Francisco: Harper & Row, 1977], 91–92). See too the discussion of Pearson: "According to the Valentinians most men are 'hylic'; less are 'psychic'; and only a few are 'pneumatic' (*Exc. Th.* 56.2). The 'pneumatics' are 'saved by nature' (*physei sōzomenoi, Exc. Th.* 56.3; *Adv. Haer.* 1.6.2). The 'hylics' cannot be saved at all; they 'perish by nature' (*physei apollytai, Exc. Th.* 56.3). . . . The 'psychics' occupy a position midway between the 'pneumatics' and the 'hylics,' and can extend in either direction—toward salvation or destruction" (Pearson, *Pneumatikos-Psychikos*, 80).

It is very likely that the statement in 2:14 can be attributed to *both* Paul and the Corinthians. Read this way, it is another of Paul's rhetorical double-edged swords. Quoting *their* slogan, Paul brings the Corinthians' distinction into the service of *his* argument. What they take to be an anthropological division by which they are the elevated pneumatics, Paul reverses. Now the *true* pneumatics are those whom the Spirit indwells (by interpreting the kerygma) and allows to understand the *charisthenta*. True pneumatics demonstrate this understanding in community life insofar as they identify with the crucified Lord (cf. 2:2-4).

Paul's use of the same antithetical pair *psychikos-pneumatikos* in 1 Cor 15:44-49 is illuminating for the discussion here. In v 45 he uses *psychikos* in connection with the first Adam and *pneumatikos* in connection with the last Adam:

> If there is a physical body (*psychikos sōma*), there is also a spiritual body (*pneumatikos sōma*). Thus it is written, "The first man Adam became a living soul (*psychēn zōsan*)"; the last Adam became a life-giving Spirit (*pneuma zōopoioun*). (1 Cor 15:44-45)

In his monograph on the *psychikos/pneumatikos* distinction, B. A. Pearson notes the obvious reference in this text to the creation account in Genesis and argues that Paul's terminology derives from the Corinthians' use of Hellenistic Jewish exegetical traditions. According to Pearson, the Corinthians, "under the influence of teachers who had grown up in Diaspora Judaism, were espousing a doctrine of a-somatic immortality, denying the bodily resurrection" and using Gen 2:7 to state their case. Their exegetical tradition (which Pearson derives principally from Philo) held that the first Adam, the heavenly man, bears the image of God (Gen 1:27) through "spiritual inbreathing" (Gen 1:17) and by this inbreathing participates in the spiritual *eikōn tou Theou* (Gen 1:27).[72] This *pneumatikos* Adam precedes the *psychikos* (*ek gēs xoikos*) Adam of 2:7. According to Pearson, the spiritualists at Corinth identify themselves with the first Adam, the Spirit of God, and thus with the incorruptibility of the image of God.[73]

Paul's own interpretation reverses this order of creation. In his sequence, the earthly being (*psychikos*) is first, and the heavenly being (*pneumatikos*) is last. By reversing the sequence, Pearson argues, Paul

---

72. Pearson, *Pneumatikos-Psychikos*, 24.
73. Pearson, *Pneumatikos-Psychikos*, 17. Pearson argues for the strong influence of the Hellenistic Jewish synagogue upon the Christians at Corinth (p. 18).

is also correcting an established line of exegetical tradition that posited a contrast between two classes of people: the *psychikoi*, who live *haimati kai sarkos hegone* (as hedonists, in blood and flesh) and the *pneumatikoi*, who live *theiō pneumati logismō* (reasonably in God's Spirit).[74] In so doing, Paul is also correcting his "opponents" at Corinth who were teaching that they had "the potentiality of becoming *pneumatikoi* within themselves by virtue of the *pneumatikōs* nature given them by God, and that by a cultivation of wisdom they could rise above the earthly and 'psychic' level of existence and anticipate heavenly glory."[75]

Theissen reaches a related conclusion and puts it into psychologically relevant language. The distinction *pneumatikos/psychikos* first arises, he argues, in Christian charismatic circles, where the experience of divine Spirit (*pneuma*) extends the otherwise limited awareness of the *psychē*, so that human beings may comprehend the divine revelation that is otherwise incomprehensible. What is most significant in Paul's corrective emphasis at Corinth, according to Theissen, is that

> the *pneumatic* is to be understood as goal not as origin; that is, that the pneumatic human being is not the primeval one of Genesis 1 and 2 but rather Christ, the new man . . . what according to others is information about our archaic derivation Paul interprets in such a way that it becomes a reference to the future. The *pneuma* points to the new world.[76]

Theissen's interpretation has the advantage of highlighting the perceptual transformation Paul associates with *pneumatic* experience. The *pneumatic* is engaged in a process of transformation toward

---

74. Pearson, *Pneumatikos-Psychikos*, 19, citing Philo, *Quis Her.* 55. Insofar as Pearson attempts to locate Paul's *psychikos/pneumatikos* distinction per se in Hellenistic Jewish exegetical tradition on Gen 2:7, his work has received resounding criticism; Theissen puts it bluntly: "One must . . . already know in advance the opposition of *pneumatikos* and *psychikos* if one wishes to impose it on Gen 2:7" (Theissen, *Psychological Aspects*, 362).

75. Pearson, *Pneumatikos-Psychikos*, 39. On this matter, M. DeBoer makes a related observation: "In 15:45, 47-49, . . . the contrast is once again between two *anthropoi*, the first, earthly Adam, the living *psychē*, and the last, heavenly Adam, the making alive *pneuma*. Paul's pointed reversal of the relationship between 'the natural' and 'the pneumatic' implies that the Corinthians addressed here in some sense held the contrary view." M. DeBoer, "The Defeat of Death: Paul's Apocalyptic Eschatology in 1 Corinthians 15 and Romans 15:12-21" (Ph.D. diss., Union Theological Seminary, 1983).

76. De Boer, *Defeat of Death*, 365.

God's new creation, and not in a regression to origins.[77] To be sure, Paul is concerned (as he demonstrates elsewhere in 1 Corinthians) to emphasize the *future* aspect of spiritual fulfillment *(teleios;* 13:10; 15:42-50). Yet the new perception he associates with pneumatic disclosure in 1 Cor 2:6-16 is a decisively *present* phenomenon.

The Spirit and the Downward Moving Power of the Cross

It is at this point that Paul's argument is most vulnerable to misinterpretation at Corinth, where the present realization of spiritual gifts (including knowledge, *gnōsis*) is the pride of the enthusiasts. To the extent that he associates the spirit with present *gnōsis* or cognitive transformation, he opens himself to misinterpretation by those who consider themselves already transferred by their *gnōsis* into glory. Paul's problem in 2:6-16 is to keep the present reality of pneumatic transformation tied to the kerygmatic disclosure of the "depths of God," that is, the saving, and *downward moving* power of the cross.[78] He addresses the problem in part by linking God's "gifts" (*charisthenta*) to the cross kerygma through the Spirit and in part by showing the advent of God's new creation in the realities of Corinthian community life, especially in God's choice of what the psychic world deems insignificant (2:14a).

The *psychikos*, for Paul, is one whose experience of spirit is informed neither by the cross event in the past nor by God's new creative activity in the present. The dislocation that the psychic experiences does not bring him into the transforming reality of new creation. Rather, it catapults him out of the created world in a retrogressive plunge toward his origins (which perhaps he calls the "depths of God"). The mystery he knows moves him, not to ministry *in* the world, but to withdrawal *from* it.

---

77. See the alternate reading of the relation of first to last creation in Scroggs, "New Being," 175. Scroggs finds in Paul's Adam typology in Romans the view "that God's intent in the original creation, frustrated by the disobedience of Adam and Eve, will be brought to fruition in the eschaton, which is viewed as the restoration of humankind to that original (but now faithful) life before God in the Garden of Eden."

78. In an essay based on this text, Henri Nouwen develops the expression "upwardly mobile religion" which he contrasts with Christ's "downward mobility." I mean to suggest a related notion; the one transformed by the Spirit is turned "downward" in service and obedience, not upward into the heights of spiritual attainment. Henri Nouwen, "Ministry and Spirituality," a lecture delivered at the Yale Divinity School, April 1981.

The distinction *psychikos/pneumatikos* in 2:14 must thus be read with present eschatological nuance: the *pneumatikos* is able through the Spirit's revelation of the cross to live authentically in the new creation, both understanding God's *charisthenta* and interpreting these "gifts" to the world.[79] The *psychikos*, whose intent is to rise *above* the world, actually remains enslaved to it. Having received *gnōsis* without *pneuma*, the psychics remain ignorant in the clutches of the world and its wisdom. Because they fail to receive the Spirit, they do not perceive *what is revealed* (2:9-10) by the Spirit, namely, the crucified Christ. They therefore misperceive the critical interpretive power of the cross for eschatological life in the present. Because their eschaton has arrived outside the realm of the Crucified, they have missed the call to faithful living in the world at the turn of the ages.

Here, as throughout the letter, Paul's driving concern is to demonstrate the vital connection between the Spirit and the cross in the life of the community. By this means, he hopes to restore unity in the church.[80]

A principal impediment to unity, however, comes to light in v 15. The verse carries an ambiguity similar to that found in v 14. It may be either a Corinthian slogan or Paul's own formulation. In either case, the thought of the verse is a clear continuation of the ideas of v 14, to which it is joined by a copulative *de*:

> The spiritual person (*pneumatikos*) judges (*anakrinetai*) all things but is himself judged by no one. (1 Cor 2:15)

As elsewhere in 1 Corinthians, the verb *anakrinō* is used here with the sense of "evaluating," for example, apostolic authority.[81] If the

---

79. Cf. Sturm, "Apokalyptō/Apokalypsis," 152. "The true pneumatikos is not one who has recovered a pure and perfect condition of humanity, but one whose hearing of the word of the cross in faith allows to receive the Spirit of God." But compare the different perspective of Scroggs: "What Paul is attempting to describe is new and yet creation, a word that cannot be divorced from the topos of the original creation by God. Both the original and the new creations are *creatio ex nihilo* (see 1 Cor 1:26-31), and both aim at the same reality: a faithful humanity living before the gracious, creative God. Thus Paul also understands salvation to be not out of, but back into humanity" (Scroggs, "New Being," 175).

80. F. Büchsel, "*Krinō*," *TDNT*, 3:944, "The community is not a pneumatic democracy; it is a pneumatic organism." Evidence that the misunderstanding of spirit has disrupted koinonia at Corinth abounds in the letter. It is implicit from the first mention of divisions along party lines (1:10-17), to the abuses of the Lord's Supper (11:17-34), to the excesses of charismatic showmanship in chapter 14, to the denial of bodily resurrection in chapter 15.

81. In 1 Cor 4:3, Paul writes, "It is a small thing to me to be judged (*anakrithō*) by you or by any human court. I do not even judge myself. . . . It is the Lord who judges me." And in 9:3 he writes, "This is my defense to those who would examine me (*anakrinousin*)." In 1 Cor 14:24 the term *anakrinein* bears a slightly different nuance,

thought expressed in 2:15 is the Corinthians' own formulation, it may be that they claimed to be empowered by the Spirit to judge who was truly *pneumatikos* and who was *psychikos*, and yet be immune to reciprocal judgment by others.[82] The uses of the term *anakrinō* in 4:3; 9:3; and 14:24 suggest that they were indeed applying this gift of discernment toward a negative evaluation of Paul! Yet Paul applies the expression to his own purposes by the addition of v 16. Here, as in 14:24, he will place the gift of discernment under the qualifying influence of the mind, in this case, *nous tou Christou*.

HAVING THE MIND OF CHRIST

We have now reached the capstone of Paul's argument, the enigmatic ending of the discourse at 2:16:

"For who has known the mind of the Lord so as to instruct him?" But we have the mind of Christ.

The verse brings Paul full circle to his opening exhortation and the call for unity that underlies the entire discourse: "I appeal to you . . . be united in the same mind (*tō autō noi*) and the same knowledge (*tē autē gnōmē*)" (1:10). Here the central themes of the discourse converge in a single image of transformed perception; the new world revealed in the cross and communicated by the Spirit now comes to consciousness. What was begun in the dismantling of intellectual and social structures by the rhetoric of the cross now reaches its completion in the consciously cruciform mind.

We must first determine what Paul *means* by the expression "mind of Christ" (*nous tou Christou*) and, second, examine the *function* of the expression in Paul's overall aim to promote reconciliation in the Corinthian church.

---

but in a context very similar to that of 2:14-15. In a discussion of the proper use of the charismatic gifts for the upbuilding of the community, in which he insists that charismatic expression in public be balanced by the exercise of what he calls "the mind" (1 Cor 14:15-19), Paul writes, "But if all prophesy, and an unbeliever or outsider enters, he is elected (*eklegchetai*) by all; he is judged (*anakrinetai*) by all" (1 Cor 14:24).

82. Wilckens writes, "Only insofar as the receiver of revelation has received the Spirit of God and been instructed by him can it be said that he can judge all things." For Gnostics, according to Wilckens, "receiving of Pneuma transforms the receiver into the essence of Pneuma so that as pneumatikos he becomes identical with the revealer" (Wilckens, *Weisheit*, 81). Here again Wilckens sees Paul's view and the gnostic view in dangerous proximity.

What Paul Means by Mind (*Nous*)

Most interpreters give 2:16b very brief comment. Conzelmann's approach is to make mind (*nous*) the equivalent of *pneuma* and leave it at that.[83] Barrett, equally reticent to venture into this noetic territory, notes simply that "Paul and his spiritual colleagues have the mind of Christ."[84] Bornkamm, without explanation, changes *nous* to *pneuma* to render, "We have the *Spirit* of Christ (crucified)."[85] Even Wilckens backs away from this verse.[86] There is considerable suspicion that Paul's use of the term *nous* is polemically directed against another, perhaps mystical or protognostic use of the term which he deems to be in error. Indeed, the fact that it appears as the culmination of a series of rhetorical strikes against the Corinthians' favored self-designations leads one to suspect that the expression "mind of Christ," used only here in Paul's letters, is meant to displace another notion of *nous* operative in Corinth.

In any case, the place of the "mind of Christ" in the culminating sentence of this section of the discourse demands close consideration. The sentence is introduced by the citation from Isa 40:13, a verse that is typically used in apocalyptic formulae to state cognitive resignation in the face of God's mystery and to confess humility in the service of praise for revelation.[87] Although our text is also apocalyptic, the motif functions somewhat differently here. First, it does not appear in a doxology formula (as it does in Rom 11:34); the theme of thanksgiving is not in the context. Second, in our text (1 Cor 2:6-16) the citation occurs in a polemical discourse. The state of ignorance Paul identifies is not simply that which is characteristic of all humanity before God. Rather, he seems to call into question a specific claim of the supposed *pneumatics* to know the mind of God. The disjunctive *de* ("but") in 2:16b adds to our suspicion that in 2:16 Paul has opponents in mind. The formula "Who has known the mind of the Lord?" leads him to the final apocalyptic disclosure: "But we have the mind of Christ."

---

83. Conzelmann, *1 Corinthians*, 69.
84. Barrett, *The First Epistle to the Corinthians*, 78. In an afterthought, Barrett cites Wendland on the trinitarian character of the paragraph (2:6-16) but concludes that "the matter is obscured by the introduction of the word *mind!*"
85. Günther Bornkamm, *Paul* (Minneapolis: Fortress Press, 1994), 163.
86. Wilckens gives this verse no individual treatment. See Wilckens, *Weisheit*, 287.
87. Elizabeth Johnson demonstrates that this apocalyptic background provides the clearest parallel to Paul's use of the nearly identical citation in Rom 11:34: "Who has known the mind of the Lord, or who has been his counselor?" (Elizabeth Johnson, "The Function of Apocalyptic and Wisdom Traditions in Romans 9–11" [Ph.D. diss., Princeton Theological Seminary, 1987], 243).

What strikes the reader immediately about v 16 is the shift from the emphasis on spirit (*pneuma*) in vv 10-15 to a new emphasis on *nous*. That Paul intends a shift in *meaning* is likely, since he might have retained *pneuma* in his citation of Isa 40:13 by using the Hebrew text which refers to the *ruah* ("spirit") instead of the Septuagint which refers to the *nous*. Precisely what shift in meaning Paul intended is not immediately clear. Although the expression *nous tou Christou* appears nowhere else in Paul's works, he does use noetic language fairly frequently. We turn now to a review of those other uses.[88]

Nous and Related Terminology in Paul's Letters

Paul uses *nous* and its cognates relatively frequently in three of his letters, Romans and 1 and 2 Corinthians (Romans: *nous*, six times; *noeō*, once; 1 Corinthians: *nous*, five times; *nomizō*, twice; 2 Corinthians: *noēma*, five times). Two other terms for "mind" or "thinking" are used in these same letters and in Philippians: *phronēma* and its cognates, and *dokimazō*. All of these terms, in their basic meanings, concern the processes and "organs" of thought per se, as opposed to those terms of perception that are not obviously cognitive (i.e., *apocalypsis, sophia, pneuma, psyche*).

Yet noetic language in Paul is not concerned merely with rational thought; it involves, rather, what Robert Jewett calls a "constellation of thoughts and beliefs which fills the consciousness and provides criteria for decisions."[89] In Paul's writings, noetic expressions sometimes overlap pneumatic expressions (especially where the *pneuma* affects perceptual and behavioral changes in human beings) without rendering the *nous* equal to the *pneuma*.[90] But a survey of other uses of *nous* in Paul's letters confirms that, for Paul, the term carries more than intellectual or even spiritual meaning.[91]

---

88. In this discussion I will avoid complex metaphysical distinctions concerning the *nous* and the perceiving faculties generally. Such subtle distinctions as make up the philosophical discourse on perception and rationality in the ancient world are not likely to be central to the argument of an apostle who passionately defends the gospel before a largely uneducated congregation.

89. Robert Jewett, *Paul's Anthropological Terms* (Leiden: E. J. Brill, 1971).

90. This identification is found in our text by those who see Gnosticism there.

91. In Rom 1:28 and 12:3, the mind is a neutral faculty subject to influences of both Flesh and Spirit. In 1:28 the *nous* is "given up" to *adokimon*; in 12:2 it is transformed. Bultmann finds similar neutrality about the *nous* but goes on to suggest that the *nous*, for Paul, is itself the agent of choice between the two alternatives, Spirit and Flesh, or between *nous tou Christou* and *adokimos nous* (Bultmann, *Theology of the New Testament*, 211–12). I depart from Bultmann in seeing Paul's use of the *nous* more as that part of the human being subject to warring powers which invade and overtake it than as the free agent of choice between conflicting possibilities. In either case, the *nous* is involved in human action in the world.

Nous in 2 Corinthians: Taking Thoughts Captive

That Paul's understanding of *nous* is determined also by his apocalyptic perspective is reflected with special clarity in the *noēma* language of 2 Corinthians where the *nous* is shown to be subject to invasion by either Spirit or Flesh. In 2:11, the thoughtful mind is alert to Satan's attempt to gain advantage; in 4:4, the minds of the unbelievers are blinded by the "God of this world"; in 10:5, the apostle announces his mission to "take every thought captive to obey Christ" in the war which does not belong to the Flesh (10:3). The apocalyptic dimensions of Pauline epistemology are most sharply expressed in 2 Corinthians. But we should keep in mind that the battle lines in the 2 Corinthians debate have already been drawn in 1 Corinthians and that in both cases the power of the cross to reconcile the community of God (and to bring an end to human boasting) is in view.[92]

Nous in Romans: Transformed Mind, Dedicated Body

In Rom 8:5-8, apocalyptic is again in view as Paul narrates the battle between the Spirit and the Flesh. Here, as in 2 Corinthians, thoughts (*phronēma*) are at stake. Since the advent of the Spirit, the world has been divided into two ontological camps: the being (*onta*) of one is determined by the thinking of the Flesh, the being of the other is determined by the thinking of the Spirit. As in 1 Corinthians, so here: one's noetic disposition (toward Flesh or toward Spirit) brings life or death. The way of thinking that characterizes the Flesh is death, but the way of thinking that characterizes the Spirit is life and peace (Rom 5:6).

The *nous* in Rom 12:2 is more the object of transformation than the object of capture. Here, too, the transformation of mind is intimately linked with the body (*sōma*): the body is to be presented as a "living sacrifice" to God and the mind is to be renewed (Rom 12: 1-2).[93] This text must be viewed in parallel with Rom 1:18-31 [94] where

---

92. See 2 Cor 10:7-18.

93. Considerable controversy surrounds Paul's use of the term *sōma*. Here I take the term to denote at least the organ of human action and relationship. Whatever our noetic or spiritual orientations, we live these out bodily.

94. Scroggs defines Rom 12:1-2 as the "leitmotif or superscript to the entire parenesis" which "assumes a central place in Paul's description of the new obedience possible to believers" (Scroggs, "New Being," 178).

nearly identical language is used to describe the relation of *nous* and *sōma* to the will of God.[95]

In Rom 1:18 the opposite of the "sacrificial *sōma*" and "transformed *nous*" is in view. The Gentiles' way of knowing God (Rom 1:21) results in their being "given up" by God to the dishonoring of their *sōmata* and to undiscerning or reprobate minds (*adokimos nous*) (12:28). As in the Corinthian correspondence, also in Romans, Paul struggles to demonstrate that knowledge of God may be true or false depending on the powers that rule the *nous* and the *sōma*. The claim to know God does not necessarily mean that one stands in a genuine relation to God. Saving knowledge requires the total reorientation of *sōma* and renewal of nous described in 12:1-2.[96]

Nous in 1 Corinthians: The Mind and the Body of Christ

A similar relation of *sōma* to *nous* is found in 1 Corinthians. *Sōma* language abounds in 1 Corinthians,[97] the letter most emphatically concerned with the matter of reconciling life in the "body of Christ." It is most prominent in 1 Corinthians 12 where Paul describes the church as one (*sōma*) with many members (12:12-27). That the Spirit is reflected particularly in the manifold gifts of the body members bears important implications for the *nous/sōma* connection. In 1 Corinthians 14, for example, the expression of the *charismata* is said to require the participation of the *nous* in order to be edifying for the church. Here we encounter a *nous* and a *sōma* whose context is communal. Both Romans and 1 Corinthians demonstrate boldly and repeatedly that for Paul the distinction "individual versus communal" is

---

95. The relation of the *nous* to the *sōma* is problematic. As Bultmann sees it, the *sōma* is more than the corporeal aspect of the human being, hence his own exposition of *sōma* as the "ego" or "self." For Bultmann, the *nous* is a subcategory of the ego, namely, that aspect of the self which is the subject of its own willing and doing. Such distinctions are unnecessary for understanding 2:16. I take *nous* to be the perceptive capacity that characterizes life in the *sōma* whether *sōma* is conceived in corporeal or psychological terms. See Bultmann, *Theology of the New Testament*, 192 ff. and 211f.

96. Scroggs finds behind the "renewal" image in 12:2 the "original noetic possibility, which Paul has described in Romans 1." On the ethical implications of this renewal, Scroggs writes: "[The mind] is now adequate to know what is, in fact, God's will. Here the renewed mind is called upon to learn and act upon its new ability to discern what God calls the person to do. Thus an essential dimension of the transformed self is the transformed mind, and it is out of this transformed mind that the ethical (as well as religious) insights of the believer emerge" (Scroggs, "New Being," 179). What Scroggs calls the "ethical" is roughly equivalent to my understanding of the transformed "somatic" or "bodily" life.

97. The term *sōma* occurs 40 times in 1 Corinthians compared to 13 times in Romans, 9 times in 2 Corinthians, once in Galatians, once in 1 Thessalonians, and twice in Philemon.

a false one. In 1 Cor 1:10, as we have seen, Paul calls the divided minds of the Corinthians into the unity of the same mind, just as in 1 Corinthians 12 he insists on the unity of the body despite its diversity of members, all of whom are, as individuals, *sōmata tou Christou* (6:15).[98]

The coincidence of noetic and somatic terminology in Romans and 1 Corinthians suggests that, for Paul, life in Christ is always marked by the orientation of the whole person and whole community in obedience to God. Such unity in obedience demands the continuing renewal of mind and dedication of body.[99] While in both Romans and 1 Corinthians, the *nous* may function as only *one aspect* of the *soma*, *nous* is never separated from its somatic context. In 1 Cor 2:16, where *nous* appears to be separate, it actually recalls Paul's opening exhortation to the divided church to "be of the same mind" (1:10), that is, to unite as church in one body (cf. 1 Cor 12:12-27).

Phronein in Philippians

One other use of noetic language speaks forcefully to the concerns in 1 Corinthians. Although we do not find the word *nous* in Philippians, the uses of the related term *phronein* ("to think" or "to consider") in Phil 2:2 and 2:5 contribute to our understanding of Paul's

---

98. It is important to note with Käsemann that "for Paul, unity in the body of Christ does not mean the sameness of all the members; it means the solidarity which can endure the strain of the differences" (Käsemann, "On Paul's Anthropology," 3).

99. Käsemann's work on sōma is particularly helpful here. True to his understanding of apocalyptic thought as both eschatological and cosmological and consonant with what he takes to be the central apocalyptic question, "To whom does the sovereignty of the world belong?", Käsemann defines *sōma* as "God's creation and the organ of our service in creation." For him, corporeality entails belonging to another as in sexual dependency on the other. To recognize one's own "bodiliness" is to see that in the body one is always ruled by someone, that everything depends on one's belonging to another. As sōmatic beings we are images of the power that determines us, either the power to which we truly belong or the power to which we have fallen prey. In neither case is somatic life a private affair; we exist bodily as historical, political beings. For Paul, as Käsemann understands him, the Easter affirmation is a political hope which (because it concerns the *sōma*) tolerates neither private existence here nor private existence in heaven: "The Christian message becomes religious utopia when it talks about spirituality without considering that the Holy Spirit wills and creates redemption of the world and therefore breaks into our corporeality and makes it into the field of our everyday worship of God of the revelation of the daily self-renewing freedom of the children of God" (Käsemann, "Lieblichkeit bei Paulus" [Paper presented at Union Theological Seminary, 1984]).

concept of transformed cognitive activity.[100] Paul prefaces his quotation of the Christ hymn with the exhortation at 2:5:

> Let this way of thinking be among you which was in Christ Jesus. (Phil 2:5)

From the context, we gather that the hymn to follow will draw Paul's audience into the "same way of thinking, the same love, full accord and of one mind" to which he exhorts them in Phil 2:2. Except for the change of vocabulary from *nous* to *phronein*, the exhortation is very like the exhortation to "be of the same mind" in 1 Cor 1:10. In Phil 2:3-4, Paul almost seems to be thinking of the Corinthians when he warns the Philippian congregants to "do nothing from selfishness or conceit." In Philippians too, as in 1 Corinthians, what follows the exhortation about "thinking" is a kerygmatic statement that emphasizes the cross (Phil 2:5-11).

While the Christ hymn rehearses the whole of the Christ myth—his descent, death, and exaltation—Paul has put the descent/humiliation/death theme, as it were, in bold print. This he does by placing the hymn in the context of exhortation to humility in the community and by emphasizing the scandalous mode of Jesus' death in Phil 2:8, "even death on a cross."

The cognitive activity that Paul calls for in the preface to the Philippian hymn is closely related to the phrase *nous tou Christou* in 1 Cor 2:16. In both texts, the cross event is closely associated with a state of mind. To be of the "one mind" or "one way of thinking" is to be cognitively identified with Christ's death on the cross. To have the "mind of Christ" is to have a cruciform mind. This "mind," moreover, is not centered on propositions about the cross or even kerygmatic statements per se; the cognitive identification with Christ's death on the cross is, rather, both internal and experiential.[101]

---

100. A related text in Philippians, although lacking our specific vocabulary, is Phil 1:9-11. Paul writes in the Thanksgiving section, "And it is my prayer that your love (*agapē*) may abound more and more, with knowledge (*epignōsei*) and all discernment (*aisthēsei*)." This text makes explicit a connection between love and perception that is implicit elsewhere in Paul's noetic language. On this text Scroggs argues that "mind" belongs between love and knowledge: "Paul means that love frees the mind so that more accurate perception of the other can happen." Moreover, as Scroggs views it, what lies behind love is "some act of God," namely, God's act of justification through Christ. This act "enables love—that is, the transformed self—to exist" in "caring perception" of others (Scroggs, "New Being," 180). The act of God implied here is, of course, the subject of the noetic text, Phil 2:5-11.

101. See R. T. Wallis, "Nous as Experience," in *The Significance of Neoplatonism* ed. R. B. Harris (Norfolk, Va., 1976), 121–23. In Homer, according to Wallis, *nous* never

Summary Observations on *Nous*

What these Pauline noetic passages have in common is significant for our understanding of the *nous tou Christou*. In every case the *mind reflects the orientation of the whole self toward or away from God*. This noetic self may be "taken captive to obey Christ" (2 Cor 10:5) or it may be ruled by the Flesh (Rom 8:5); it may be renewed to the service of God (Rom 12:2) or it may be fallen, *adokimos* (Rom 1:28). It may be conformed to this world or conformed to the mind of the crucified Christ (Phil 2:5). In Philippians and 1 Corinthians the *nous* is associated with the Spirit. Thus in Phil 2:1-2, to share in the same way of thinking is to participate in the Spirit; in 1 Corinthians 14, to temper one's ecstasy by the *nous* is to be an effective minister of one's gifts.

In every case, *nous* and its cognates denote more than *intellectual* or spiritual orientation. *Noetic disposition determines one's relationships with God and with others in body, mind, and spirit.* Themes of reconciliation, service, unity, and humble regard for others surround Paul's references to the *nous*. Thus when the *noēmata* are "captive" to Christ, obedience to God results. When the mind is renewed, service to God follows. When the mind of Christ is embraced, unity in the church is regained (Phil 2:5; 4:2).

TRANSFORMED PERCEPTION AND RECONCILIATION

When Paul proclaims, "But we have the mind of Christ," he speaks a performative word if that word, in fact, is received by the hearer as the culmination of the larger speech act in which Paul has been engaged. For here, the cross, the *pneuma,* and the noetic self are joined in an image that defines a new social relationship.[102] One who receives this mind perceives anew who God is, that is, the self-giving God of the cross, and is thus reoriented toward reconciling service to God and the world.

The disjunctive "but" at the beginning of the sentence supports this interpretation. Paul shows by his use of the particle *de* ("but")

---

means "reason" or purely intellectual thought but is uniquely associated with sense perception. It reflects "a kind of sixth sense which penetrates deeper into the nature of the objects perceived than the other senses." It involves "the realization of a situation." My understanding of Paul's noetic language brings it close to Homer's use of the term.

102. On the social dimensions of speech act theory, see the helpful discussion by Sandy Petrey, *Speech Acts and Literary Theory* (London: Routledge & Kegan Paul, 1990), 27ff.

that the *nous tou Christou* is the final and full opposite to the world's ways of knowing God. There is but one way to know the "mind of the Lord"; one must receive the mind of Christ. This receiving is the subject of the discourse in 2:4 and 2:10-14. There the *pneuma* is the mediator of the mystery of God and the "things given by God" (*charisthenta*), that is, the kerygma of Christ crucified. To whomever receives this Spirit, it is revealed that God is the one who saves through self-giving love apart from human merit. The understanding of these things, supplied by the Spirit, brings about a fundamental change in perception (2:12).[103] One who now knows God, self, and world *kata stauron* ("according to the cross") has thus received the *nous tou Christou.*

This pattern of transformation, together with our conclusions on the relational aspects of noetic language, suggests the reason for Paul's substitution of *nous* for *pneuma.* The *pneuma* facilitates the transforming of the human *nous* to the *nous tou Christou.* The transformed *nous* now consciously *embodies* (i.e., brings to relational life) the ministry of the Spirit.

But what does the *nous tou Christou* allow one to perceive? What does the world look like when one takes one's bearings from the death of Jesus? And what is the perceiver to do with the new vision? We may begin to answer these questions by recalling that, in our text, the power of the cross and its proclamation lies in what it reveals about God. The God of the cross is the one who gave life to the world through the death of his son and by that act made weakness into power, suffering into redemption, and folly into wisdom. When one sees that this God is the *source* of life (1:30), then *all* of life (cognitive and relational) comes into new perspective (3:22-23). Indeed, one now sees that God has created a new world on the model of self-giving love. To enter into this world is to perceive that one is loved by the Creator *without qualification.* For Paul, this truth is demonstrated in the makeup of the church, the concrete image of the new creation:

> For consider your call, brethren; not many of you were wise; not many were powerful; not many were of noble birth. But God chose what is foolish by the world's standards in order to shame the wise; God

---

103. For Koenig (who follows Ardnt and Gingrich, *A Greek-English Lexicon of the New Testament,* 219), *eidōmen* in 2:12 denotes a "change in consciousness" (Koenig, "Ministry," 169).

chose what is weak by the world's standards to shame the strong; God chose what is low and despised by the world's standards, even things that have no being, to bring to nothing things that have being. (1 Cor 1:26-28)

To recognize *oneself* in this narrative of new creation is to see that no circumstance of birth or being qualifies God's election. In this recognition there is freedom from the tyranny of attainment and an end to all human boasting (1:31). To be possessed of this freedom is, in Paul's understanding, to "have the mind of Christ." When this mind and the Spirit that gives it birth characterize community, the new world is realized, however provisionally. There, the reign of God which consists "not in talk, but in power" comes in (1 Cor 4:20).

Conclusion:
Living the Transformed Mind

In chapter 1 we overheard a debate among modern interpreters of Paul about the implications of his apocalyptic vision for ethics. On one side of the debate were scholars like Käsemann and Martyn who resist applying ethical categories to Paul's thought lest Paul's insistence on the sovereignty of God be compromised by overestimating human choice. These scholars prefer to speak of God's power invading the cosmos and drawing human beings into its orb where it works through them to accomplish God's purpose. For Martyn, apocalyptic is an epistemological, not an ethical category; it is about seeing the new creation and one's place in it as God's sovereign act of election apart from any human decision. Viewed through Paul's apocalyptic spectacles faith involves, in Martyn's words, "the certainty that neither the future transformation, nor the new way of seeing both it and present developments, can be thought to grow out of conditions in the human scene."[1]

Others, like Beker, see things somewhat differently. They find in Paul's apocalyptic vision of the coming triumph of God a strong, specifically *ethical* imperative to join up with God's redeeming action, to participate in the establishment of God's reign: "The world's need for redemption inspires both the sighing of Christians and the imperative of their redemptive activity in the world."[2] The two positions are characterized by differing emphases on the events of Jesus' death, resurrection, and parousia. Martyn emphasizes the death as the locus of perceptual shift, the point at which God's new and pre-

---

1. Martyn, "Apocalyptic Antinomies in Paul's Letter to the Galatians," *NTS* (31) 410–24, 424 n.28.
2. J. Christiaan Beker, *Paul the Apostle: The Triumph of God in Life and Thought,* (Philadelphia: Fortress Press, 1984), 277.

sent reality is first seen for what it is. Beker emphasizes the resurrection and especially the parousia as the focal points of hope that call the believer into God's redemptive activity in the world.

EPISTEMOLOGY AND ETHICS ACCORDING TO THE CROSS

In his debates with the scholastics in the sixteenth century, Martin Luther anticipated many of questions that still dominate discussions of Pauline epistemology and ethics. While 1 Corinthians is well represented in the literature of the church from the Apostolic Fathers to the present, it has been particularly prominent in theological discussions since the Reformation. Today, however, many scholars are beginning to call for relief from the heavily Lutheran cast of Pauline scholarship, by which they usually mean an emphasis on "justification by grace" to the exclusion of other aspects of Paul's thought, especially his ethical imperatives. Others continue to see the doctrine as central to Paul's thought everywhere, not least in 1 Corinthians. In both cases, Paul's apocalypticism gets center stage, but the implications of apocalyptic are drawn quite differently. A fresh hearing of Luther will illuminate options for ethics that have arisen from the predominantly Lutheran readings of Paul's theology of the cross since the Reformation. I will then review the rhetorical strategy of Paul's discourse and suggest that by reading 1 Corinthians 1–2 as an instance of performative language we may begin to integrate the epistemological and ethical claims biblical theologians are currently making for Pauline theology.

Luther's *Theologia Crucis*

First Corinthians 1–2 was a formative text for Luther, most obviously so in the 1518 Disputation at Heidelberg, where, principally on the basis of 1 Cor 1:18 ff., he developed his celebrated *theologia crucis.* Following Paul's lead, Luther found in the cross the substance of a way of knowing which he set polemically against the speculative theology of his day. Selected passages from the Disputation reveal theological and epistemological themes derived from 1 Corinthians that have continued to dominate theological exegesis of Pauline texts to the present day.

In the Disputation, Luther took up the rhetorical question, "Who is a theologian?" and answered it in language reflecting the themes of 1 Corinthians 1–2:

> That person does not deserve to be called a theologian who looks upon the invisible things of God as though they were clearly percepti- ble in those things which have actually happened. He deserves to be called a theologian, however, who comprehends the visible and mani- fest things of God seen through suffering and the cross. (*LW* 31:40)[3]

The cross, then, for Luther, is a paradoxical instrument of knowing. On the one hand, it forbids every attempt to know God directly, "as if the things of God were clearly visible"; on the other hand, it is only in the cross event that God is truly revealed. True perception comes only by way of the revelation of the cross which leads the believer to a totally new way of knowing God. The true theologian (for Luther, every true Christian), comprehends God only through the suffering and cross of Christ. For one who knows God in this way, the cross is not merely an *aspect* of theology, a dark part of a story that ends hap- pily in the resurrection, but the lens through which the whole story must be read. The cross determines not only *what* one sees, namely, "the things of God" but *how* they are seen, namely, "through suffer- ing and the cross." When Luther opposed the "visible and manifest things of God seen through suffering and the cross" to the "invisible things of God looked upon in error as though clearly perceptible," he argued that what one can know about God is arrived at not through reason, another instrument of the fallen will, but only in what God clearly reveals in the cross. Here he echoes Paul's words: "For since in the wisdom of God, the world did not know God through wisdom, it pleased God through the folly of what we preach to save those who believe" (1 Cor 1:21). From his reading of Paul, Luther gathers that any route to knowledge of God other than the revelation of the cross is not only ineffectual for salvation, but leads to self-exaltation and a false "theology of glory."[4] The epistemological

---

3. *Luther's Works, American Edition*, vol. 31: *Career of the Reformer I*, Harold Grimm, ed. (Philadelphia: Fortress Press, 1957), 40.
4. In his discussion of Thesis 21 in the Heidelberg Disputation, he elaborates fur- ther on these two ways of knowing—the one based on the cross, the other on glory— again with obvious reference to 1 Cor 1:18-25:

> A theology of glory calls evil good and good evil. A theology of the cross calls the thing what it actually is. This is clear: He who does not know Christ does not know God hidden in suffering. Therefore he prefers works to suffering, glory to the cross, strength to weak- ness, wisdom to folly, and, in general, good to evil. These are the people whom the apostle calls "enemies of the cross of Christ" (Phil 3:8), for they hate the cross and suffering and love works and the glory of works. Thus they call the good of the cross evil and the evil of a deed good. God can only be found in suffering and in the cross, as has already been said. Therefore, the friends of the cross say that the cross is good and works are evil, for through the cross works are dethroned and the old Adam, who is especially edified by works, is cru- cified. It is impossible for a person not to be puffed up by his good works unless he has first been deflated and destroyed by suffering and evil until he knows that he is worthless and that his works are not his but God's (*Luther's Works*, 31:53).

cast of the argument is clear: The cross causes Luther to see things for what they are, among them, the tendency of good works to mislead and corrupt.

Knowing 'What God Wants to Give'

Luther's cross-based epistemology is further clarified in the distinction he makes between "general" and "particular" knowledge. General knowledge, "the knowledge that God is, that he has created heaven and earth, that he is just, that he punishes the wicked etc.," is available to all. But "particular knowledge", "what God thinks of us, what he wants to give and do to deliver us from sin and death and to save us" comes only through the cross.[5] This is the redeeming knowledge by which we know God to be giving himself *for us* in suffering and death. Because it is revealed through the cross alone, however, "in the very things which human wisdom regards as the antithesis of deity," it is also hidden knowledge, unveiled in things reason cannot recognize as divine—weakness, poverty, suffering, and the cross. Only insofar as God is recognized in *these* things, Luther insists, is God truly known.

In some ways, Luther's analysis sounds strikingly modern, especially insofar as he articulates what is at stake perceptually and psychologically in the cross. For Luther, it is the cross that compels one to see God's love, and thus to be liberated from the dominating structures, intellectual and moral, of the old world. But the power of Luther's insight, which must always be read in its sixteenth-century ecclesial context, issued in a doctrine so wary of the language of good works that for many who accept Luther's premises, any talk of ethics, particularly Pauline ethics, is anathema. Yet Luther, like theologians in every generation who struggle with the tension between works and grace, lived out his insight in concrete relationships. The love of God revealed by the cross empowered a new existence, not just a new perception. Despite the strength of his argument against works righteousness, Luther was no gnostic.

Distortions of the Theology of the Cross

The psychological insight that we are enabled to love by the experience of *being* loved is at the core of Luther's reading of Paul, but he

5. *Luther's Works, American Edition*, vol. 26: *Lectures on Galatians 1535*, Chapters 1–4. Jaroslav Pelikan, ed. (St. Louis, Concordia Publishing House, 1963), 399–400.

articulates this truth in ways that leave the theology of the cross vulnerable to misinterpretation. For example, one may take salvation by grace, that is, the undeserved love *of* God, so far as to neglect the love *for* God and other and the participation in God's redemptive work that Paul himself demonstrates. Or one may become so intent on knowing the sufferings of Christ that one becomes again a slave to the false self that seeks to earn God's favor through suffering. Perhaps the most dangerous distortion is drawn to our attention by feminist theologians; a theology of the cross read merely as self-emptying sacrifice may effect bondage to false powers rather than liberation from them. Some who counsel victims of domestic violence, for example, recount the often used rationalizations that God calls some to suffer for suffering's sake or that God's love requires submission to God's wrath. In her book on the cross and feminist ethics, Sally Purvis summarizes the problem:

> Contemporary feminists, including Christian feminists have been wary of the cross as a symbol for community. As several scholars have cogently and persuasively argued, the cross has been used to justify, even glorify, suffering in ways that are damaging to persons. It has also distorted persons' understanding of responsibility, guilt, sin—that is, the cross is theologically and ethically dangerous.[6]

Purvis herself goes beyond this wariness to offer an alternative and more consistently apocalyptic reading of the cross as "power" and to reclaim it as "an intellectual, spiritual, and communal resource for radical change." The cross, she says, "can only be used to harm and suppress within certain shared assumptions about power . . . . properly understood, the 'power of the cross' subverts its own nature as harmful and oppressive."[7]

What I have tried to demonstrate here—namely, that in 1 Corinthians 1–2 Paul strives through preaching the cross to dislocate common worldly conventions, including conventions about power—bears directly on Purvis's reclamation project. For Paul the reordering of consciousness by the power of the cross generates neither obsessive self-humiliation nor glorification of suffering itself. Rather, for Paul, the real power of the cross proclamation is to reveal that divine love overcomes worldly power and thereby redefines power it-

6. Sally Purvis, *The Power of the Cross: Foundations for a Christian Feminist Ethic of Community* (Nashville: Abingdon, 1993), 14. See also the book Purvis cites by Joanne Carlson Brown and Carole R. Bohn (eds.), *Christianity, Patriarchy, and Abuse: A Feminist Critique* (New York: The Pilgrim Press, 1990).
7. Purvis, *Power*, 14.

self. By refusing to play the world's power game, God has begun already in Christ to invade territory held by worldly powers and to draw the liberated as participants into the new and continually growing realm of freedom. It is the seizure by this apocalyptic truth, and not just by the horror of one's sinfulness and inadequacy, that compels the hearer to dislocate from the world of sin and death and to be relocated in the new creation. One who has been thus seized is no longer enslaved to the corrupt and lying powers of the "present evil age." Although suffering continues or even intensifies for believers who now stand definitively against the ways of the world, the suffering is not that of despair and helplessness. In the surrender of the self to divine love, one becomes aware for the first time of love's power to create life in the very midst of suffering and death.

Reclaiming the Theology of the Cross

My inquiry into the power of the Word of the Cross is grounded in a linguistic model borrowed from speech-act theory. But throughout my argument there flows a related psychological undercurrent; Paul's rhetoric works or does not because of certain psychological operations that attend the appropriation of language. In order to move from merely theoretical discussion of perceptual transformation to describing the actual life such transformation makes possible, some have found it helpful to be more explicit about the psychological aspects of perceptual change.

Pauline theologians who take human psychology explicitly into account sometimes come very near articulating what is emerging here as an ethic of apocalyptic perception. In an innovative exegesis of 1 Corinthians 1–2, for example, Gerd Theissen uses psychological theory to explain how the cross, acting as "counter-wisdom" to the dominating wisdom of the world, breaks through "an inner limit to understanding . . . , allowing the pneumatics (the genuine "spirit people" in 2:6-16) to emancipate themselves consciously from the compulsive standards of this world." With new-found freedom from the world's system of sanctions, they are filled with the divine spirit, and, simultaneously, a "new solidarity with the whole creation."[8] Now they are able to participate in what is perfect, namely, "intrinsically

---

8. Gerd Theissen, *Psychological Aspects of Pauline Theology*, translated by John P. Galvin (Philadelphia: Fortress Press, 1987), 379 and 385–86 (originally published as *Psychologische Aspekte paulinischer Theologie* [Göttingen: Vandenhoeck & Ruprecht, 1983]).

motivated love," that love which has overcome the reinforcement system based on domination.[9]

Similarly informed psychological insights about the power of the cross proclamation both to liberate perception and motivate behavior are found in Robin Scroggs's interpretation of Paul. On the theology of the cross in 1 Corinthians, Scoggs writes,

> In God's act in Christ, clearly revealed in the self-giving and radical love of the cross, Paul is forced to acknowledge that the god he had known was not the God who gave so selflessly through his Son. The cross shows what God had always been. The cross also revealed to Paul what true power is. As a result, Paul knows himself differently, not as a person defined by performance, but as a person secured independently of performance in the divine relationship. Such a new person participates in the cross, because he or she participates in that new world, re-created according to the image of God "who did not spare his own Son but gave him up for us all" (Rom 8:32).[10]

Here and elsewhere, Scroggs uses Freudian theory to explain the doctrine of justification by grace. Transformation has to do with recovering the "authentic" self from the tragically impossible project of securing one's own existence. The self-securing will works on the "performance principle" that the parent (God) is basically hostile and requires the child to earn or justify his or her own life before God. The child thus becomes defined by the striving to win God's love through perfection. But in the cross, Paul sees that he has been wrong about who God is. The God who dies for sinners justifies the imperfect, the ungodly, and does so out of profound and unconditional love for humanity, willing its liberation from the lie of self-securing existence.

One strength of this analysis is that it shows how human relationships may be transformed by the new perception. A person who is dominated by the self-concern of winning God's favor, Scroggs says, is also apt to be in hostile relations with the neighbor: "Our lives *do* become projects for securing our place in the sun. We *do* use other people as part of this project."[11] But persons transformed by the recognition of God as love and thereby freed to love God will live out that freedom in life that celebrates the mutuality of love and service in the community. Paul puts the matter this way to the quarrelling Corinthians:

---

9. Theissen, *Psychological Aspects*, 372.
10. Robin Scroggs, *Christology in Paul and John* (Philadelphia: Fortress Press, 1988), 31.
11. Scroggs, *Paul for a New Day* (Philadelphia: Fortress Press, 1977), 9.

> But God has so composed the body, giving the greater honor to the inferior part, that there may be no discord in the body, but that all members may have the same care for one another. If one member suffers, all suffer together; if one member is honored, all rejoice together. (1 Cor 12:25-26)

But how does this look from the "underside," that is from the side of the one being used for the securing of another's project? Is the theology Scroggs recommends prescriptive only for the "strong"? Certainly, his language is cast to address the role of the "user" most directly. But the theory applies as well and perhaps even more powerfully to the one being used. This one, too, has arrived at his or her position through certain tragic distortions, some would say obliterrations, of the self that leave one defenseless against oppression and abuse. To such persons Paul's liberating word is empowering. The love of God demonstrated in the cross is a love that keeps saying "no" to the forces that twist and destroy the self. To the victim of abuse, Paul's Word of the Cross says, "Do not be deceived into accepting a broken self as God's will for you. The powers who claim to have defeated God through their murderous violence and who now would shackle you have no real power. They are already in fact defeated by the love that refused to return violence for violence. That love is your powerful security against every violation of the whole self you were intended to be." When Paul calls the cross "power in weakness," he addresses both extremes of the distorted self.

These psychological interpretations bear rich implications for a speech act reading of 1 Corinthians. We have learned from the letter that Paul's first line of attack against division is epistemological. To use a phrase from the second letter to Corinth, he seeks to promote unity by "taking thoughts captive" for Christ (2 Cor 10:5). His first move is neither to moralize nor to outline a course of human action, but to challenge false perception by presenting the new conditions effected in the cross as a matter not of choice, but of reality. The presentation is deliberately stark and jarring; the Word of the Cross calls into question every dimension of the old way of being, especially conventional ways of knowing God.

It is clear that Paul expects the new perception to render behavior which reflects the dissolution of standard epistemological convictions and conventions. The Corinthian division demonstrates to him that what the Corinthians proudly claim to know is not yet the reality inaugurated by the cross. In particular, they have missed the central message of Christ's cruciform reign, namely, that the body is for the Lord and the Lord for the body (1 Cor 6:13). Insofar as division rules them, they refuse to acknowledge the radical advocacy of God for the body against the powers of sin and death. Insofar as they miss this point, they deny God's sovereign love and forfeit love's power to overcome all that would thwart the new creation. Such persistence in blindness among those to whom the truth has been revealed is a vexation and a mystery to Paul. But he does not simply give them up to blindness. Possessed by the love he proclaims, he returns to preach the Word of the Cross again.

THE PERFORMATIVE DRAMA IN REVIEW: EPISTEMOLOGY AND ETHICS RECONCILED

The relinquishing of the false self, Paul's letter to Corinth tells us, demands both the perception of the cross as power through its performative proclamation and the living out of that power in the action of love. These transforming powers of the Word of the Cross in 1 Corinthians 1–2 can be summarized under three headings. The first two, "dislocation" and "revelation," are epistemologically focused; the third, "reconciliation," tells us what the transformed life looks like. Here, transformed perception finds renewed life in the body.

Dislocation[12]

First Corinthians 1–2 demonstrates that for Paul the cross and its preaching create cognitive dissonance[13] so great as to press certain previously held cognitions about God, self and world to collapse.[14]

---

12. It is somewhat artificial to separate effects of the cross which in actual experience occur simultaneously. The first two powers, *dislocation* and *revelation* are especially difficult to delineate as separate events. While I do treat these powers as three elements of the experience of the cross, I do not mean to suggest that they are isolated events.

13. On cognitive dissonance theory, see Leon Festinger's *A Theory of Cognitive Dissonance* (Stanford: Stanford University, 1957). By "cognitive dissonance" Festinger means the psychological discomfort "that arises in the presence of an inconsistency." For example, a person who enjoys smoking but knows that smoking is bad for him likely experiences some dissonance, which he may or may not be able to rationalize. Rationalization brings consistency or consonance to prevail over inconsistency or dissonance. Festinger's hypothesis about cognitive dissonance is, briefly, that dissonance will motivate a person to try to reduce dissonance. In trying to reduce dissonance, a person will actively avoid situations and information which would likely increase the dissonance. I am particularly indebted to Festinger's definition of dissonance as "the existence of non-fitting relations among cognitions" where cognitions are defined as "any knowledge, opinion, or belief about the environment, about oneself, or about one's behavior," (pp. 2–3).

14. Theissen stresses cognitive dissonance as the first and most important function of the cross. *Psychological Aspects*, 387.

When Paul himself was apocalyptically confronted by the crucified and risen Christ (Gal 1:17), he was fundamentally dislocated; where he once stood he could stand no longer.[15] All that Paul tells us about his own experience of the risen Christ and all that he writes to his churches presupposes the dislocating power of the cross.[16]

So, too, are the Corinthians meant to be dislocated by the word Paul preaches. From the beginning of the letter his language is saturated in dissonance.[17] At 1:18, he confirms his intent to disorient the schismatics:

> For the word of the cross is folly to those who are perishing, but to us who are being saved, it is the power of God.

In images of salvation and destruction, this topic sentence sets the whole discourse in the context of the most dislocating of ancient traditions, apocalyptic. The Word brings the last judgment; the end of the world is at hand. But the proclamation dislocates even the apocalyptic tradition it reflects. Where one expects to hear that in the future there *will be* salvation for the *wise* and destruction for the *fools,* one hears instead that salvation is already, provisionally here and concerns not types of human beings (wise and fools) but *perceptions of the cross event* as power (not wisdom) or folly.

We have been concerned throughout with the interplay of wisdom and apocalyptic "ways of knowing" in our text. This interplay reflects Paul's attempt to dislocate the Corinthians from a type of wisdom epistemology dominated by worldly concerns and to relocate them in a way of thinking that is newly formulated in light of the cross event. The first step in Paul's effort, as we have seen, is to challenge the patterns of knowing that constitute the Corinthian "wisdom" and thus to leave his hearer perceptually unbalanced. Suddenly the opposite of folly is not wisdom but power, and those who seek wisdom are fools. Cognitive dissonance theory tells us that a hearer con-

---

15. In this respect at least, Luke's account of Paul's transformative experience fits Paul's own. He was dislocated, knocked off his feet by the apocalypse of Christ crucified (Acts 9:4).

16. See Paul's account of his former life in Judaism and his post-apocalypse assessment of the accomplishment of that life at Philippians 3:4–11.

17. In 1:7 Paul congratulates the congregation for their utter fullness in the gifts of Spirit while he reminds them that they have not "arrived," but await the ultimate fulfillment of the end-time apocalypse. In 1:9 he affirms their *koinonia* (fellowship) in Christ, but in the next sentence he appeals to them to avoid the dissensions he knows to be present already. Just after he calls them to unity of mind (1:10) he quotes their divisive slogans (1:12). Acknowledging the power of both baptism and baptizer in the estimation of the Corinthians he denies having baptized any of them (1:13-16). Having begun with reference to their fullness he closes this section (1:1-17) with a warning of the emptying that threatens the cross of Christ.

fronted by Paul's linguistic reversals will try to rationalize his way back to consonance.[18] A similar insight comes from speech-act theory; if an utterance does not engage accepted norms, it cannot "do what it says." Paul's Word must do more than *reflect* an alternative reality in order to "work;" it must also begin to *create* that new reality by challenging and rearranging the conventions of its hearers.[19]

A further step toward new perception involves the cross per se as the dissonant image. The cross testifies to a crucified messiah; whoever has other expectations about the messiah (or about divine power) will see this as scandal or folly (1 Cor 1:18, 22). But this dissonance too may be resisted. "This man," the scandalized person may say, "could not have been the messiah. In his cross is every necessary dis-confirmation of that claim."[20] "This act," the conventionally wise person may say, "shows us a god so weak or a god so violent as to be at best unworthy of praise or devotion, and at worst, a dangerous model for human emulation."

What is it, then, we must ask, that makes the observer of the hearer of this subversive Word abandon the old world rather than resolve its dissonances? In the first section of the discourse (1:18-25) Paul presses previously held cognitions about God and the world to the point of collapse but he does so in a way that allows the hearer to maintain enough critical distance to deflect the dissonances initially presented. At this critical juncture, however, Paul reminds the Corinthians that the cross calls even their own self-identity into question. At a crucial transition point in the argument he writes:

18. He may assume, for example, that the speaker is confused, insane, or from a foreign culture in which power is the natural opposite of folly.

19. On the potential of ritual both to reflect and to create social reality see Mary Douglas, *Purity and Danger* (Harmondsworth: Penguin, 1970) cited by Wayne Meeks in his discussion of the baptismal formula in Galatians 3:28 as an instance of "performative" utterance. Meeks, "The Image of the Androgyne," *History of Religions* 13 (1973–74), 165–208.

20. The offense of the cross to human sensibilities in the ancient world is well documented. By the standards of the world of values common to Jews and Greeks, a crucified man cannot also be a Messiah, a redeemer. For example, see Cicero: "Let even the name of the cross be kept away not only from the bodies of the citizens of Rome, but also from their thoughts, sight and hearing." Cicero, *Pro Rabirio* 5:16. Also on this matter see J. Louis Martyn who writes: "On a real cross in this world hangs the long-awaited Jewish Messiah. How can that be anything other than an epistemological crisis?" in "Epistemology at the Turn of the Ages: 2 Corinthians 5:16," *Christian History and Interpretation:* Studies Presented at John Knox (eds. W. R. Farmer, C. F. D. Moule, and R. R. Niebuhr; Cambridge: Cambridge University Press, 1967), 286. Compare the similar judgment of Theissen that cognitive dissonance is "triggered" by the presentation of an executed man as mediator of salvation. Theissen, *Psychological Aspects*, 387. See also Alan Segal's opinion that "no pre-Christian view of the messiah conceived of the possibility of his demise at the hands of the Romans." *Paul the Convert: The Apostolate and Apostasy of Paul the Pharisee* (New Haven: Yale University Press, 1990), 56.

> For consider your call, brethren; not many of you were wise according to worldly standards, not many of you were powerful, not many were of noble birth; but God chose what is foolish in the world to shame the wise, God chose what is weak in the world to shame the strong, God chose what is low and despised in the world, even things that are not, to bring to nothing things that are, so that no human being might boast in the presence of God. (1 Cor 1:26-31)

This real-life example calls the Corinthians to recognize their utter dependence on God's creative and redemptive power. The strategy that began in a disruption of language and ideology thus leads the perceptive reader to the knowledge of his own un-knowing, indeed his non-being (*ta mē onta*) before God. This recognition, it seems, is required for true perception of the cross and hence for reconciliation to God, self, and other.

Once Paul's conventions have done what they can do by destabilizing the hearer, creating cognitive dissonance that prepares for transformation, then *what* the Word *reveals* can have its effect. From the rubble left by the destruction of the conventional cosmos and conventional notions of the self within that cosmos arises a unifying image of the One who not only calls and creates *ex nihilo* but, by a self-giving act of love, sanctifies and empowers "things with no being."

Revelation

We may assume that everyone in the Corinthian church has at some past time encountered the cross in Christian proclamation and has responded to it according to available perceptual paradigms. We may also assume, given Paul's polemical stance in the letter, that the controlling paradigm for the Corinthian understanding of the cross is one he finds inadequate. His polemic is designed to re-present the cross in such a way as to relocate the Corinthians in a new paradigm. If his cross theology is apocalyptic in the ways I have suggested, it will function to *reveal* something that causes the hearer not merely to be dislocated but to be moved from one world to another.

In order to understand the revelatory power of the cross, one must recognize both the world it calls into question and the alternative world it offers. I have suggested that the Corinthian theology belongs to a symbolic world in which a certain wisdom epistemology—one that seems both to borrow from and to modify hellenistic Jewish wisdom traditions—provides the context for the success or failure of the Word as speech act.

The Corinthian Epistemology. The Corinthian "wisdom," Paul's polemic suggests, was associated with signs (1:22), tradition (1:20), persuasive, eloquent, and propositional speech (2:1, 4), and with attributes such as nobility (1:26), power (1:26), spiritual identity (i.e., as *pneumatikos* 2:14), and perhaps "perfection" (if *teleios* comes from the Corinthian vocabulary, 2:6).[21] If our analysis of 2:6-16 is correct, the Corinthians may also have drawn a close relation between human spirit and divine Spirit and may have stressed the human capacity for self and world transcendence through spiritual ecstasy. Here, perhaps, lies the key to the material and spiritual attainments sought and cherished by the Corinthians. If one's knowledge of truth depends on one's capacity to transcend the constraints of earthly life and to reunite with the divine Spirit, it follows that the circumstances of existence should reflect that transcendence. The qualities of perfection, nobility, royalty, wealth, and immortality in this life should attend and demonstrate one's advancement in wisdom.

Foundation for this portrait of the Corinthians is provided by Richard Horsley's studies of parallels in Philo to the language of 1 Corinthians 1–2. The division of humanity into levels according to spiritual status, the demonstration of status by means of claims to nobility and eloquence,[22] and the attainment to immortality of one who is advancing on the Royal Road[23] find striking parallel in language associated with the Corinthians in our text. In a study dedicated to the problem of *psychikos/pneumatikos* terminology in 1 Corinthians,[24] for example, Horsley notes Philo's development of two types of humanity: those who are characterized by possession of the "earth-born and body loving mind,"[25] and those who are characterized by the "mind existing after the Image which has no share in corruptible earthly re-

---

21. See my analysis of 1:26-31. See also Paul's concern with problems that seem to reflect social elitism in his discussions of strong and weak Christians in Chaps. 8–10, and of disturbances at the Eucharist that arise, according to Theissen, from social and economic class divisions. Gerd Theissen, *The Social Setting of Pauline Christianity* (Philadelphia: Fortress Press, 1982), 121–143.

22. Richard Horsley notes that eloquent speech is highly valued in the Jewish wisdom tradition. "In literature such as Proverbs 1–2, Sirach, and Wisdom 6–9—writings which have been important for tracing the development of wisdom speculation and wisdom christology—eloquent speech is a prominent motif" ("Wisdom of Word and Words of Wisdom in Corinth," *CBQ* 39 [1977], 224).

23. See Philo, *De post.*, 101–102.

24. Richard Horsley, "Pneumatikos vs. Psychikos: Distinctions of Spiritual Status among the Corinthians." *HTR* 69 (1976): 269–88.

25. According to Horsley, Philo tends to understand *anthropos* (allegorically) as referring to "mind" or the highest part of the soul. "Pneumatikos vs Psychikos", 277.

ality."[26] The *sophoi* and the *teleioi*, often interchangeable for Philo, belong to the latter group.[27] The *sophos*, Philo writes in "On Sobriety,"

> is a friend of God rather than a servant . . . . but he who has this allotment has passed beyond the bounds of human happiness. He alone is nobly born (*eugeneis*) . . . , not only rich, but all rich . . . , not merely of high repute, but glorious . . . , sole king . . . , sole freeman. . . .[28]

Moreover, the speech of the *sophos* is marked by its boldness. Horsley cites Philo's "Who is the Heir?":

> Keeping quiet is advisable for the ignorant, but for those who desire knowledge and also love their master, bold speech (*parrēsia*) is most necessary . . . those who have put their faith in the divine love of wisdom should speak . . . with a great cry (14). Moses reaches such a courage even to reproach God. He reaches such a limit "because all *sophoi* are friends of God . . . . And *parrēsia* is akin to friendship (20-21).[29]

Teleios status also entails, Horsley notes, the gift of eloquent speech.[30] While Philo has much to say (as does Paul) on the matter of empty sophistry, he highly values the gift of *eulogia* (eloquences).[31]

The passages from Philo are valuable to our study because they demonstrate developments in hellenistic Jewish wisdom that have strong *terminological* affinities with what we know of the Corinthian theology. But at Corinth, Philo's theological depth is lacking. If the Corinthians have access to traditions similar to Philo's (as I have argued they do), they have developed these traditions toward an episte-

---

26. Horsley cites *Leg. all.* 1.31–33; 2.4–5; *Leg. all.* 1.53–55; 88–89, 90–95, *Plant.* 44–45. "Pneumatikos vs Psychikos," 277.

27. Horsley notes: "As is the case with one's status as *teleios*, the *sophos* is constituted rich, nobly born, king, glorious, etc., by virtue of intimacy with Sophia (e.g. Her. 313–315) "Wisdom of Word," 235. Note also that Philo writes of the *teleios* as one who has exceeded the boundaries of the merely human. This one is "neither God nor man but . . . on the borderline between the uncreated and perishable form of being"; indeed the *teleios* not only bears God's image (*Leg. all.* 1. 94) but has seen the "Absolutely Existent."

28. Philo, Sob 56, cited by Horsley in "Pneumatikos vs. Psychikos," 283n.32. See 1 Cor 4:8, "Already you are filled! Already you have become rich! Without us you have become kings! And would that you did reign, so that we might share the rule with you!"

29. Philo, Her. 14–21, cited by Horsley in "Wisdom of Word," *CBQ* 39 (1977): 228.

30. For Philo, perfection (*teleiōtes*) was a spiritual status that could be attained through intimate relation with *sophia*. See *Leg. all.* 3.159 and Agr. 165, cited by Horsley in "Pneumatikos vs Psychikos: Distinctions of Spiritual Status Among the Corinthians," *HTR* 69 (1976): 269–88. See also the valuing of eloquence in the Wisdom literature; Sir 6:5, 18:28–29; 38:33; 39:1–6 and Wis 8:8, 12, 18.

31. See Horsley, "Wisdom of Word and Words of Wisdom," 227 and Philo, *Mig.* 70–85.

mology of spiritual and social exaltation that we suspect would have been foreign to Philo. Had Philo been the visiting theologian at Corinth, perhaps he would have encountered one problem Paul met there—the use of his language toward purposes other than his own.

Paul's Alternative Epistemology. Paul's Word is apocalyptic in part because it calls for an end to the world defined by the Corinthian categories of wisdom and power. We need only to glance at 1 Corinthians 4:8-13 for a list of characteristics of the wise in Christ that are very different from the Corinthian ideal. Paul and his co-workers are "exhibited as last of all, like men sentenced to death, a spectacle to the world, to angels and to men." But the Word he offers can move his hearers into the transfigured wisdom and power of the cruciform existence only if it *both* creates cognitive dissonance (dislocation) *and* provides the positive impetus to *re*-locate in the new world it prescribes. To see how it might do the latter we must consider what *content* the cross reveals that would compel a Corinthian hearer to relocate in the new world it constitutes rather than to rationalize the dissonance it presents.

Paul writes in his letter to the Roman Christians that the cross reveals the love of God: "God shows his love for us in that while we were yet sinners, Christ died for us" (Rom 5:8). But the revelation has not been effective for the Corinthians in the way that Paul expects. Their division reflects a community driven not by love, but by conventional, worldly power. By setting before them the intrinsically motivated love revealed in the cross, he means to point them toward a new reality governed by a new image of God.[32]

Martin Luther echoed Paul when he argued that the cross changes us by revealing for the first time *who God is*. The moment of transformation for Luther was the moment one realized that God is love and that God's righteousness (demonstrated supremely on the

---

32. In recent essays on the theology of 1 Corinthians, both Gordon Fee and Victor Paul Furnish have emphasized the element of divine self-disclosure in the cross. Fee writes, "Thus in his crucifixion Christ not only effected salvation for the called, but ultimately revealed the essential character of God, which is revealed further in the servant character of Paul's apostleship (3:5; 4:1-2, 9-13). In "Toward a Theology of 1 Corinthians," *Pauline Theology, Volume II* (Minneapolis: Fortress Press, 1993), 42. There is a similar emphasis in Furnish's statement that "[Paul's] point is that specifically the crucified Christ discloses the nature of God's power and wisdom. The cross is thus definitive for a properly Christian understanding of God." In "Theology in 1 Corinthians," *Pauline Theology, Volume II*, 68.

cross) seeks to justify and not to condemn. For Luther as for Paul, this revelation transfigures power. The impotence of human beings to save themselves is answered not by divine judgement, but by the willing power of God to justify sinners through love. Transformation comes as one sees for the first time that salvation is not a human possibility but a divine gift and surrenders all pretense of self-saving power to the transcendent power of God. This revelation, Luther maintained, depends entirely on the cross.[33]

We have seen that the emphasis in Protestant theology on the cross as a symbol of self-sacrifice has struck feminist scholars as a dangerous doctrine. But Paul's own theology of the cross as revelation is far from the culture-bound ideology of oppression feminists rightly criticize. Indeed for Paul the cross is an *em*powering, not a *dis*-empowering symbol, provided that now we speak of the power of divine love. What the cross reveals in Christ's own struggle for us against systemic sin and thereby God's loving will to stand with the suffering world against the "rulers of this age" (1 Cor 2:8). The insight is deeply apocalyptic. At the end time, with the victory of God over the enemy certain, the skirmishes continue, and yet, in the assurance of God's presence and loving power to save, the suffering are emboldened to stand firm. True power is born not of control or force, but of solidarity in divine love.

Reconciliation

I have argued that the cross links the two principal sections of Paul's discourse, 1:18—2:5 and 2:6-16, so that the "Word of the Cross" in 1:18, the "mystery proclaimed" at 2:1 and the "wisdom we speak among the perfect" at 2:6 all share the same content, namely, the message of the cross. The development in Paul's argument has to do not with what is being proclaimed or revealed (this is always the cross), but with how the Word is empowered to enter the hostile territory of the archons to liberate and transform human consciousness from within. The closing affirmation, "But we have the mind of

---

33. Luther, "The Heidelberg Disputation, Thesis 24." *Luther's Works*, 31:53.

Christ" proclaims the arrival of the Word into consciousness where it can govern not only the mind but the heart and its intentions.[34]

Having the mind of Christ describes more than an intellectual position; it reflects the comprehensive condition of unity in the Body of Christ, or reconciliation, toward which the entire discourse labors. This final movement of the Word into consciousness depends, however, on the presence and power of another actor introduced at 2:4, the Spirit of God. At 2:10, Paul makes explicit just how the Spirit relates to the message: What the rulers of this world did not know, blinded as they were by false wisdom, "God revealed to us through the Spirit." The wisdom of the cross Paul preaches finds its way into the heart only by agency of God's Spirit who alone has power to claim for God the hearts of "those who love God" (2:9).

From the Spirit's claim on the heart follows transformation and the perfecting power of love. In the Spirit-taught knowledge that one is claimed for God, indeed indwelled by God's liberating Spirit, one is for the first time free to love God and the other. By the power of this new and mystical alliance, the spiritual person (the true *pneumatikos*) now enters into the reconciling work of the Spirit. Freed from the dominating powers of the world, this one is remade in Christ. The apocalyptic transfer from the realm of this world (elsewhere in Paul called the "flesh") to the new creation is most obvious in Romans:

> But you are not in the flesh; you are in the Spirit, since the Spirit of God dwells in you. Anyone who does not have the Spirit of Christ does not belong to him. But if Christ is in you, though the body is dead because of sin, the Spirit is life because of righteousness. (Rom 8:9-10, NRSV)

---

34. Gerd Theissen writes persuasively of the Corinthians' enslavement to the *archons* of this world who represent social and political power. A strong impediment to the hearing of the Word in Corinth is the inner resistance to divine wisdom produced by external and internal censorship of the world's system of convictions. Theissen reads the "narrative" behind 1 Corinthians 2:6-16 as follows:

> Something that was accessible to no one has penetrated the heart of the Christians. God has revealed it to them—against the embittered resistance of the archons of this world. The archons thus become hostile guards in front of the human heart. Formulated in our language, this means that the kerygma forced its way into the unconscious depths against an inner resistance.

Gerd Theissen, *Psychological Aspects*, 379–80.

As the passage continues, Paul discloses the vital connection between spiritual and bodily life:

> If the Spirit of him who raised Jesus from the dead dwells in you, he who raised Christ Jesus from the dead will give life to your mortal bodies also through his Spirit which dwells in you. (Rom 8:11, NRSV)

So too in 1 Corinthians mystical union with the Spirit leads to transformed bodily life. Anyone united to the Lord "becomes one Spirit with him" (1:17), the body is now "the temple of the Spirit" (1:19); or again, "the body is for the Lord and the Lord for the body" (6:13). One who is joined to the Spirit of the crucified pours out the Spirit's compassion, prays with the Spirit for the groaning creation (Rom 8:22-28), lives out the Spirit's love (1 Cor 13), and teaches the ways of the Spirit (2:13) by word and example. In other words, for Paul, where the Spirit is, there is present that connecting, interceding force that links human beings to the compassionate love of God and hence in that same love to one another and to the whole creation.[35]

At 2:16, Paul's discourse comes full circle as his initial call for unity at 1:10 is echoed in the closing appeal to a common mind, "the mind of Christ." For Paul the mind marks the orientation of the whole person, not just the intellect, toward the ways of the Spirit. As we have seen in the vocabulary of Romans and 1 Corinthians, while the *nous* (mind) may function as only one aspect of the *soma* (body), *nous* is never separated from its somatic context. Mindful life, in other words, is also *bodily* life. To have "the mind of Christ," is to embody the life of the Spirit in loving obedience to God and service to the other. Possession of this mind is what makes possible the unity Paul

---

35. Elizabeth A. Johnson seems to reflect Paul's assessment of the Spirit as agent of transformation through divine compassion when in her discussion of the suffering God she characterizes the anti-conventional power of divine wisdom:

> Thinking of Holy Wisdom's "almighty power" . . . leads to a resymbolization of divine power not as dominative or controlling power, nor as dialectical power in weakness, nor simply as persuasive power, but as the liberating power of divine connectedness that is effective in compassionate love. We can say: Sophia-God is in solidarity with those who suffer as a mystery of empowerment. With moral indignation, concern for broken creation, and a sympathy calling for justice, the power of God's compassionate love enters the pain of the world to transform it from within.

See Elizabeth A. Johnson, *She Who Is: The Mystery of God in Feminist Theological Discourse* (New York: Crossroad, 1992), 270.

calls for in 1:10, the mindful servanthood outlined in 1 Corinthians 3–4, and the mindfulness in prayer and praise to which Paul exhorts the worshippers in Corinth (1 Cor 14:13-16).

SEEING AND ACTING IN
THE POWER OF THE CROSS

The resolution of the multiple problems in Corinth depends on the apocalyptic, performative power of Paul's Word of the cross to promote perceptual transformation in and reconciliation among all its members. That is to say, in 1 Corinthians, Paul calls for an integration of epistemology and ethics, of knowing and acting "according to the cross" without which there can be no genuine Christian existence. Like the transformations in Austin's performatives, but on a radically different plane, this speech act, too, is manifestly social, issuing in changed relationships to God and others that reach deep into the life of the church and the world. The insights gained from speech act theory lead me to conclude that for Paul the action that follows perceptual transformation is not a human decision to do what the Word says (as ethical action may follow ethical imperative) but rather a living out of what the Word has done *in* the saying. Like Austin's illocutionary acts, the Word of the Cross has the capacity to act *in* the saying and thereby to enlist its hearers for service in the redemptive activity of God. In other words, when the Word of the Cross reveals the love of God, it also makes that love available to the world through those who are drawn into its service. These are the ones who are joined with God's redemptive activity.

First Corinthians turns out to be very promising ground for the integration of epistemological and ethical interpretations of Paul's apocalyptic theology. On the one hand, more than any other letter, it is concerned with the death of Jesus and power of that death to reveal the present reality of the new creation. On the other hand, this letter is unusually dedicated to explicitly ethical matters within the church and ends with a discourse on the final triumph of God in which Paul insists on the bodily and not merely spiritual reality of the general resurrection. Now it becomes clear that the perceptual shift inspired by chapters 1–2 finds purpose in the resolution of real community discord (chapters 3–14) and looks ahead to the final unity of the Body of Christ in the general bodily resurrection (chapter 15). Perception of the new creation in the cross, bodily action in that creation, and participation in God's final triumph are inextricably linked.

The middle of the letter spells out by concrete example what the first two chapters call for; namely, the re-conceiving of all life, especially the moral dilemmas of life, in the light of the cross. Paul demonstrates his own transformation not least in dedicating himself fully to the Corinthian questions. As one deeply aware of belonging to the Body of Christ crucified, he is able to "become all things to all people," in other words, to see the needs of the other with such clarity as to take them up, one by one, as a servant, in pastoral discourse (4:1). As one who has known the emptying of the false ego by the power of the cross, Paul is able to withstand attacks on his own person and character. Embodying the truth that God alone is judge, he allows the false ego to be replaced with the divine power of service to the other, even to the other who rejects or mocks that service. Bearing the cruciform mind, he is able to bless the reviler, endure the persecutor, rejoice in becoming the refuse of the world; indeed, in this mind, he sees that the dominating powers of this world are passing away (1 Cor 7:31).[36]

This is what apocalyptic ethics looks like. It is both perception and action, both assurance of the power of God's reign now and active hope for its culmination in the future. To use Paul's own language, it is having the presence of mind to live "as if" free although one is a slave, to live "as if" not mourning although one is in grief, even to live "as if" not rejoicing although the world may give its reasons to rejoice (7:25-31). It is to create a small realm of liberty in the midst of

---

36. For a fuller treatment of Paul's determination to be "all things to all people" as a result of his cross-based apocalyptic perception see Barbara Hall, "All Things to All People: A Study of 1 Corinthians 9:19-23" in *The Conversation Continues: Studies in Paul and John in Honor of J. Louis Martyn,* eds. Robert T. Fortna and Beverly R. Gaventa (Nashville: Abingdon Press, 1990), 137–157.

the world's "no" to freedom.[37] On both personal and corporate levels, as Paul himself demonstrates in "fear and trembling" (2:3), it is to be drawn into freedom's orb by the revelation of the new creation and then, despite every conventional claim to the contrary, to live the freedom one sees.

Near the end of the letter in the resurrection discourse (chapter 15), Paul writes of the parousia as the time when *all* will be subjected, not to the world nor to any ideology of the world, but to God (1 Cor 15:28). Although there are many who do not perceive, many for whom the cross remains folly, many who tragically misunderstand its power to transform human existence, Paul continues to preach the Word of the Cross. In the conviction that God wills and already inaugurates the salvation of all, Paul preaches as he lives, the gospel of the cross of Christ, entrusting its transforming power to "God who gives the growth" (1 Cor 3:6).

---

37. There are examples all around us of the power that comes of living "as if" free. One of the most impressive because it has issued in profound political change in our time is the Solidarity movement in Poland. Well before the collapse of the Soviet bloc an observer of the movement wrote in language very like Paul's in 1 Cor 7 of Solidarity's determination to act "as if" Poland were already a free country:

> [Solidarity's] style has been to act "as if" Poland were already a free country and once those in opposition began to that way, something unexpected happened. As soon as they started to act "as if," the "as if" started to melt away. Then they really were defending the worker (and often with success), or giving the lecture, or publishing the book. It wasn't "as if" it were a book, it *was* a book, and soon people were really reading it. Of course in the country at large the "as if" did not melt away. That became clear when the book was confiscated, or the lecture was broken up by a government goon squad, or the innocent worker was sent off to prison in spite of the opposition's best efforts to defend him. Nevertheless, in the immediate vicinity of the action—and that vicinity expanded steadily as the movement grew—the "as if" was no pretense. There a small realm of liberty was created. (Schell, Jonathan. "Reflections: A Better Today," *The New Yorker*, February 3, 1986, 47–67.)

Similar ideas are expressed in other liberation movements. Leaders in the civil rights movement in America and the anti-apartheid movement in South Africa, for example, were masterful in their ability to inspire active hope by calling their hearers proleptically into freedom's realm.

Select Bibliography

Austin, J. L. *How to Do Things with Words.* Cambridge: Harvard University Press, 1962.

Barrett, C. K. *The First Epistle to the Corinthians.* New York: Harper & Row, 1968.

Bateson, C. D., J. C. Beker, and M. Clark. *Commitment Without Ideology.* Philadelphia: United Church Press, 1973.

Beker, J. C. *Paul the Apostle: The Triumph of God in Life and Thought.* Philadelphia: Fortress Press, 1980.

———. *Paul's Apocalyptic Gospel: The Coming Triumph of God.* Philadelphia: Fortress Press, 1982.

Berger, P. and T. Luckmann. *The Social Construction of Reality: A Treatise in the Sociology of Knowledge.* Garden City, N.Y.: Doubleday & Co., 1966.

Brueggemann, W. "The Epistemological Crisis of Israel's Two Histories (Jeremiah 9:22-23)." In *Israelite Wisdom: Theological and Literary Essays in honor of Samuel Terrien.* Eds. J. G. Gammie, W. A. Brueggemann, W. L. Humphreys, and J. W. Ward. Missoula: Scholars Press, 1978.

Cousar, C. B. *A Theology of the Cross: The Death of Jesus in the Pauline Letters.* Minneapolis: Fortress Press, 1990.

Conzelmann, H. *1 Corinthians,* Hermeneia. Philadelphia: Fortress Press, 1975.

———."Paulus und die Weisheit," *NTS* 12 (1965–66): 231–44.

Dahl, N. A. *Studies in Paul.* Minneapolis: Augsburg Publishing House, 1977.

Davis, J. A. *Wisdom and Spirit: An Investigation of 1 Corinthians 1:18—3:20 Against the Background of Jewish Sapiential Tradition in the Greco-Roman Period.* Washington, D.C.: University Press of America, 1984.

Fee, G. *The First Epistle to the Corinthians.* Grand Rapids: Eerdmans, 1987.

———. "Toward a Theology of 1 Corinthians." In *Pauline Theology, Vol II.* Ed. D. M. Hay. Minneapolis: Fortress Press, 1993.

Feuillet, A. *Le Christ Sagesse de Dieu: D'Apres les Epitres Pauliniennes.* Paris: Gabalda, 1966.

Fiorenza E. Schüssler, "Rhetorical Situation and Historical Reconstruction in 1 Corinthians." *NTS* 33 (1987) 386-403.

Funk, R. *Language, Hermeneutics, and the Word of God.* San Francisco: Harper & Row, 1966.

Hamerton-Kelly, R. G. *Pre-existence, Wisdom, and the Son of Man.* SNTSMS 21. Cambridge: Cambridge University Press, 1973.

Hanson, P. *The Dawn of Apocalyptic: The History and Social Roots of Jewish Apocalyptic Eschatology.* Philadelphia: Fortress Press, 1979.

Hays, R. B. *Echoes of Scripture in the Letters of Paul.* New Haven: Yale University Press, 1989.

Horsley, R. A. "Pneumatikos versus Psychikos: Distinctions of Spiritual Status Among the Corinthians." *HTR* 69 (1976): 269–88.

———. "Wisdom of Word and Words of Wisdom in Corinth." *CBQ* 39 (1977): 224–239.

Käsemann, E. "1 Korinther 2:6-16." *Exegetische Versuche und Besinnungen 1.* Göttingen: Vandenhoeck & Ruprecht, 1965.

———. "On the Subject of Primitive Christian Apocalyptic." In *New Testament Questions of Today.* Translated by W. J. Montague. Philadelphia: Fortress Press; London: SCM Press, 1969.

———. "The Saving Significance of the Death of Jesus." In *Perspectives on Paul.* Translated by M. Kohl. Philadelphia: Fortress Press, 1971.

Keck, L. "Paul and Apocalyptic Theology." *Int* 38 (1984), 229–241.

Koch, K. *The Rediscovery of Apocalyptic.* London: SCM, 1972.

Koenig, J. "The Knowing of Glory and Its Consequences (2 Corinthians 3–5)." In *The Conversation Continues: Studies in Paul and John in Honor of J. L. Martyn.* Eds. R. T. Fortna and B. R. Gaventa. Nashville: Abingdon Press, 1990.

Lang, F. *Die Briefe an die Korinther.* Göttingen: Vandenhoeck & Ruprecht, 1986.

Luz, U. "Theologia Crucis als Mitte der Theologie im Neuen Testament." *EvTh* 34 (1974): 116–141.

Mack, B. *Logos und Sophia.* Göttingen: Vandenhoeck & Ruprecht, 1973.

Marcus, J. and M. Soards, eds. *Apocalyptic and the New Testament.* Sheffield: JSOT Press, 1989.

Martyn, J. L. "Apocalyptic Antinomies in Paul's Letter to the Galatians." *NTS* 31 (1985): 410–24.

———. "Epistemology at the Turn of the Ages: 2 Corinthians 5:16." In *Christian History and Interpretation: Studies Presented to John Knox.* Eds. W. R. Farmer, C. F. D. Moule, and R. R. Niebuhr. Cambridge: Cambridge University Press, 1967.

———. "Paul and His Jewish Christian Interpreters." *USQR* 42 (1988): 1–15.

MacRae, G. "The Jewish Background of the Gnostic Sophia Myth." *NovT* 12 (1970): 86–101.

Minear, P. "The Crucified World: The Enigma of Galatians 6:14." In *Theologia Crucis—Signum Crucis: Festschift für Erich Dinkler zum 70 Geburtstag.* Eds. C. Andersen and G. Klein. Tübingen: J. C. B. Mohr, 1979.

Mitchell, M. M. *Paul and the Rhetoric of Reconciliation: An Exegetical Investigation of the Language and Composition of 1 Corinthians.* Louisville: Westminster/John Knox Press, 1991.

O'Day, G. "Jeremiah 9:22 and 1 Corinthians 1:26-31: A Study in Intertextuality." *JBL* 109 (1990): 259–267.

Osten-Saken, P. von der. *Die Apokalyptik in ihren Verhaltnis zu Prophetie und Weisheit.* Munich: Kaiser, 1969.

Pearson, B. A. *The Pneumatikos-Psychikos Terminology in 1 Corinthians.* Missoula, Mont.: Scholars Press, 1973.

Petrey, S. *Speech Acts and Literary Theory.* London: Routledge & Kegan Paul, 1990.

Pogoloff, S. *Logos and Sophia: The Rhetorical Situation of 1 Corinthians,* Atlanta: Scholars Press, 1992.

Purvis, S. *The Power of the Cross: Foundations for a Christian Feminist Ethic of Community.* Nashville: Abingdon, 1993.

Rudolf, K. *Gnosis.* San Francisco: Harper & Row, 1977.

Scroggs, R. *Christology in Paul and John.* Philadelphia: Fortress Press, 1988.

————. *The Last Adam: A Study in Pauline Anthropology.* Philadelphia: Fortress Press, 1966.

————. "New Being: Renewed Mind: New Perception. Paul's View of the Source of Ethical Insight." In *The Text and the Times.* Minneapolis: Fortress Press, 1993.

————. *Paul for a New Day.* Philadelphia: Fortress Press, 1977.

————. "Paul: Sophos and Pneumatikos." *NTS* 14 (1967–68): 33–55.

Segal, A. *Paul the Convert: The Apostolate and Apostasy of Saul the Pharisee.* New Haven: Yale University Press, 1990.

Stuhlmacher, P. "The Hermeneutical Significance of 1 Corinthians 2:6-16." In *Tradition and Interpretation in the New Testament: Essays in Honor of Earl Ellis.* Eds. G. F. Hawthorne and O. Betz. Grand Rapids: Eerdmans, 1988.

Sturm, R. "Defining the Word 'Apocalyptic.'" In *Apocalyptic and the New Testament: Essays in Honor of J. L. Martyn.* Eds. J. Marcus and Marion Soards. Sheffield: JSOT Press, 1989.

Theissen, G. *Psychological Aspects of Pauline Theology.* Translated by J. P. Galvin. Philadelphia: Fortress Press, 1987.

————. *The Social Setting of Pauline Christianity: Essays on Corinth.* Philadelphia: Fortress Press, 1982.

Vos, J. S. *Traditionsgeschichtlich Untersuchungen zur paulinischen Pneumatologie.* Assen: Van Gorcum, 1973.

Weiss, J. *Der Erste Korintherbrief.* Göttingen: Vandenhoeck & Ruprecht, 1925.

Wilckens, U. *Weisheit und Torheit: Fine exegetische-religionsgeschichtliche Untersuchung zu 1 Kor 1 und 2.* Beiträge zur historischen Theologie. Tübingen: J. C. B. Mohr [Paul Siebeck], 1959.

Wilken, R. *Aspects of Wisdom in Judaism and Early Christianity.* Notre Dame: University of Notre Dame Press, 1975.

Yamauchi, E. *Pre-Christian Gnosticism: A Survey of the Proposed Evidence.* London: Tyndale Press, 1973.

Scripture Index

Modern Author Index

28372873R00117

Made in the USA
Middletown, DE
11 January 2016